THE DYNAMICS OF THERAPY
IN A CONTROLLED RELATIONSHIP

THE
DYNAMICS OF THERAPY
IN A CONTROLLED
RELATIONSHIP

BY

JESSIE TAFT

With a New Introduction by
VIRGINIA P. ROBINSON, Ph.D.
*Emeritus Professor of Social Casework and
formerly Assistant Dean of the University of
Pennsylvania School of Social Work*

GLOUCESTER, MASS.

PETER SMITH

1973

Reprinted, 1973, by Permission of
DOVER PUBLICATIONS, INC.
ISBN: 0-8446-3045-4

INTRODUCTION TO DOVER EDITION

THIS book, which Dover Publications is republishing in a new edition, has been out of print since 1945 and copies of the original edition still in existence are hard to come by. Loaned sometimes by owners who have valued them greatly, they disappear inexplicably. Recently it has been microfilmed for the use of a library. The present edition meets a need expressed by therapists, psychologists, social caseworkers and counselors for the description and illustration of what is sometimes known as relationship therapy and sometimes as Rankian therapy.

When this book was written in the years 1930 to 1933 psychoanalytic therapy was comparatively new in this country. The great pioneers in the field, Freud, Jung, Rank, Adler, were living—practicing, writing and publishing. The powerful, far-reaching effect of their discoveries concerning the nature of man, his inner life, his projections upon the world around him in art, science, religion and all forms of culture, will not be fully comprehended and appraised in many generations. The immediate effect of these contributions, however, on the professions and enterprises dedicated to helping people in trouble, on psychiatry, psychology, religion and social work, was dynamic and revolutionary. Introduced into the United States by distinguished psychiatrists, under the name of Mental Hygiene, this movement was permeating social work and psychiatry by the time of World War I. Outstanding among the leaders in social work at that time,

Jessie Taft found in this movement the support for her own thinking and practice as well as the dynamic for further development.

She brought to social work a philosophic background acquired in doctorate study in the University of Chicago under the teaching of Dewey, Mead, Tufts, and Angell, and training in the techniques of psychological testing. In 1918, in a newly created position in Philadelphia as Mental Hygienist in a child placing agency, she found unlimited opportunity to know children and constant challenge to find ways of helping the child in trouble. She had extended help to many children in child placing agencies and institutions and to others brought to her by their parents and referred by psychiatrists, but her growing awareness of their problems and her dissatisfaction with her own inability to help in some cases turned her thoughts to psychoanalysis in search of "the secret of helping."

Rank first came to the United States in 1924 and Jessie Taft was present when he spoke to a meeting of the Psychoanalytic Society in Atlantic City. In the fall of 1926 with a leave of absence from her position in the Children's Aid Society of Pennsylvania, she was in therapy with Rank in New York and by January, 1927 she was practicing therapy in Philadelphia in continuing contact with Rank in a seminar and in individual conference on her own cases. In these years she translated two of Rank's books, *Will Therapy* and *Truth and Reality,* which, published by Knopf in 1936 and republished in one volume in 1945, have become the source book for understanding Rank, so much of whose writings (extremely difficult in the original German) still remains untranslated.

The secret of helping. This she experienced herself in therapy with Rank and found it validated and illum-

inated in her own practice, teaching, and writing throughout a long professional life. When she gave up the practice
of therapy in 1934, it was to accept a full-time position on the faculty of the University of Pennsylvania
School of Social Work, where she was free to clarify
further her conception of therapy in contrast with the
process of helping in social casework and to explore its
similarity to and difference from the teaching process.
Because she was essentially a therapist in her personal
development and dedication, many students knew what
it was to take help from her, while she maintained
responsibility for her function as teacher and for the
purpose and goals of the training process in social casework.

This book, *The Dynamics of Therapy,* as she says in
her foreword written in 1933, grew out of the "combined
results of work and thought written at different times
during the past three years . . . and therefore without
the unity of a book conceived and brought forth as a
whole." She adds, however, that "there is, nevertheless,
the integration of a consistent interest and viewpoint,
together with the continuity which characterizes any record of developing experience in which a conscious psychology and philosophy are interacting with immediate,
yet controlled contacts."

Part I of this book consists of a paper entitled "The
Time Element in Therapy" which had been given at a
meeting of the National Conference of Social Work in
May, 1932 in Philadelphia. It describes her concept of
therapy and of time as the medium in which therapy
takes place and for which the therapist is responsible.
She spoke in 1932 to a social work audience whose practice was intimately known to her and whose attitude
towards the use of time might be said to have been naive
and irresponsible. Social caseworkers were moved by this

paper and the concern for the use of time that it aroused has been an important factor in the development of case-work agencies whose practice today is highly time-conscious. But the attitude towards time that Dr. Taft is describing in this paper and illustrating in records of therapy with two children goes deeper than what one can find in the literature of casework today; and while the use of a time limit deriving from Rank has been found to be valuable in many schools of therapy, its value is still controversial. Dr. Taft's attitude on this is fundamental in her thinking and practice. She states it at the end of Part I:

> While the topic of this paper is Time, I end as I began, not so much with concern for limiting treatment in time, although that is one of the most valuable single tools ever introduced into therapy, but with the necessity for accepting deeply, not merely intellectually, but emotionally and organically in our daily living, the reality of personal as well as functional limitation. A time limit is a purely external, meaningless and even destructive device if used by someone who has not accepted limitation in and for himself. It becomes then merely a weapon turned on the other, or a salvation to be realized through and by the other. In order to use time as a major element in therapy one must first have come to grips with it in oneself, otherwise the limitations which it introduces as a therapeutic agent are unbearable and what the therapist cannot bear in and for himself, the patient cannot learn to bear either, at least if he does, he succeeds in spite of, not because of the therapist.

This concept is illustrated in Part II of this book in the record of her work with two children where "the effect of limitation in time, in space, and in practical possibility is clearly indicated both in its immediate thwarting of child and therapist and in its ultimate value for the growth process." While she never fails to acknowledge her debt to Rank for her understanding of the growth process and its movement in a therapeutic rela-

tionship, she is careful to warn against having these
records used as equivalent to a record of a Rankian
therapy since Rank had had no experience in analysis
of children. It is inevitable that they will be used as
illustrative of Rankian therapy today, since Rank's books,
Will Therapy and *Truth and Reality,* while they present
full and detailed exposition of his theory of therapy,
contain no description of technique and no actual record
of his work with a patient.

Dr. Taft's work with Helen, a seven year old girl,
and Jack, a seven year old boy, was done in the days
before the tape recording machines had made of record-
keeping an easy, mechanical affair. Dr. Taft admits to the
awkwardness of her note-taking in pencil during the contact and recognizes the child's reaction to it as a factor
to be dealt with. Her records, however, though not verbatim, need no apology. One cannot read them without the
conviction that this is the way it was, these two experiences for the child and for the therapist; this is the
actual changing process that was going on between them.
The children live in their individuality and in their
different use of the experience as the therapist lives in
her spontaneous and disciplined responses, as well as
in the frank and honest discussion that follows of the
problems involved for her, particularly in undertaking
the first case, of which she says, "this case was for me
purely experimental and as open to doubt as if I had
never before undertaken an analysis."

A very brief statement of the child's reason for being
there precedes the record: Helen brought by her father
because of her bad behavior in school, in his words, "she
ain't afraid of nothing—nothing in the world"; Jack
referred for this experience because of his attachment
to his mother, who had placed him in a child placing
agency for "a year or two," and his extreme fearfulness

that made it seem problematic to try to find a foster home for him. The absence of a diagnostic statement or of elaborate background history is striking. Nor is the record weighed down with a summary and prognosis at the end. Each child lives in the experience for himself and for the reader who can involve himself in it with the child.

There is a plethora of records of therapy available today on tape, and in print, recorded for purposes of studying technique, for research on the make-up of the patient, on methods of therapy, on outcome, on progress. But one would look far to find, in this era of sophisticated scientific research, records which show as simply and convincingly as these records of Helen and Jack the actual experiences of two children in a therapeutic process undertaken not for scientific purposes but in the interest of and from the viewpoint of the child. Their differences emerge not through any effort on the part of the therapist to describe them or their social situations past or present, but in the actual use they make of this new situation and relationship. The controls are immediately apparent, first of all in time limits, in the materials offered, and in certain conditions which the child must respect. Certain playthings can be used in the room and cannot be taken home; some belong to others and cannot be destroyed. All these controls are inherent in the situation and are not imposed artificially, but they are felt immediately by the child as the imposition of the other person, of the other will upon his. Dr. Taft makes a fundamental statement about her own concept of therapy in summarizing Helen's reaction to these controls when she says:

This brings me back to what is after all the only essential in analysis, to speak statically, the bare bones of the process stripped of all content, whether it be drawn from past, present, or future, and this is the meeting of two wills; in this case the actual clash with the child, the living immediately present action and reaction of her will upon mine, which constitutes whatever of reality, therapeutic or otherwise, there may be in the relationship.

This clash of wills is common enough in ordinary living experience for every child and one must ask oneself what makes the difference that the therapist introduces into the experience. In Dr. Taft's words, "The therapeutic function involves the most intense activity but it is an activity of attention, of identification and understanding, of adaptation to the individual's need and pattern, combined with an unflagging preservation of one's own limitation and difference."

The difference between this concept and practice of therapy and those of other schools of therapy is obvious in these statements just quoted. As one follows the records, the focus in the experience, the absence of other content, the increasing involvement of the child hour by hour, are impressive. The child, we are reminded, has been brought into this situation, does not know why he is here, has made no choice to take this help. He will stay only if his own will becomes engaged and if he begins to feel his own wants and needs met by the therapist's understanding and response. The deeply compassionate relation of the therapist to the needful, unfound child, her sensitivity to his changing feelings, which she recognizes at the same time that she holds firmly to the conditions that provoke them—to the inexorable limitations of the hour, the pencil that writes, the hard refusals—sustain the process to the end. The therapist is sustained, too, by her own unshakeable belief in change and movement, by a conviction that underneath the constantly changing ambivalence of feeling, a movement with direction towards an ending is taking place. The child, if he gets something more of himself in his relation with the therapist, will want to leave the experience in spite of his reluctance and protest. This belief in a growth process as universal in a therapeutic relationship—a belief that can support the therapist in setting an ending for the experience—perhaps more than any other aspect distinguishes this practice of therapy from that of other schools.

In a brief conclusion Dr. Taft gives a moving statement of her philosophy of life, of growth and of therapy. She says of therapy: "Therapy is a process in which a person who has been unable to go on living without more fear and guilt than he is willing or able to bear, somehow gains courage to live again, to face life positively instead of negatively." And in answer to the question she puts herself "How is this possible?" confesses "I do not know; . . . at bottom, therapy of this kind is a mystery, a magic . . . never comprehended in itself or controlled scientifically any more than the life process is comprehended and controlled." It can only be described as it has been described in this book, in philosophic and psychological terms. Each reader will find acceptance or difference with this description only in his own inner experience.

VIRGINIA P. ROBINSON

Flourtown, Pennsylvania,
August, 1961.

FOREWORD

In this volume I have combined results of work and thought written at different times during the past three years as experience crystallized, and therefore without the unity of a book conceived and brought forth as a whole. There is, nevertheless, the integration of a consistent interest and viewpoint, together with the continuity which characterizes any record of developing experience in which a conscious psychology and philosophy are interacting with immediate, yet controlled contacts.

Therapy as it relates to the balance of forces in the organization of personality has always been of prime importance to me, but my concept of what such therapy involves has undergone a complete revolution in the past twenty-five years. It has developed from the notion of a reform of the "other" through superior knowledge of life and psychology, a concept closely allied to that of scientific control in the field of emotions and behavior, to my present acceptance of therapy as presented in this volume, a therapy which is purely individual, non-moral, non-scientific, non-intellectual, which can take place only when divorced from all hint of control, unless it be the therapist's control of himself in the therapeutic situation.

While many words could be written in the abstract

about what I mean by therapy as growth, and the
therapeutic relationship as dynamic, it seemed to me
that only a verbatim or nearly verbatim recording of
the content and interchange in such a relationship
could give meaning and life to my explanations. I
have used two records therefore, not to prove anything,
but to give my abstractions a chance to come alive
for those who want to understand emotionally. I have
chosen records of contacts with two children, first
because they are brief enough and simple enough to
serve as immediate experience for the reader without
entangling him in symptoms and interpretation and
second, because therapeutic contacts with children were
new enough and problematic enough for me, to sharpen
every theoretical issue and to challenge whatever I
might possess of technical skill. My own uncertainties
regarding the nature of the therapeutic relationship
seem to have been lodged in children, and there only
was I able to settle them; which is not to say that I
think of direct therapy for children as non-problematic
or frequently indicated, but merely that in these experiences I have satisfied myself and answered my own
doubts as to the possibility of setting up the therapeutic relationship with a child without detriment to him,
regardless of its effectiveness or desirability as a method
for solving environmental problems. I am not, therefore, advocating analysis of children or any other form
of direct treatment for their behavior and personality
problems, I am merely using the therapeutic relationship with two particular children to illustrate my conception of therapy.

It is necessary to make one more explanation in

terms of my own peculiar experience since for me psychological therapy, as a profession, includes not only the various forms of psycho-analysis but also the direct treatment undertaken by social case work in which, justifiably or not, the client's relation to the case worker is utilized more or less consciously and responsibly for the amelioration of emotional and behavior difficulties. This assumption of responsibility by social case work for healing as well as practical aid has developed rapidly in the eastern part of the United States, stimulated by the growth of mental hygiene and child guidance clinics. It has come to a climax in so-called "psychiatric social work" where the function of the case worker is usually recognized as primarily therapeutic. The efforts of social agencies organized for a particular function such as relief, health, child placing, to keep step with this growing emphasis on psychological understanding, interpretation, and treatment have resulted in the confusion to which I refer in the first chapter between social work as therapy and social work with some other practical goal. Although, technically speaking, I am a psychologist, I have always been associated with social agencies and have never divorced my interest in therapy from its application to case work where the problem is even more compelling because it is undefined theoretically, complicated practically, and seems to imply a discipline as exacting as that which psycho-analysis requires. The first chapter, "The Time Element in Therapy," was written at the close of the second case, and represents from one aspect, the net result of my thinking about the relation of this type of therapy to the case work of the two social agencies with which the children were connected. In both of these agencies, but particularly in the second, time is important not only theoretically and philosophically but actually, as a vital factor, determining the possibilities of any treatment.

The term "relationship therapy" is used to differentiate therapy as I have experienced and practiced it, from psycho-analysis or any process in which either the analytic or the intellectual aspect is stressed or the immediacy of the experience denied or confused with history. It was only gradually that I became sufficiently confident of my own difference to want to give it a label, but it now seems necessary to use some name to designate a philosophy and technique which have little in common with psycho-analysis as generally understood, but are, on the contrary, antipathetic to the Freudian psychology and practice. My quarrel with case work, however, is not that it is psychoanalytic, but that it undertakes therapy under the guise of practical help, without becoming responsible for it overtly, or it fails, for lack of understanding, to be therapeutic incidentally within the limits of a concrete function.

My thanks are due first to Otto Rank, who above all others has understood the psychology and philosophy of helping, without which no therapy can succeed except by chance; second to my friend Virginia Robinson, on whose clarification of the case work relationship much of my own thinking is based; and finally to the Children's Aid Society of Pennsylvania and the Child Guidance Clinic of Philadelphia without whose understanding and coöperation the two records could not have been obtained. I am also indebted to the *Psychoanalytic Review*, the *National Conference of Social Work* and the *American Journal of Orthopsychiatry* for permission to use material previously published, and to Karl de Schweinitz and Dr. Frederick Allen for their careful reading and criticism of the manuscript.

JESSIE TAFT

Philadelphia,
April, 1933.

CONTENTS

xix

THE DYNAMICS OF THERAPY
IN A CONTROLLED RELATIONSHIP

PART I

THE TIME ELEMENT IN THERAPY

I. THE TIME ELEMENT IN THERAPY *

THE *word* "therapy" is used instead of "treatment" because in its derivation and in my own feeling about the word, there is not so much implication of manipulation of one person by another. To treat, according to the dictionary, is to apply a process to someone or something. The word "therapy" has no verb in English, for which I am grateful; it cannot do anything to anybody, hence can better represent a process going on, observed perhaps, understood perhaps, assisted perhaps, but not applied. The Greek noun from which therapy is derived means "a servant," the verb means "to wait." I wish to use the English word "therapy" with the full force of its derivation, to cover a process which we recognize as somehow and somewhat curative but which, if we are honest enough and brave enough, we must admit to be beyond our control. In fact if it were not so, life would be intolerable. No one wants another to apply any process to the inmost self, however desirable a change in personality and behavior may seem objectively. We may be willing to let the physician cure a bodily ill, although even that is not so sure, but the self is defended against every encroachment, even the most benevolent. Resistance to cure, however, is not necessarily open, conscious or violent. The most docile patient is often best

* Read at the National Conference of Social Work in Philadelphia, May, 1932. Reprinted by permission of the *Journal of Orthopsychiatry*.

able to demonstrate the worthlessness of the remedy and the helplessness of the doctor. In the face of my own personal realization of the impotence of the other to help me unless I let him, in fact of my necessity to keep him impotent lest he use his interest in my welfare to interfere with me, I am forced to accept the full limitation which this recognition implies, in my own power to help others. I know in advance that no one is going to experience change, call it growth or progress if you have the courage, because I think it would be good for society, good for his family and friends or even good for himself. I know equally well that no one is going to take help from me because someone else thinks it desirable. The anxious parent, the angry school teacher, the despairing wife or husband, must bear their own burdens, solve their own problems. I can help them only in and for themselves, if they are able to use me. I cannot perform a magic upon the bad child, the inattentive pupil, the faithless partner because they want him made over in their own terms.

This means not only a limit put upon those seeking help but a genuine limitation in myself, an impotence which I am forced to accept even when it is painful, as it frequently is. There is a beloved child to be saved, a family unity to be preserved, an important teacher to be enlightened. Before all these problems in which one's reputation, one's pleasure in utilizing professional skill, as well as one's real feeling for the person in distress are perhaps painfully involved, one must accept one's final limitation and the right of the other, perhaps his necessity, to refuse help or to take help in his own terms, not as therapist, friends or society might choose. My knowledge and my skill avail nothing, unless they are accepted and used by the other. Over that acceptance and possible use, I have no control beyond the genuineness of my understanding of the difficulty with which anyone takes or seeks help, my respect for the strength of the patient, however negatively expressed, and the reality of my acceptance of my function as helper not ruler. If my conviction is real, born of emotional experience too deep to be shaken, then at least I am not an obstacle to the person who needs help but fears domination. He can now approach me without the added fear and resistance which active designs for his cure would surely produce and can find within the limitation which I accept thus sincerely, a safety which permits him to utilize and me to exercise all the professional skill and wisdom at my command. On the other hand, the person who seeks the domination of another in order to project his conflict and avoid himself and his own development by resisting the efforts of the other to save him, is finally brought to a realization of the futility of his striving, as he cannot force upon me a goal which I have long since recognized to be outside my province and power. Whether such a person will ultimately succeed in taking over his own problem, since I cannot relieve him of it, can be determined only by what actually happens. There are those who are unwilling or unable to go further, an outcome every therapist must stand ready to admit and respect, no matter how much his professional ego is hurt or his therapeutic or economic aim defeated. This is in no sense to be designated as passivity in treatment. As I conceive it, the therapeutic function involves the most intense activity but it is an activity of attention, of identification and understanding, of adaptation to the individual's need and pattern, combined with an unflagging preservation of one's own limitation and difference. With this preliminary explanation of the choice of the word "therapy" in preference to treatment, because of its original connection with serving or waiting upon, not in the moral or religious sense, but in the realization of a psychological fact of limitation which must be accepted before therapy is possible at all, I am ready to discuss time in relation to the therapeutic process. It might have been discreet to limit my title to therapy as exemplified in social case work since I intend to consider it for the most part in that connection, but what I have to say about time is true, as I see it, for all therapy.

It is the type of work found in the child guidance clinic which comes nearest to what I mean by case work as individual therapy, and it is this kind of case work which I wish to consider in its relation to time. Here where there is no practical barrier, where the agency is set up to offer therapy, we are faced with the full responsibility for the time factor, on the one hand the problem of unlimited time, on the other equally, the danger of cutting off too soon something that might have eventuated in therapy if only the worker had held on a little longer. In the therapeutic case work with which I am acquainted it seems to me that the case worker has finally accepted at least intellectually the fact that she can be of no use unless the client wants something, is willing to take her help and actively seeks it; but she is not yet rid of her feeling of responsibility for his improvement. Why go on week after week if nothing happens to indicate progress; how justify herself for this piling up of time; how recognize when there has been enough therapy except by results. Yet for results she cannot be responsible without putting pressure on the client. As soon as she decides what ought to happen must she not take command and decide however tactfully that the client should come longer, or has come long enough? Responsibility without control is the dilemma of therapeutic case work as now practiced. Then there is the worker who has given up responsibility for the client's behavior in the world, for any final shaping of his personality, but who still cannot free herself of responsibility for the interview in which she takes part. How can she go into it blindly and passively? She may be willing to be silent, to be very slow and patient, but is she not there to guide the process somehow to a result which will be therapeutic? If the whole affair is to be left to the client where does she come in? It is no wonder she clings to history and the value of catharsis. If she cannot show the patient how to live, if she cannot give him moral, religious or ethical instruction, at least she can see to it that he empties himself of his past, and even that he learns to interpret in ways he never thought of. In other words she can use the hour or two of the weekly conferences to bring out material.

That this preconceived idea of what the interview should sooner or later bring forth, tends just as much to the control and domination of the client as if she had tried to reform his habits or his morals, very few case workers ever realize because if they did they would be greatly at a loss as to what function remains for them. Moreover, the reliving or rehearsing of the past plus the worker's interpretation of it, seems to offer some kind of rational limit to an otherwise unlimited affair. If it is dangerous to use the disappearance of symptoms as a criterion, then what can be used? Perhaps the fact that all the material from the past seems to have been brought out and understood, will provide a natural ending. But, as I know only too well from my own earlier efforts, it is a very baffling experience to see your patient with his past apparently clear to him and you, all his involved relations to his parents finally revealed and neatly interpreted, but his problem of living as unsolved as ever. "Yes, I understand," he says, "but what can I do about it? I don't find it any easier to live." If you decide that he should continue to come what happens next? There is always something, there always will be something to be discovered in his past that he has not brought out before. There is really no limit to the past with this approach, and the client may well go on until he rebels or you grow too weary to bear it, and end the struggle with or without therapy.

The futility of this type of relationship to the client has led certain case workers to the recognition of two other factors which may be determinative of therapy and perhaps contain an inherent time limit or criterion for ending. The one recognizes the relation between worker and client as dynamic and present, the other recognizes time as a qualitative as well as a quantitative affair, valuable in and for itself when it is actually utilized in the passing moment without dependence on a next time. The first factor, the recognition of the reality of the relationship between worker and client and its dynamic changing quality has been quite completely accepted, at least verbally, among the more radical group of case workers. But the cloven hoof remains, in my opinion, in the fact that the dynamics of the immediate relationship is often obscured by the concept of living out, reliving or solving past relationships on the worker. According to this concept, the worker is being used in the present but only as a lay figure on which to project experiences and feelings from the client's past. An utter confusion results, a practical denial of the reality of the present which is functioning for the sake of the past. Once more the worker is effectively hidden behind the screen of father, mother, brother, sister, while all the time her value for the client is that she is none of these and he knows it. He may be using patterns which were developed by him in birth, nursing, weaning, toilet training, Œdipus situation and what not, but he is using them now, with all the changes wrought by years of living, using them afresh as they are in the present hour, in immediate reaction to someone who behaves as no one has ever behaved to him before; someone who understands and permits a use of herself, which determines for the client a new experience valuable, if at all, in and for itself. He does not want a father or a mother, but he does want someone who will permit him ultimately to find himself apart from parent identifications without interference or domination; someone who will not be fooled, someone strong enough not to retaliate. The client may feel toward the worker attitudes which recall his earlier ties to mother or father as they developed biologically, but the moment the worker confuses her own relation to the client with his relation to anyone else past or present, that moment she has again entangled herself with history, with external fact, with the static goal of definite material, and also has escaped her own responsibility for the present. The relation may be dynamic but the client is unable to avail himself fully of its therapeutic possibilities because it is predetermined, set in advance, without creative opportunity.

According to this doctrine, which I am criticizing, the client is not really "cured" or through, until he has lived out all the faulty biological and sociological relationships. If he has apparently exhausted his use of the worker as a mother, he is not safe to go until the father relation has been lived through also and so on. How long it should take before one can be sure that everything essential has been reëxperienced consciously is as uncertain as material and relationships from the past are unlimited. Once more therapy is defeated by the setting up of an external norm or purpose for which the case worker must assume responsibility willy nilly but which, unfortunately, again contains no inherent time limit.

Driven into a blind alley by this limitless possibility in long-time treatment, certain groups have taken refuge in what has come to be known as "the short contact." Here, for the first time in the history of case work as far as I know, a few case workers are struggling with the fundamental problem of therapy. It is interesting to see that they have been able to come to grips with the real issue only when they have set up for themselves an arbitrary limit in time. What happens, they ask themselves, to make a single or short contact meaningful, as it often is, for client and worker even if they never meet again. The fascination which the study of the short contact holds indicates that somehow it contains the whole problem of therapy, if only it can be mastered. I find the significance of this concentration on the short contact by individuals who represent the experimental emphasis in case work to be threefold. First, it indicates a self-confidence which has freed itself to the point of taking responsibility for its own part in a process. Second, it points to a growth and achievement in case work which can afford to admit a limitation. Third, it is a recognition of the fact that whatever takes place between worker and client of a therapeutic nature must be present in some degree in the single contact if it is ever to be there. If there is no therapeutic understanding and use of one interview, many interviews equally barren will not help. In the single interview, if that is all I allow myself to count upon, if I am willing to take that one hour in and for itself, there is no time to hide behind material, no time to explore the past or future. I myself am the remedy at this moment if there is any and I can no longer escape my responsibility, not for the client but for myself and my rôle in the situation. Here is just one hour to be lived through as it goes, one hour of present immediate relationship, however limited, with another human being who has brought himself to the point of asking for help. If somehow this single contact proves to have value for the applicant, how does it happen? What in the nature of my functioning permits this hour to be called therapeutic at least qualitatively?

Perhaps one reason we find it difficult to analyze what takes place in the short contact, is that here we are brought face to face with a present from which it is

hard to escape and which in consequence carries symbolically and really our own personal pattern as it relates to time and the self-limitation which is involved
in its acceptance. Not only is the client limited by this
brief period of time, not only is he facing the possibility
of being turned out too soon or kept on after he is ready
to go, but I also am forced to admit my limited function
as therapist, dependent as I am upon his right to go
when he must or to deprive me of a second opportunity
no matter how willing I may be to continue the contact,
no matter how much he may need the help I have to
give from an objective standpoint. My only control,
which is not easy to exercise, is my control over myself
in the present hour if I can bring myself to the point of
a reasonable degree of acceptance of that hour with all
of its shortcomings. The fact that our personal reaction to time gives a clear picture of the real nature of
our resistance to taking full responsibility for therapeutic case work, makes it necessary at this point to
consider time and its relation to therapy more philosophically.

Time represents more vividly than any other category
the necessity of accepting limitation as well as the inability to do so, and symbolizes therefore the whole
problem of living. The reaction of each individual to
limited or unlimited time betrays his deepest and most
fundamental life pattern, his relation to the growth
process itself, to beginnings and endings, to being born
and to dying. As a child I remember struggling with the
horror of infinite space, but the passing of time was even
more unbearable. I can remember my gratitude for
Christmas, because at least presents remained, some-

thing lasted beyond the moment. There was deep depression in adolescence over the realization of this flow of time. Why go to a party since tomorrow it will be over and done with? Why experience at all, since nothing can be held? On the other hand, there is equal fear of being permanently caught in any state or process. Fear of being bored is perhaps its most intellectualized form, panic in the face of a physical trap or snare its most overwhelming and instinctive expression. As living beings we are geared to movement and growth, to achieving something new, leaving the outworn behind and going on to a next stage. Hence we do not like a goal that can never be reached nor yet a goal that is final, a goal beyond which we cannot go. In terms of this primary double fear of the static and of the endlessly moving, the individual is always trying to maintain a balance, and frequently fails because of too great fear either of changing or of never being able to change again. To put it very simply, perhaps the human problem is no more than this: If one cannot live forever is it worth while to live at all?

We see this problem and this double fear reflected in every slightest human experience from birth to death and consequently also in the case worker's as well as the client's attitude toward the long or the short contact. Whether or not she can face the reality of either, depends on whether life to her can be accepted on the terms under which it can be obtained, that is, as a changing, finite, limited affair, to be seized at the moment if at all. The basis for believing that life can be thus accepted, beyond the fact that all of us do more or less accept it if we continue to exist, lies in this: that we are, after all, part and parcel of the life process; that we do naturally abhor not only ending but also never ending, that we not only fear change but the unchanging. Time and change, dying and being born, are inner as well as outer realities if fear of external violence or compulsion does not play too great a part. Life is ambivalent but so are we, "born and bred in the briar patch." And on this fact rests the whole possibility of therapy. We cannot change the fundamental biological and psychological conditions of living for others, nor for ourselves, but somewhere within each individual is this same life process which can go on for and of itself, if the fear which has become excessive primarily in birth and the earlier experiences can be decreased in quantity sufficiently to permit the inherent normal ambivalence to function and hence to provide its own checks and balances. Time in itself is a purely arbitrary category of man's invention, but since it is a projection of his innermost being, it represents so truly his inherent psychological conflict, that to be able to accept it, to learn to admit its likeness to one's very self, its perfect adaptation to one's deepest and most contradictory impulses, is already to be healed, as far as healing is possible or applicable, since in accepting time, one accepts the self and life with their inevitable defects and limitations. This does not mean a passive resignation but a willingness to live, work and create as mortals within the confines of the finite.

I know of no more poignant presentation of the release which comes from yielding to life as it is, with its inevitable endings than is given in an article by Gertrude Carver in the October 1931 number of the *Atlantic Monthly,* entitled "Early Holiday," which gives the ex-

perience of one who faces death from a fatal disease
with ample time for realization and no sustaining belief in immortality to blur the immediacy. "In this
literal acceptance of death," she says, "I now find the
only authentic preface to living. . . . I should have
expected to share in the face of death the panorama of
life that proverbially presents itself to a drowning man,
but the scroll of the years refused to unfurl. The
hidden record betrayed them, however, by burdening
the present moments with an anonymous significance.
Repeatedly I was made aware that every impression,
every contact had incorporated itself into myself by a
law of mysterious but complete assimilation, until my
previous selves with their contemporary experience had
endowed my present self with dimension. They were
myself but so unified, so drawn into the present, that
there could be no separation of episode. Time, necessary as an impulse and chart to memory, did not exist.
Therefore, not only was my future, by the imminence
of death removed, but in a strangely satisfying way my
past no longer existed, except in the expanded vitality
of the present. With the future denied, and with the
past automatically denying itself, it was as though
the moment, transient and ephemeral in the laws of
time, challenged those very laws and reaching out
across boundaries dissolved by the removal of past and
future, became reality, infinite and precious. A concentrated urgency impelled each second into aeons and
frustrated time. In a present so powerfully weighted,
where was there room for even a thin thread of concern about immortality?"

I have never come across anything in literature

which so perfectly explains the use of a time limit in therapy. Since death is so much more final and compelling than any time limit man can set and difficult to take into the self, so complete an experience is seldom granted, but the principle is the same and however strange it may seem, all endings, all partings, being more or less shadowed with the fear of death, become important and fearful out of all proportion because their value is symbolic. Perhaps the ending of a long-time therapeutic relationship, agreed to by the patient from the beginning, takes on more of this compelling quality than any other situation where threat of death is entirely absent; hence its therapeutic worth, which consists primarily in this fear-reducing heightening of the value of the present and the releasing discovery that an ending willed or accepted by the individual himself is birth no less than death, creation no less than annihilation.

So literally true even in the slightest situations is this description of our relation to time and particularly to a time limit that in any therapeutic interview where in coming the individual admits a need for assistance, it is possible to see the operation of this person's particular pattern, his own way of reacting to time or if you like to the life problem itself. This one is at your door fifteen minutes too soon, the other keeps you waiting, or perhaps fails to turn up at all. The very one who makes you wait at the beginning of the hour may be equally loath to go at the end and leaves you to be responsible for getting him out. The other who comes before you are ready is on edge to be gone before the time you have allotted to him is up. Neither can bear the hour as it is, with limits set by the other, even though he has agreed to them beforehand. The one makes *you* bear the burden of his lateness and his lingering, the other tries to bear too much, both his own responsibility and yours depriving himself of what is his, and you of the chance to contribute what you have already assigned for his use in terms of time. And so it goes, for every individual a slightly different pattern but with the same motivation which is so deeply symptomatic of the individual's problem that one might fairly define relationship therapy as a process in which the individual finally learns to utilize the allotted hour from beginning to end without undue fear, resistance, resentment or greediness. When he can take it and also leave it without denying its value, without trying to escape it completely or keep it forever because of this very value, in so far he has learned to live, to accept this fragment of time in and for itself, and strange as it may seem, if he can live this hour he has in his grasp the secret of all hours, he has conquered life and time for the moment and in principle.

Here then in the simplest of terms is a real criterion for therapy, an inner norm which can operate from the moment the person enters your office to the moment at which he departs more or less finally, whether he comes once or a hundred times. It is a goal which is always relative, which will never be completely attained, yet is solved in every single hour to some degree however slight if the client really wants help and I offer a contact in which limitation is accepted and acted upon, at least for myself. If I believe that one hour has value, even if no other follows; if I admit the client's right to go as well as to come, and see his efforts and resistances in both directions even when he cannot; if I maintain at the same time my own rights in time as well as my responsibility and limitations and respect his necessity to work out his own way of meeting a limit even when it involves opposition to mine as it must, then I have provided the essentials of a therapeutic situation. If with this personal readiness, I combine self-conscious skill and ability to utilize the elements which make for therapy, the client may if he choose, in greater or less degree, learn to bear this limited situation which, as he finally comes to realize, is imposed by himself as truly as by me, by his own human nature, no less than mine, or if you like, by the nature of the life process itself.

I have often heard discouraged case workers with much—perhaps too much—psychoanalytic information, question the value of case work, since only psycho-analysis seems to offer real therapy. The problem, as I see it, lies not so much in the case worker's lack of equipment for carrying on psychoanalytic treatment with her clients as in her failure to comprehend the nature of therapy and what she undertakes when she sets out to help other people, either practically or personally and psychologically. There is no question in my mind as to the value of case work once it learns to utilize within the limits of a practical function the psychological insight to be gained from an understanding of the therapeutic process. Therapy is a matter of degree, of depth, and may be present anywhere but the quantitative element must be controlled in terms of the ostensible function otherwise it becomes either a waste or a detriment. In my opinion the basis of therapy lies in the therapist himself, in his capacity to permit the use of self which the therapeutic relationship implies as well as his psychological insight and technical skill. If this is true, therapy is potentially present wherever the therapeutic attitude is maintained, whether the contacts be one or many, and whether the vehicle be case work or some form of professional therapy. However, to offer individual therapy directly and frankly involves a training, personal discipline and responsibility for self as well as a willingness to take payment which the majority of case workers have not achieved.[1] Yet they are being forced into a kind of long-time, intensive case work which seems to be nothing unless it is professional therapy in disguise; relationship deliberately set up with therapy as its goal, carried as far as the case worker knows or dares under conditions involving practical responsibility for the patient which no professional therapist would accept. Few case workers are willing to be entirely responsible for this type of work. Either they do not let themselves know what they do or they rely upon a supervisor or psychiatrist to soften the responsibility which they are not able to carry. The alternatives seem quite clear to me. Either the case worker should prepare herself to do individual therapy responsibly and proclaim it as a function to the client

---

[1] The fact that it seems not only possible but natural that the social worker should receive no compensation from the client for the therapy derived from the relationship, implies that the client has no responsibility, and the "will to health" is largely the will of the worker directed toward the client's improvement.

or she should learn to differentiate social case work with a practical goal from case work with a therapeutic function and to value it for itself.

Relationship therapy as a technical process dependent upon repeated contacts as well as a conscious control of the dynamic thus set up, with a definite beginning and ending in time, is a highly specialized discipline which the case worker has no more right to practice than any lay person unless she has prepared herself adequately.[2] But she has a right, nay more, an obligation to understand the interplay of forces in a helping relationship, so that the mere repetition of interviews will not precipitate her into a process that she cannot stop but cannot utilize, nor the shortness of the contact deprive it of the therapeutic quality which the acceptance of its functional limitation would ensure.

While the topic of this paper is Time, I end as I began, not so much with concern for limiting treatment in time, although that is one of the most valuable single tools ever introduced into therapy, but with the necessity for accepting deeply, not merely intellectually, but emotionally and organically in our daily living, the reality of personal as well as functional limitation. A time limit is a purely external, meaningless and even destructive device if used by someone who has not accepted limitation in and for himself. It becomes then merely a weapon turned on the other, or a salvation to be realized through and by the other. In order to use

[2] It is difficult to say what constitutes preparation for practising relationship therapy; certainly one requirement is that the would-be therapist should first have experienced in himself what it means to take help, to be a patient.

time as a major element in therapy one must first have come to grips with it in oneself, otherwise the limitations which it introduces as a therapeutic agent are unbearable and what the therapist cannot bear in and for himself, the patient cannot learn to bear either, at least if he does, he succeeds in spite of, not because of the therapist.

In the last analysis, therapy as a qualitative affair must depend upon the personal development of the therapist and his ability to use consciously for the benefit of his client, the insight and self-discipline which he has achieved in his own struggle to accept self, life and time, as limited, and to be experienced fully only at the cost of fear, pain and loss. I do not mean that knowledge is not necessary, that technical skill is not necessary; they are, but they are of no value therapeutically without the person. To make case work therapeutic, incidentally or deliberately, one must *be* a therapist and only to the extent that this is true are the relationships one sets up therapeutic, regardless of the label, the number of visits or the interpretation recorded in the dictation.

We do not think of the physician as conceited or egotistic because he admits his ability to heal the sick. In fact, we would consider him reprehensible if he did not offer conscious skill and power to those depending upon his professional ability. When it comes to a therapy which is internal and rests upon strength of will, freedom to feel, and an ability to lend oneself to the use of the other, we shrink from the position into which we are put by admitting that we are able to offer these things in addition to knowledge and skill. Apparently we cannot face this degree of self-assertion easily or if we can, perhaps we are not justified, but are merely determined to do what interests us even if we have no real understanding of the therapeutic process into which we plunge so recklessly. The case worker who accepts her therapeutic function, as it were surreptitiously, is actually denying responsibility, refusing to develop or accept the self which is required by her job, a self with real strength to be utilized therapeutically by the client. On the other hand, the case worker who must help, who plunges into involved relationships from which she can hardly be extricated because the case is so interesting she cannot resist it, is not really accepting responsibility any more than the one who plays safe. She is only pursuing her own reflection, seeking the solution of her own problem by trying to force salvation upon someone who seems to exemplify her unrecognized, unassimilated, emotionally unaccepted conflict. The one denies strength, the other weakness, while to be any use as therapists each must admit and become responsible for both, not in the client, but in herself.

The social worker who makes no claim to therapeutic case work but sticks to a concrete function other than individual therapy certainly runs less danger of being destructive when she refuses the self-conscious responsibility which therapeutic case work demands but the fact remains that she can never realize the full possibility even of the practical goal, can never attain to conscious guidance of the relationships with which she deals, can seldom contribute incidental therapy except by the happy accident of personality, unless she brings to her task an understanding of therapy through relationship which enables her to avoid it, to limit herself in terms of her agency function and the best interest of her clients. The next step for case work, as I see it, is not to become more psychological but rather to become responsible for therapy, for practicing it overtly or for refraining deliberately, but in any case, for knowing and bearing its strength as well as its weakness, in other words, for accepting itself.

Since my own experience does not provide first-hand material for analysis of the case work situation, I must content myself with a presentation and discussion of the long-time, overt therapeutic relationship as exemplified in the two records of children which follow, where the effect of limitation in time, in space, and in practical possibility is clearly indicated both in its immediate thwarting of child and therapist and in its ultimate value for the growth process.

PART II

AN EXPERIMENT IN A THERAPEUTICALLY LIMITED RELATIONSHIP WITH A SEVEN YEAR OLD GIRL

Reprinted by permission of the *Psychoanalytic Review*
October, 1932

I. INTRODUCTORY STATEMENT

THE title of this section is not as clear as I should like it to be but it does describe with some accuracy exactly what I wish to present. My contacts with Helen P. which took place under the auspices of a child guidance clinic are in no sense a child analysis as Melanie Klein or Anna Freud would define it. Throughout the sixteen visits which she made to the clinic twice a week for eight weeks, no attempt was made to unearth or analyze unconscious content or to give to the child anything in the nature of Freudian interpretation. The relationship between us was taken simply and immediately for itself and developed according to what the child found in it and did to it of her own will both positively and negatively, under the pressure of the deprivations and frustrations imposed by the time limits, the reality situation, and the lack of projection on my part. The interviews, or rather the contacts, for there was much more action than verbalization, were carried through, as far as I was humanly able, in terms of the child as she actually was at the moment, and my recognition of her immediate will, feeling or meaning. Everything centered in her, was oriented with regard to her. This does not mean that there were no checks but that even when my response was a prohibition, it was also a seeing of her, never a denial of the nature of her impulse or her right to have it. Where my own curiosity as to her behavior symptoms or my interest in bringing out certain material got the better of me, as it did occasionally, I abandoned it, as soon as I became conscious of my folly. This was to be her situation, not mine, and I held to that even when I felt that nothing interesting therapeutically or psychologically could come of it. Interpretation there was none, except a verbalization on my part of what the child seemed to be feeling and doing, a comparatively spontaneous response to her words or actions which should clarify or make more conscious the self of the moment whatever it might be.

The reason I have called it a therapeutically limited relationship instead of a therapeutic relationship, is that I wish to assume nothing as to the nature or value of the results, either for Helen herself, or for her suffering family and school. I do not know how much a child might get out of so brief and perhaps superficial an experience as this or how much it would affect her social adjustment for the better but I do know that the stage was set, as far as I could control it, in terms of the child herself and her freedom to make what use she could of a type of contact never before experienced by her, that is, I set up within this brief period a true analytic situation in the Rankian sense,[1] therapeutic in possibility if not in actual result. My interest here then, is largely in the form and method which this skeleton-like material shows so clearly and in the light it throws upon certain fundamental doubts which I have harbored in regard to child analysis in general.

---

[1] For the elaboration of the viewpoint indicated in this material see "Technik der Psychoanalyse" (particularly Part 2), by Otto Rank.

While my psychological work with children covered a ten year period, my analytic work of the past five years has been confined to adults, with one exception. Therefore this case was for me purely experimental and as open to doubt as if I had never before undertaken an analysis.

From the point of view of clinic policy, there was a question whether direct treatment for Helen was indicated at all, inasmuch as the father's relation to her behavior seemed almost more important than her own use of it. But since she came with him in the first place and seemed so eager to return, advantage was taken of her unusual willingness to become responsible for her own visits. Knowing that I had only nine weeks to give before vacation, I thought no great harm could come to the child and seized this opportunity for an experiment thus safeguarded in advance. The application interview which follows will give the setting of the case and the arrangement with the clinic. The case worker saw the father on every visit of the child. Periods were limited to about fifty minutes for both. The father was prompt and meticulous in his payment of the moderate fee.

May 6, 1931

Mr. P., a small and harassed looking man, neatly dressed, came rather apologetically into worker's room and immediately started out by saying, "Mr. M., principal of Grant School, sent me down here because, he said, in all of his 500 children in that school, he ain't got none like my girl. She tears her clothes all to pieces because she says she won't go to school. He says you will help me down here, and God knows I need help." Worker asked if Mr. M. had told him anything about the kind of help this clinic was able to give and in answer to his negative reply told him of the general plan of the clinic,—working through with the parent what seemed to be involved in this particular difficulty and sometimes, too, working along with the child.

Worker brought up the fee and in response to father's comment that he would expect to pay but was worried about his wage cut and heavy responsibilities, indicated that we had a sliding scale. Father interrupted this to go on with a further description of the child's behavior. She tears her copy books, she tears all her clothes, she is now beginning to tear the curtains and other things in the house. "It ain't as if it was my house. I'm living with the grandmother— I mean my mother—and my brother. (Several times he referred to his mother as "my grandmother.") My wife left me four times, and now I have the two children. My brother won't have Helen any more because when I threaten to whip her, she runs out in the yard and screams that I'm lickin' her. My brother lets me have our board very cheap, so he won't put up with this. I ain't going to let the Cruelty get me because of something I never done. I want to put her away—in an institution or a school where she will have to be afraid. The trouble with her is—she ain't afraid of nothing—nothing in the world." Worker asked, "Are you sure of that," and Mr. P. replied—"Well, anyway I want her to act as if she was afraid when she ought to. It ain't natural for a seven year old girl to look the principal in the eye and tell him she won't sit on the bench."

Discussion followed on the possibility of institution or private school placement, foster home placement, or having her continue to live at home if the father decided to go on with the clinic. He discussed each one in turn. Private schools were too expensive—he really wanted her in an institution where she would be "made to fear," but there are no institutions for so young a child.. He couldn't bear the idea of going to a child placing agency because they "investigate" and that was not necessary "where a man knows his mind and is asking for what he wants." He also questioned whether he could afford to pay for such a home. Anyway the mother might get hold of the children that way and she would neglect them. He rather vaguely mentioned a possibility of taking his two children and starting a new home, getting an old lady from an old ladies' home to keep house, but he promptly dismissed this, saying that his wages had been cut ten percent and might at any time be cut more so that he could not afford such a venture. Worker said, "Well, you seem to be clear about these other possibilities. What do you want to decide about the clinic?" Following this, father talked quite vehemently against the child, saying that his brother was through, that he had said she would have to go away and that the first thing he knew he and the other child would be out of a home too. Then, too, he was a poor man and couldn't afford to be sending her torn clothes to a tailor all the time. His mother refused to mend Helen's clothes any more, so that he himself had tried the best he could to sew on her buttons and darn the long rips, but at night she would come home with the same garments torn from top to bottom. He spoke of how hard this was for him since he works fourteen hours every night and gets almost no sleep because of her. Every time he talks to her about it she says she will tear all her clothes so she won't have to go to school. He put a great deal of emphasis on the torn clothes, particularly as it affected cost and what the school and neighbors would think of him when she went out so ragged. Father said, "It's terrible to talk so about your own children, but it's certainly got me." He then turned to worker and said, "You tell me what to do. You know what I'm up against and I want your advice." Worker said that she was sure he would see how futile it would be for her to decide for him, because he had so complicated and difficult a situation that no other person could be sure of just what would be right for him. This discussion continued for some moments and finally father said, in response to worker's query as to whether he wanted to talk the matter over with his brother and see how he would feel about having Helen stay on for a time,—"Well, I just want you to see that child. I'm going to bring her in."

Father then brought Helen in from the waiting-room. She walked straight over to worker and stood in front of her as if she were to be "talked to." Her eyes were wide open and filled with tears. Her upper lip was caught between her teeth as if she were trying to keep from crying. Her face, neck and hands were very dirty and her soiled dress was torn down the front. Father said, "Tell the lady who tore your dress." "I tore it," Helen replied. "Why?" "Because I won't go to school." Father then sent her out for her coat and when she returned had her show worker how she had ripped it, though it was only two days old. He then said, "You're filthy—why didn't you wash when I told you to?" "I didn't want to. I washed my legs anyway." She then showed her legs which were quite clean. She was wearing new silk stockings which she leaned over to fix. Helen then said to worker, "Can I take that book home, out there in the other room?" Worker replied that we couldn't give the things in that room away because sometimes other children had to wait a long time just as she had, and that it was nice to have some things for them to do. Sometimes we loaned a book to children who were coming back because then they could bring the book back for other children to read. She turned to her father and said, "Well, ain't I coming back, Daddy?" "Do you want to?" "Sure, I want to live here." Worker said, "None of us stay here at night." "Where do you go at night?" "Home." "Well, I could go home at night, too, and be here in the day and not go to school." Because the father had said so much about school and the torn clothes and because Helen was standing waiting for worker to say something about them, worker said to Helen, that we have doctors here that children can talk to if they want to, about the things that are pretty hard, like all this about the school and clothes. "Would you want to have a chance to talk over with a doctor how you feel about it all?" She turned her back to father and came over to worker with her eyes full of tears and said, "Sure, I'd like to. Only there was a girl out there that didn't want to see the doctor." Worker said, "I wonder if she had ever been here before." Helen said, "Sure, I guess so." Worker said, "That seems strange because only the people who want to come, come here. No one has to see a doctor if she doesn't want to." There was a little more conversation about the book and clothes, and finally worker said to father, "Suppose you let me know what your decision is after you have had a chance to think it over." Father replied, "Well, I'm set to go on. She's my kid and I can fix it up with my brother." He then said, "That book will be torn when she brings it back. It ain't safe to let her have it." Worker said nothing and Helen answered, "I won't tear it—Didn't I say I'd bring it back?"

To the environmental and relationship situation brought out quite clearly in this initial interview, should be added these additional points which became clear as acquaintance with Mr. P. progressed. The mother, who has deserted the family, was never deeply attached to Helen. In fact, Helen had always turned to her father but the mother's departure seemed to have increased the jealousy problem with the brother, two years younger, since he too now depended on the father for care. We suspected that part of Helen's objection to school resulted from the fact that little brother was at home with Mr. P. who slept in the day time. Mr. P's use of Helen's behavior grew increasingly apparent as we knew them better. He obviously enjoyed her fearlessness and defiance of authority, even her ability to defeat him. He always wanted her to conquer and yet he was shocked and guilty over her success. When she went so far as to involve him with the school, the neighbors, and his brother, he was driven to do something in his own defense but even when enraged and desperate, he was powerless to discipline or resist her. His coming to the clinic, then, was a last throw, a final threat, which he had been holding over her. Helen, with her determination to outdo him, immediately took all punishment out of the situation by finding the clinic the most interesting of places. It was one more failure for the father, one more triumph for her.

She came then, not so much a child in trouble as a child who is determined to find pleasure and a new world to conquer. The fact that it meant a special trip with her father twice a week, a trip from which little brother was excluded, as well as absence from school, added to her satisfaction. A psychological examination given before she came to the clinic rated her as just average (intelligence quotient 102). A physical examination showed nothing out of the ordinary except that she was somewhat underweight. The record of her visits which follows was derived only in part from notes. Although I dictated in every case immediately after the hour, much escaped both notes and memory. While there is nothing scientifically accurate in this recording, I think it represents faithfully the feeling-tone and movement which can be clearly perceived.

It is obvious that Helen came with me in the first instance somewhat fearfully and with no desire of her own to see me or any other doctor, but, except for the first bit of pressure which I exerted enough to realize at least one contact, there was no effort to keep her coming. I was ready to let her leave me at any point, although I should have been disappointed if she had. It seems fairly clear too, that her first few visits were not so much from any desire to confine her attention to me as from her determination to find the clinic interesting, to keep on coming. I was her only avenue of approach, as everything else was intentionally cut off. There was a point when I thought her desire to wander through the various rooms in search of adventure and kinder adults who would give her what she asked for, would prove too strong and destroy all possibility of relationship but, to my relief and surprise, she soon settled down to me and the section of the building where we were located.

I have hesitated to present so long a record in full and yet in no other way is it possible to show the almost contentless process in relationship which really took place. For the same reason I have decided not to interrupt the flow of the material with technical discussion, but to leave the reader to make the effort of going back to the particular points which are necessary for the final theoretical consideration.

II. RECORD OF CONTACTS

May 14, 1931, Thursday—First hour

Helen is found in the waiting-room reading. Is apparently startled at the idea of going with a strange person. Says that her father is talking to a doctor and that she would have to stay there. I say that she is going to talk with the doctor, too, and that I am the doctor. She wants to know where she would have to go. When she realizes it is in another direction from where her father is, she thinks she would rather stay right here in the waiting-room. I suggest that she leave her coat and hat in the waiting-room and come upstairs with me; that her father would not go home without her, because he would have to take her, as she couldn't go alone. Whereupon she follows me without any great reluctance. When we arrive at the office she stands in the middle of the room and at no time does she sit down and make herself comfortable. She begins at once asking rather apprehensive questions: "Do you live in this room? What do you do at twelve o'clock? Where do you go at five o'clock? Do you stay here all the time?" I tell her that I do not stay in the room all the time, that I came here just to see her. She sees two nurses crossing the yard below and says, "Who are those nurses? Do they put you to bed?" "If you are sick they do. You aren't sick, are you?" I ask. "No, I am never sick," she says.

"Weren't you coming here to-day to talk to somebody, Helen?"

"Yes, I was coming to talk to a doctor."

"Well, I am the doctor, only I am not the kind of doctor that gives medicines. You don't need any medicines anyway, do you, because you are not sick?"

"Sometimes when I go to the bathroom I feel sick. Then

36

when I come out I am all well again. Then I have to go back again, and then I am late for school. I take water, but it doesn't do any good."

"Do you mean that it is hard to go to the bathroom?"

"Sometimes it is and sometimes it is loose. Once I went to the hospital."

"What did you do that for? Were you sick?"

"No, I wasn't sick. I just went to see if I was sick. My ear hurt. My father is up here, isn't he? Right in there?" pointing to the next room.

"No, I think your father is in the other building."

"But I saw him. I saw him smoking." Apparently she refers to Dr. P., whom she passed. "How long have I been here? Is it time to go?"

"It is twenty-five minutes to ten. I can stay until ten. Can you stay that long?"

"Well, I was late to school when I was here before."

"Yes, you will be late for school. I think there is no doubt about that. But perhaps you can wait until ten o'clock."

During this conversation she is slowly taking in things in the room, but not moving from the spot where she stands. I had asked her sit down, but she had paid no attention to the invitation.

"Do children play here?" she says.

"Yes, I think they do. They come to play with another lady who uses this office."

"What are these papers?" pointing to the shelves where the psychological tests are kept.

"They belong to the other lady. They are not mine, but you can use the papers on the other table if you want to."

It is interesting that the attraction seems to be entirely for the forbidden shelves. She edges up to them and picks up the most obvious and harmless object, which is a baby's rattle. I say nothing. Then she picks up another toy. I pay no attention. Finally she selects Healy A., which is loose from the other tests, takes it over to the table, and begins taking the blocks out and putting them in.

"I know this game. This is a game I played once. You have to put them in right."

I do not interfere with this in any way since it is not disturbing the main pile of tests, but I suggest again that these shelves do not belong to me but to the other lady. She picks up a box of blocks, also loose, and looks at them. Then she sees the drawing paper and the paints, and her interest is diverted from the shelves. The paints interest her most, but there is no water. I am not anxious to involve myself with water and painting, so I suggest that there are crayons there that do not take water. I can see that she is not satisfied, but she does not protest. Finally I say: "If you really want to paint very much, we will try to get the water." She says rather reluctantly that she would like to draw with the crayons, which she proceeds to do, making some blocks of each color. Then she sees the doll. Asks if she may take off the shoes. "If they will come off," is my response. She takes off the shoes. Begins to take off the other clothes, but finds that they do not come readily and gives it up. There is quite a little conversation about the doll that she once had, and a doll coach that was taken away, but she does not respond to the question, "How did you happen to lose them?"

She goes over to the shelves again and asks what is in the big boxes on top. I tell her that they do not belong to me and that I do not know. I add that I think we ought not to do anything with them. She gives this up without further protest and in the meantime has returned the first objects she took from the shelves to their proper places. Then she returns once more to the paints and says almost to herself that she wishes she had some water. At that I give in, and we get the water. When she finally has the equipment, she realizes she does not know how to use it, although she had said she had painted at school. She lets herself be shown very nicely, but is not particularly free in her way of going at it.

She begins to talk a bit about school. There is a place where she went where they used to sing, and when your turn came you wrote on the blackboard. This isn't the school where she goes. It is a place she went to just once. She doesn't say that she does not like her school. She just says that she likes to come here and to go to school too. "Miss Jones is my teacher." At one point in the middle of the period she says, "Oh, I forgot to bring back the book I took from here."

"You bring it when you come next time. You are coming to see me again, aren't you?"

"Yes, I would like to come back. Can I take another book? The lady said I could when I brought this one back."

"If it is all right to take one, you can."

The telephone rings in the next room, and we both seem to get the idea that perhaps the time is up. She starts out to find her father. I suggest that we put the things away first, which she does very sweetly, and we go down together.

Her father is very pleasant and gentle with her, but when I ask whether he will come at nine or a little later than that next time, he says the reason he was late is that Helen had torn her coat so badly that he had to go to borrow one from his brother. Helen doesn't seem to react to this, and I pay no attention except to say perhaps next time she will want to come earlier so we can have more time and therefore will not tear the coat. I say this in a perfectly matter-of-fact way. Mr. P. remarks that Helen has said she would like to stay here all night. When he told her there would not be anybody in the building she had said she would not care. She is rather inclined to stay longer, but I say that we both have to go,—that it is ten o'clock.

May 18, 1931, Monday—Second hour

Helen is doing arithmetic on the blackboard when I come for her. She is quite willing to go with me and thinks she can learn the way so that she can come upstairs alone next Thursday. When we get to the room she says, "This is a new dress I have on. It is the very first day, and my father got me a new hat too. Can I take the crayons home with me this time? I brought the book back. I do not have any crayons at home. My brother has crayons, but he won't let me use them."

"Does that make you mad at your brother?"

"Oh, no, but I would like to take these crayons home."

"I do not think that is possible, because other children have to use them."

"I took the book home."

"Yes, I know you did, but books are easier to take care of. Crayons would get broken or lost."

"I have nothing to do at home. I haven't anyone to play with. I don't even clean the house."

"Don't you go to school?"

"Yes, but then I have all Saturday and Sunday without anything to do."

"Don't you help at home?"

"No, I don't do anything."

"Who lives at your house?"

"I have two daddies and one mother and my brother."

"Two daddies? How does that happen?"

"I have one daddy who works at night and one daddy who works in the day and one mother who works night and day, just like other mothers."

"What do you mean? Your mother works at night, too?"

"She doesn't go to bed until nine o'clock and she gets up at four. She has to get breakfast for me and my other daddy. The daddy who works in the daytime isn't the one who brings me down here. I have a green and red and yellow dress. That is new, too, and I have to get a new coat. The coat I had last time belonged to my uncle." (She seems to recognize the difference between daddy and uncle.)

"Why did you have to wear the coat that belongs to your uncle?"

"I didn't have any."

"Didn't you have any coat?"

"No, I didn't have any. Can I take the crayons home?" The same answer is gone over.

"I am going to get some water and paint."

"All right."

As soon as she has the water she begins to fool with the paint box, but shows no real interest in drawing or painting.

"It's a nice day. I would like to play out front."

"I'm sure it is a nice day, and I do not blame you for wanting to be outdoors, but if you were home you would have to go to school, wouldn't you?"

"Oh, sure."

The table isn't quite near enough to the light, so we move it together. I have brought a little chair down for her to use, but she doesn't have any interest in it and puts the big chair in front of the table.

"I am coming down Tuesday."

I have already told her I cannot see her until Thursday, so I say, "But I shall not be here then. I cannot come until Thursday."

She gets into the big chair.

"I have a table at home, and my uncle has it."

"You mean your uncle took your table?"

"No, it is his table."

She begins to try to get the paint out of the containers and spends most of the time prying them out with scissors and putting them back. Apparently her interest is taking things to pieces rather than using them.

"Do you have any book that I can take home?"

"I do not know, but we'll find out."

"My brother has a book, but he didn't have the one I took home. He isn't allowed to."

"What is your brother's name?"

"His name is Walter. My father's name is Walter, too, and there is a girl next door I play with, and her name is Walter."

"What? Her name is Walter?"

"I mean her father's name is Walter. Her name is Anna." She then goes on to tell me about a neighbor who gives children everything—pretzels and candy and all.

"Who is going to be here to-morrow?"

"The lady who belongs in this room."

"Does she know me?"

"I don't think she does. Helen, did you want to come this morning?"

"Sure."

"What did you want to come for?"

"Oh, I wanted to play. Can I take the doll home?"

"I'm afraid not. The doll belongs here, too, just the same as the crayons."

"Could you come to my house?"

"I don't go out of the office, Helen. I stay in the office all day long."

"Then do you go home at five?"

"Yes. What did you want me to come to your house for?"

"Oh, I wanted to show you all the things I have. I don't let crayons drop."

"Why don't you save your pennies and get yourself some crayons if you want them, Helen?"

"My father never gives me any pennies. I don't have anyone to play with at home. Sometimes they let you take crayons home from school."

Once more I explain that we cannot let her take the crayons home, but that she can take a book if we can find one. She is perfectly cheerful through all this. There is this insistent pressure to take something home which is never for a moment forgotten. She doesn't really enter into play. It is as if she were determined to get something from me.

When I say, "It is time to go," she isn't ready to go. She would like to continue fooling with the paints, which by this time she has begun to use with water, but very badly, so that they are messed all over. However, she is careful about her dress. Takes great pains to wash her hands so that she will not get paint in her pocket. When she realizes that I am going she is pleasant enough about it and cleans up. After I bring her to the waiting-room she begins on the book that ᴤhe is to take. Her last remark is, "If somebody gave me five cents I could get some crayons." I say it would be a good idea—that perhaps her father will.

At one point in the interview I again refer to the reason why she came. Didn't she want to talk to the doctor? She says she did want to come, but it was to play with crayons. Then I refer to the first time she came, and she says that was because she wanted to get a book. One is very much aware of the pressure which this child puts toward getting something from the other person. There is no appearance of any problem which is pressing her to talk. It is all activity and possession.

This interview began and ended with the forbidden shelves. Her first attention on entering was almost automatically in that direction. I went over the statement about their not being for us. She went toward them for a second and then turned away as if accepting the prohibition. At the very end she went over and quickly picked up an envelope of blocks, which she put down at my request.

From Father's Interview with Case Worker

Father is to pay fifty cents a visit.

Reports Helen eager to come. Has been talking about Monday ever since her last visit. Has been behaving better.

In the Waiting-room

Helen returns book. Father reports torn page and makes Helen show it. She shows no feeling. When asked if she intended it she says it was an accident. Father offers to pay.

Helen complains of no crayons with which to finish her drawing. Father tells how she breaks and loses them. She is given a magazine to take home.

May 21, 1931, Thursday—Third hour

Helen comes up the stairs by herself and is quite pleased with the fact.

"You said I was to come up. I know my way." We arranged the table over by the desk. She sees a wooden giraffe on the mantel. "What's that?" I give it to her. She calls it something preposterous, like a tiger. Opens the paint box. "Has anybody had these paints?"

"I think they are the way you left them."

"No, I didn't leave them just like this."

"Perhaps some other child has had them."

Helen takes possession of the situation this morning. Is much more at home. She goes to get the water, and then at once goes over to the forbidden shelves, where she picks up a rattle, puts it on her table. At first she does not sit down, but begins to write, standing at the end of the table. She has the same dress on that she wore last week, and I comment on how clean and fresh it looks. "I only wear it to come down here," she says. "I can go home alone from here."

"What do you mean, Helen? All the way from here?"

"Oh, I don't mean to my own home. I mean downstairs. Did you think I was lost? I came up all alone."

I chuck her under the chin. "No, I didn't think you were lost."

There is quite an exchange of feeling in this remark, a little atmosphere of familiarity and friendliness. She shows me the spelling that she has been writing on the paper. Says she can read a little. "Did you take a book home last week?"

"Yes I did, but I'm not through with it yet, so I didn't bring it back."

She now settles herself in the little chair and begins on the paints.

"Will you be here to-morrow?" she says.

"No, will you?"

"I think so. When will *you* be here?"

"Not until Monday, when I come to see you." She is drawing a red streak across her paper, and I ask her what kind of picture it is going to be.

"I am going to make the rain come down and the sun come out." She picks up the rattle and shakes it, as if to bring it into the situation. Then she picks up the crayons and begins to use them in place of paints. She draws a little, and finally goes over and gets the doll. She puts it in the chair.

"I could take this shoe home and sew it and make it so it would fit, and I could fix the dress too."

"Oh, can you sew? Perhaps you could bring a needle down and sew it here."

"Yes, I sew on dolls' dresses at school. They are not real dolls. They have pencil faces and we stuff them. We are going to make some hair for them, too."

She begins to put the rattle under the doll's dress where the arm is, so that it looks as if the doll were holding the rattle. She is quite amused with this. Then she starts to place the rattle between the doll's legs, but quickly withdraws it. I say, Oh, is it a boy?"—laughing a little, but she does not respond. I say again, "Do you think the doll is a boy?"

"No, it's a girl," she says, "because it's got dresses." "Is there any other difference?" "Well, the hair does look like a boy. Perhaps it is a boy," she says.

She returns to her drawing and makes a picture which she brings to me. It is a lady holding an umbrella. "Is it you?" I say.

"No, it's a lady."

"Is it I?"

"Sure." She continues to add touches to the lady. "That's you," she says laughingly.

"Helen, were you mad at me last week?"

"No."

"Weren't you mad—just a little? I should have been in your place—because I wouldn't let you take the crayons home."

"I wasn't mad. I like to come down here to draw." She shows me the picture again.

"You could make a funnier one of me, couldn't you? Just as funny as I am!"

Helen, with enthusiasm: "I am going to make a great big one without any arms or legs. Did you ask the lady if I could take the crayons home?"

"No, I asked her if you could take the book home."

"It is going to be a sunny day and blue sky."

"How is that? Oh, I see you are making it."

"When do you come down again?"

"Not until Monday."

"When do you have to go?"

"About ten o'clock."

"Can I take the dress home?"

"Some other little girl might want to play with the doll, and it wouldn't have any clothes on. Supposing I bring a needle and thread in next time, so you can sew it here." She brings me a picture of a woman without arms and legs. "You got even with me, didn't you, Helen?"

"No, I just made it funny so you would laugh."

"I think you made a picture without any arms and legs to get even with me for last week."

Helen, with a good deal of pleasure: "You got runned over." She draws a picture, which she says is a man in an automobile. "He is going to run over you."

Then I say, "Am I bad?" She laughs.

"I will put your arms on."

And I say, "So you can take them off, I suppose."

She laughs assentingly. "He is going to go to jail." Then she draws a picture of a plant with flowers which I am supposed to be picking. "The man is just kidding you."

She begins to get a little restless, and it is time to go. I suggest that we clear up. She goes promptly over to the shelves and begins to investigate. She looks in the bag which she wasn't allowed to take last time and finds the pieces of a puzzle. I say firmly that we are not allowed to take them. She makes one or two efforts to get into the other material in spite of my firmness, but there is nothing unpleasant in her attitude, just persistence. Then to divert her, I suggest that she can have a box of plasticine which is on that shelf. She opens it and is rejoiced to find she can get out some little pieces of it which she can take home. Her whole joy seems to be the thought that here is something that can be taken home, and she goes back to the box after it has been closed and put away to get one more little piece. She also takes the drawing that she has made. She would like to come every day and stay all the time.

During the period a reference is made as to how long she will be coming. I say, "Perhaps you will want to come until your school is out, until you have vacation."

"Then can I come back again?"

"If you want to, but perhaps you will get tired."

"I like to come," she says.

"Yes, I know you do, but you may feel differently some day."

Father, Worker and Helen in Waiting-room

Father reports Helen has torn her coat again (perhaps to nullify my suggestion last time that maybe she wouldn't do it again). He shows the coat to worker. Helen seems unimpressed. Father adds that she has not torn her dress since coming to clinic.

The secretary reports that Helen tries to see if Miss D. (the person she saw in the first interview) is in her office.

May 26, 1931, Tuesday—Fourth hour

Helen comes all the way to the room alone. Has on a new dress and, as she says, a new handkerchief too. She begins at once on the plasticine. I suggest various measures for keeping it off her dress.

"I can't find the picture I made last time. I left it downstairs and it was gone—the picture I made of you in the rain. I wanted to show it to my brother." She is now attracted by the typewriter which is on my desk, begins to play with the keys and finds out how to make the bell ring. I try not to make any objection to this, hoping that she will weary of it soon. After a while she says, "Where is the doll?"—and I notice that it is not present. "Did you bring a needle?" she says.

"Yes," I reply, "I have the needle, but I don't know where the doll is. Perhaps some other little girl has had it."

Helen says quickly, "Did they take it home?"

"I don't think so, because it isn't allowed."

She refers to not coming Monday. Did I send word not to come? She refuses to move her table over near mine.

She turns again to the typewriter. "I know how to put a paper in it."

"I am not sure we are allowed to use the typewriter. I will ask the lady, and if she says we can, then you can put a paper in next time, but we won't do it to-day."

She persists for a few minutes and then turns once more to the plasticine. "I got a big chunk," she says.

"What are you going to make?"

"I can't tell. I can make a big ball. My father made a cat."

"Out of that piece you took home?"

"Yes. It's lost—my brother lost it. What time is it?"

"Twenty minutes to ten."

"Do you have to go at ten o'clock? My father says, why don't you stay later? I like to stay later."

"I am going to arrange so I can stay later than ten o'clock, Helen. I will stay until a quarter past this morning."

Once more she turns to the typewriter. She is very persistent about wanting to put the paper in. Then she starts working at it quite hard, making the shift bang as loudly as possible. I pay no attention.

"I have played on this before."

"Where was that?"

"Anyway, I saw them do it down in the office."

She begins again on "How long can you stay? You used to have to go at ten o'clock."

"But I can stay until ten-fifteen this morning."

Again she turns to the plasticine and brings me a rather shapeless ball which she says is a pussy. She plays with it a little and then says, "I'm going to get a piece of paper and wrap it up and take it to my father."

"Do you mean you are going to take it now?"

"No, I am going to take it home. Can I take the crayons home?" This is as if it were a fresh new question never answered before. A child goes by with Dr. H. She is very much interested.

She is now diverted to the drawing. "I am going to make two pictures, and I am going to take them home." She draws the picture of a woman which she says is I. Then she draws a little girl.

"Who is that?"

"That is your little cousin."

"Oh, is it? Isn't it you?"

"Yes, it's me."

"What are we doing?"

"We're holding hands."

"Does the little girl like me this morning, or is she mad at me?"

"She likes you. I am going to draw a house for you to live in." She proceeds to draw a small house up in the corner, makes a chimney with black smoke coming out. "The smoke is going to come down and go in your eyes, and I am going to make it rain and the snow will come in your eyes. You haven't any coat on and you'll get all wet."

"What will that do to us if we get wet?"

"Suffer," she said.

She now remembers the paints and brings them over. "Someone's been using these paints. I cleaned them all up nice" (which was not true). I forgot to mention that when she was drawing the picture of the rain coming down, she was using green crayon and jabbing viciously at the paper. She jabbed so hard she finally split the end of it, whereupon she laughed loudly as if she had had nothing to do with the matter. It was the crayon that broke. She was tempted to poke still more viciously and break the crayon in two but did not carry out her desire. Now she drops the crayon on the floor. She is distinctly noisy and rough this morning. A little later mentions the fact that she is always dropping something.

"What time does the lady come?"

"She usually comes at ten."

"Then I will have to go downstairs."

"Do you want to?"

"No, I would rather stay up here." Dr. H. goes past. "Is he a doctor?"

"Yes."

"Does he do things to you?"

"No, not any more than I do."

"Are there playthings in his room?"

"Just about the same as in here, I think."

Her attention is now diverted to the shelves, and she picks up the envelope with blocks from the Healy Pictorial. In spite of all the discouragement I can give her, she takes the blocks out, looks at each one and tells all the things she can do with them. I insist steadily that she cannot play with them. She reluctantly returns them to the envelope. "Do you like to do things when someone says you can't, Helen?" She makes no real response to this. Then she returns to the drawing.

"I'm going to draw some more. I'm going to take it home. I'm going to make you guess what it is. You can't look at it—I can tell when you're looking." She finally comes with the picture behind her back, and I try to guess. "It's too hard, you can't guess," she says. "It's the blocks, a design." In one of the intervals she has come over to the other block tests and looks at them longingly. She begins to paint, hoping she can get another picture painted before the time is up, so she can take it home. "I'll take these paints home and hang them on the wall and I'll take them to show my teacher. Can I talk with the lady who comes in this room?"

"Yes, I think you can if she has time. Do you want to talk to the lady?"

"I want to talk to five ladies." Apparently the idea is that she would like to stay down all day. I tell her it is time to go, so we had better clear up. She does so with enjoyment of the detail and unwillingness to leave. Her greatest disappointment to-day seems to be that she has to go. She protests loudly, saying she would like to stay longer. We stop to speak to Mrs. T., who is in the next office, and Helen asks her where the doll is. She is quite taken back when we come to the waiting-room, to find a little boy and girl sitting by the table. I speak to them, and she asks me if I know the little girl.

Helen's last shot is to ask if she can take a book home, although she still has one not returned. I say when that one is returned, she can take another if we have it.

Items from Father's Interview

There has been no further tearing of clothes.

Helen was much disappointed in the change of days from Monday to Tuesday. She told her father about a dream of the first lady she met here, in which this lady gave her lots of things—everything she wanted. When father doubted its being a dream, Helen said it was not.

May 28, 1931, Thursday—Fifth hour

Went to the waiting-room to bring Helen up to the new room, since the other room had to be abandoned. She is very curious about why we have a different room. Wants to know who comes to this room, what I do with the people who were in it, where her things are. She looks to see if everything is there and finds the paints gone. I explain there is no water over here, so I did not bring the paints, but if she wants them we will try to get them next time and bring the water up. She makes for the blackboard and does a little figuring. Then she sees the doll. The shoes are gone. She begins sewing on the doll's dress, but this does not last long—she gets disgusted and pulls the thread out.

She refers to having come on Tuesday instead of Monday of this week. Apparently she has not yet gotten over the change of dates and asks again if I wrote the letter, and if I knew she was coming this morning. I say that I expected her. "How did you know?" she says. "I might not come."

As if to warn me that she could play fast and loose as well as I.

Then she starts in on the room again. "Are we going to stay in this room?"

"Don't you like the room?" I ask.

"Yes, I like it. What is this?" pointing to the inkwell. "It is an inkwell but it is empty." "I stayed here a long time last time after you went—I stayed until eleven o'clock," she says. "Were the little children there?" She shows no interest in the little children.

She now spies the open window. Fortunately the window is down from the top. She climbs on the window sill and stands in a rather precarious position, talking rapidly all the time. "I was worried about coming here." There is something about a train which I could not get clear, but the point apparently is that the last time she did not have time enough. She just came and had to go right out again. She inquires about the playground across the street. I tell her it is for colored children. She sees a ragman going by, and I ask her if she is afraid. She isn't afraid of a ragman, and I ask her if there is anything she is afraid of. "I'm afraid I'll fall out of the window." The real truth is that she wants me to be afraid.

As I give no sign of interest in her being at the window, she finally goes over to the blackboard and begins on the chalk. "Can I take the chalk home?" I explain as in the case of the crayons, suggest that she can buy a piece of chalk for a penny. She is pathetic about having no chalk at home and no money with which to buy any. She has a blackboard but no chalk; if she could just take a piece home everything would be all right. But I am firm.

Then she takes the doll and stands up in the window. I have a suspicion that she plans to drop the doll out, but this does not materialize. She again refers to my coming and going. Can't I come out to see her on Reach Street? "I want to come to your house, but I'm not allowed." I accept this as a fact—that she can see me down here but nowhere else.

"Did you go up to the other room this morning, Helen?"

"Yes, I went up twice."

"And you couldn't find me, and you couldn't find the things, could you?"

She now starts on the other window and begins to see what she can do to open it. She is very strong and very persistent. The window sticks, but she keeps at it until she finds she can both open and shut it. Then she begins turning the electric lights on and off, which gives her quite a bit of pleasure for a few minutes. Then she conceives the idea of pulling the curtains down so I can't see and can't write. Apparently she has noticed my writing and has resented it. This game goes on for quite a few minutes. I am to shut my eyes, then she surprises me by hiding under the table or putting the curtains up. She gets quite hilarious, and so rough in the play that she hits her elbow and then her head, but refuses to admit that it makes any difference.

She goes back to the window again, and this time is so daring that my heart is in my mouth, but I say nothing. She lifts herself by her forearms until her waist is resting on the lower sash, bends way out, feet off the sill. I realize that if I make a sign on this I am lost, and finally she gives it up and decides she will go down and wash her hands before drawing something.

She is gone for some time. I had warned her that I had not so very many more minutes to stay. She comes back triumphant with a piece of chalk which the girl in the office has given to her. Instead of going to the drawing which she had in mind, she tries to thread the needle, then abandons that and goes to the window again. This time she is more extreme than ever, and I am really alarmed. I bring it to an end by saying I have to go. She thereupon is determined to take home some of the drawing paper. Realizing this is going to be a fatal issue, I tell her she can take home a drawing when she has made it, but not the drawing paper. I take the paper from her and put it in the drawer. It is the first sharp opposition we have experienced.

After this she is entirely out of bounds. We go downstairs, but her father has not called, and she is all over the place. Finally she comes wandering up to the room where I am dictating, saying she wants to see the doctor, whom she refuses to recognize as having anything to do with me. She wanders through the rooms until the stenographer takes her to the stairs, telling her that her father is waiting for her.

My fear is that this is the end. She has obtained from someone else what I refused to give her, the clinic is full of exciting possibilities. I see no way of keeping her interest.

Father's Interview

Father emphasizes how good Helen has been and says she is more affectionate with him than she has been for a long time.

In Waiting-room

Helen displays chalk gleefully and insists she is coming on Friday (next day). Worker replies that the doctor will not be there until Monday. Helen also asks for a book, but the worker refuses it because the other has not been returned.

Item

Everyone at the clinic was asked not to give Helen anything, and it was arranged that the father should take her immediately after her hour to avoid her roaming through the rooms.

June 1, 1931, Monday—Sixth hour

Helen is somewhat late in arriving. I come down to the waiting-room for her.

"Are we going to the same place? I could come alone."

"You can come alone next time if you want to."

"What time is it, and how long can you stay?" she asks.

"It is twenty minutes to ten, and I can stay forty minutes."

She makes for the window the first thing, but soon jumps down and complains she has hurt her leg. She points to an old bruise. There is quite a little reference to the leg, and she limps about for a few minutes.

"Where is the doctor?"

"I am the doctor."

"No, I mean where is the man doctor? The one up in the other room."

"Do you want to see him?"

"Yes, I want to ask him about the book. It's a singing book."

"You mean you want to ask him if you can take it home?"

"Yes, I want to take it home."

"I don't think he would know whether you could take it home. Did you bring back the book you have?"

"No, I haven't finished it yet."

"When you bring that back, perhaps you can have the other one."

She is attracted to the blackboard, and then picks up the doll and notices the dress is torn more—at least, she thinks it is torn more—than it was before. Then she asks where the papers are, but does not go into the drawer to get anything. Sees that there is water in the dish for her paints, but makes no attempt to paint. Tells me about the good time she had at the parade on Saturday.

She tries the window once more, and then goes back to the board and adds for some time. Examiner is surprised at her persistence. Just as a feeler, examiner asks casually whether Helen ever dreams. "No," says Helen.

"What did you dream last night?" is my reply.

"I had a dream about you. I told you about it before— you've forgotten. Don't you know? I dreamed you were in my house."

"I didn't know that was a dream, Helen." She turns to the window and begins to play with the shade and the light.

"Now we are going to pretend it is night. We are going to close all the windows. We do that at our house."

From that time on she engages in active play, with me as the center. I expect to see her leaving me at any minute, but she never goes further than the other room. The entire play seems to be to get a response from me. I try to respond imaginatively, pretending there is somebody coming to see me, that it is Mrs. Brown and the baby. This is too much my idea, and she quickly goes on into other forms of activity. The thing she enjoys most is being Santa Claus and a mouse. As Santa Claus she gives me all the things that I have refused to let her take home, getting them out of the drawer. I say promptly, "Can I take them home?" "Sure," she says. I say, "Do you mean it?" "Oh, not for real." I say, "You are giving me all the things to take home that I wouldn't let you have, aren't you?" She doesn't persist long on any one line, and very little response comes in answer to questions or suggestions. As a mouse, she is going to eat me up, but that is quickly abandoned. Her chief pleasure is banging the door so that I will jump, and putting the light off and on.

Finally she seems to realize the time is going and she has not yet drawn any pictures to take home. She begins quite frantically at the last minute to see how many she can draw. One picture is of a little girl whose mouth was hurt by an automobile. She draws the automobile with a man. She crumples this picture up and throws it out the window with a good deal of enjoyment. I tell her it is time to go and ask her to put away the crayons. She hangs on to them until the last minute, trying to get one more picture done.

"If you begin early on the pictures, Helen, you can draw as many as you want to. It is too late this morning." As I am persistently firm, she soon gives up and comes with me, carrying the doll.

I am very much surprised at her comparatively gentle mood. It seems that something happened last time. Perhaps she feels that she has gone the limit and is repentant, anxious to get back into a better relationship. At the end of the interview she remarks, "I like to come to see you."

Father's Interview

Reports that he bought Helen two new dresses and six pairs of socks. She ripped off the pockets of her new dress, the first dress tearing since she has been coming.

June 4, 1931, Thursday—Seventh hour

Helen comes up alone to the third floor and surprises me. "I came early."

"Yes, I see you have. Isn't that nice?" Inadvertently I mention the doll which I had expected her to bring up. She immediately wishes to go down to get it, and does so, coming back promptly. Pays no more attention to the doll the entire hour.

She goes to the board and begins adding, starting with the combination seven and seven is thirteen, looking at me for confirmation. Last time we had gone over the problem of seven and seven, and she had counted upon her fingers and found it was fourteen, so I refused to answer, and she finally puts down fourteen of her own accord. "You are trying to fool me," I say. She laughs and goes on with other combinations.

Finally wearying of this, she looks up the paints and finds there is no water. I hope to divert her from getting water, but I am not successful. She toils down the stairs but comes back fairly promptly. She gets out the drawing paper and talks about the number of sheets she is going to cover so she can take them home. She keeps adding a sheet until finally she has decided on twelve. She begins with a spelling lesson which she presents to me to take home.

"Did you know I was waiting this morning? I came early." This is not true, as I had just come through the waiting-room and she was not there. She spells something to give to the teacher. "Do you like your teacher? Isn't she mean?" I ask. "No." There was no follow-up from this question.

At this point she has her eye on the fact that I am writing. She has never said anything to me about the writing, but has referred to it and tried to stop it in various ways. To-day she asks me for the pencil, and although she doesn't mention it, she is quite aware of the fact that I pick up a crayon to use instead. She tells me she is in the 1-B grade in school, and she got her card and is going to be promoted to the second grade.

"You will be a big girl, won't you? And will your brother go to school next year?"

"How do you know I have a brother?"

"Why, you told me. You said you had two daddies and a mother and a brother."

"Yes, I know I did, but it isn't a mother, it's a grand-mother."

"Where is your mother, Helen?"

"I don't have any mother."

"Do you mean that you weren't ever born like other people?" At this point she breaks into the conversation as if it were getting uncomfortable for her, shuts the door, and then goes over to the window and begins to see what she can find to talk about outside. Very shortly she starts climbing around on the chairs. I am afraid that the camp chairs will tip over with her, and I tell her she had better be careful with them. I am surprised to find that she is really very cautious and anxious not to be hurt.

She is soon back at the window again, going through the usual gymnastics to which I have become somewhat hardened.

"I see some boys out on the street."

"Do you like boys?"

"No, I like girls."

"Why don't you like boys?"

"Oh, they do things to you."

"What sort of things?"

"Oh, they're just rough and they fight and hit you. Girls

should go with girls, and boys with boys. My father says I shouldn't go with boys. They're bad and do rough things to you."

"I know boys who go with girls, and girls who go with boys. It seems all right to me."

Helen puts an end to this conversation by coming over to get out the clay. She insists it isn't the same she had before. She is always a little suspicious about a change having been made in her possessions. Her attitude toward the clay is interesting. She seems to like the feel of it on her fingers, but has no idea how to use it. It is almost as if she had an aversion to it. She starts putting a lump of it in the glass dish which holds the painting water. Something in the way she handles it makes me think she is reminded of the toilet, and I mention the fact that it makes me think of that. She laughs, but makes no response. Then she begins dropping pieces of clay into the open drawer, looking to see if I will stop her, and she slams the drawer as violently as possible.

"Helen, you must be trying to make me say, 'Helen P., stop that!'"

This amuses her greatly and she thinks up new things to do. Gets out the scissors and threatens to cut the clay with the scissors.

"Helen, it will be your job to clean it off, for I won't have time. It's very hard to get off."

Then she starts toward the furniture as though she is going to scratch it with the scissors. I pay no attention, and she threatens to drop the dish. Once more I say, "Helen, all you want is to have me say you can't do it, isn't it?"

At this point she decides to paint.

"How long can I stay?"

"You have half an hour yet."

"Can I come on Wednesday?"

"This is Thursday."

"Yes, I know—to-morrow is Friday."

"You can come on Monday."

She wanders out of the room into the next room, which makes me a bit nervous, but I do not follow her. Very soon she comes back saying, "Boo!" to surprise me. She goes into the drawer for the paint and insists it isn't there.

I say, "I'm getting used to you and I don't believe all the things you say."

Helen laughs and produces the paint. "Everything I do," she says, "is to fool you."

She runs out into the next room again, and I say, "Helen, if you want to get anything painted you will have to get at it." Back she comes and paints for a while, making a table, with chairs on each side.

"This is for you. You don't have to bring this back. You can take it home, keep it and write on it."

Quite soon she is at the window again, and this time she is the most daring she has ever been. She has her toes resting on the middle frame work of the lower sash and the rest of her is out of the window.

"Helen, if you fall out on your head, it's not my fault," I say in a most indifferent tone of voice.

"Whose fault will it be?" she asks.

"It's going to be yours. There is nothing I can do about it; just fall if you want to."

I am much surprised to find that she responds by being very careful. She sits down on the back of the chair next to the window instead of hanging out of it. As she is sitting by the window she pretends to be writing on the pane, and seems to be talking under her breath. I catch the words "I love," and say, "What's that you are saying, Helen?" A little ashamed, she says, "I love you and you love me." "Is that the way you feel?" I ask. She assents.

"Well, you don't always feel like that. Some mornings you hate me."

"No, I don't," says Helen.

"Yes you do—because I don't let you take things home."

After this an effort is made to get things put away, and Helen tries to see how many papers she can mark up so that she can take them home. She begins to put a single line to a paper.

I say firmly, "Helen, that is a mean trick. It isn't fair. You don't really draw a picture. You just put a mark on it. You can take only the ones you really draw."

She struggles to get one more picture, and draws a figure with hands that are claw-like—refers to them as finger nails. I say, "She certainly could scratch." Helen is so enthralled with this idea that she enlarges the claws. "She is scratching herself. It is a doll, scratching herself."

Finally we get everything put away. She concentrates on getting as many papers as possible, but takes none that do not have actual drawing or spelling on them. We come down amiably, Helen bringing the doll. She is much interested in what I think must have been a hearse going past the window, wanting me to come and look at it. It is the first thing she has insisted on my seeing. "It has dead people in it. They put dead people in the cemetery. I like to see that." She leaves me, as a parting gift, the sheets on which are the spelling and figuring, but I notice she has taken from me the one with the painting. I comment on this, but she does not return it, or make any sign.

Father's Interview

Refers again to ripped pockets. She pinned them so no one down here saw it. Begged her father not to tell. He sewed the pockets, but they were ripped again this morning, and again she begs him not to tell.

In the Waiting-room

Father asks worker before Helen if the Clinic will be open in summer and if the doctor will see Helen. Worker replies that she would like to talk this over. Father asks if the

Clinic has a seashore home. Would like Helen to have a vacation out of the city.

Worker (turning to Helen)—"Would you like to go away?"

Helen—"Sure. What is it like?"

Worker describes briefly some of the advantages of camp and farm life.

June 8, 1931, Monday—Eighth hour

The room was changed to the original room this morning, and Helen comes up by herself, very much interested in the fact we are in the old room.

"Why didn't we go to the other room?"

"Because the lady downstairs said we had to come up here."

"Which lady?"—and she pursues this until she settles upon the exact lady. Wants to know at first if it was the lady "who sees people,"—referring probably to Miss D.

The typewriter, which was the bone of contention when we were in this room last, is the first thing to receive her attention this morning. I give her a paper to put in it, as I have been told that the typewriter is for the children to use. It is interesting to watch the way in which she goes at the machine. She has to know everything about it. She goes at it very roughly and as soon as she finds a part she does not understand begins to wrench at it. Her chief interest is the carriage release, whose use she cannot understand, nor do I. She is so violent with it that I suggest we'd better leave it alone for the time being. By accident she discovers how to use it and is triumphant. She shows more interest in the use of the typewriter than in any other activity she has taken up. She spends almost half an hour on it, but she wants my attention most of the time. I must see everything she writes, which is chiefly letters and figures. She wants to turn the typewriter around so I can see everything as she does it, but this does not seem to be feasible.

The subject of ink comes up. She finds a bottle of ink on my desk and wants to write with it on the paper she has in the typewriter. I flatly refuse to have the ink used. Then she turns on the desk light and wants me to pull the curtain down, which I do. She begins on the articles on the desk, which so far had escaped her attention. The calendar interests her, and she asks me to explain it, and then asks me if she can write on it. When I say no, she seems to accept it. She picks up my watch and asks about the time,—does not seem to know time. As I have to forbid her using nearly everything on the desk, she finally goes back to the typewriter. Her treatment of it is extremely rough, and it seems to me that it is a reaction to my refusals. I do not bring this out because I fear for the typewriter.

Finally she turns her attention to drawing. The feeling I get is not that she wants to draw, but that drawing is a way of getting papers to take home and that she feels she has neglected it. She leaves me the typewritten sheet.

"You must look at this while I draw. You must read it."

I ask her if she has dreamed, and she says no. I ask her what she is drawing.

"I'm making a funny lady. She is laughing."

"What is she laughing at?"

"She's laughing at a yellow and brown T. She never saw one like that, but I have. I saw one on the way down."

She wants to know what time it is. Then she goes back to the typewriter. After a short time she hands me her paper and says, "Now you read this, and read it, and don't say you're through." She goes for water to paint. "I'll make a picture for you next time and it will be a big surprise. Its going to be a girl with a nice dress on." Then she begins to see what is missing in her old possessions—"Where's the rag? Where's the needle?" The rag is there but the needle is missing. "It must be in the other room." She is sure somebody has used her paints. She brings me the very rough painting which she has completed. "It is a little round blue boy."

"What's he doing?"

"He's trying to find something. He's hunting for a stick. If you want to, you can keep this picture."

"Do you want me to?"

"Yes, if you want it. What did you do with the other one I gave you?"

"It is in my desk at home."

She seems very anxious to have me want the picture. Is more interested in that, than in giving it to me on her own account.

She now centers her attention on seeing how many pictures she can finish before the time is up. "What shall we do when the drawing paper is all gone?—because I am getting rid of it fast."

"Perhaps we can find some more."

"What did you do with the paper I gave you to read?"

"It is here,—but there are only five minutes more, Helen, and we will have to begin to put things away." At the mention of a time limit she begins to draw more frantically than ever. "My father isn't downstairs yet."

"How do you know?"

"I know he isn't."

From this time on, the game is to see how much time she can get, in spite of me. I help to put everything away, but she discovers the trick of keeping me waiting while she makes use of the bathroom. She uses the toilet which she has never done before to my knowledge, and she washes her hands at great length. When I come in to see if I can make her hurry, she says she is going to wash her face too, and does so in spite of me. I remark that if it takes so long to get ready, we will have to begin earlier next time.

It seems to me the continuity has been broken somewhat by the change of rooms and the excitement of the typewriter. Possibly her hyperactivity and roughness are a reaction to the feeling climax of the last hour, plus the conversation about vacation and the thought of stopping.

From Father's Interview

Helen is reported to be much better. He can let her go out to play now with a free mind.

June 11, 1931, Thursday—Ninth hour

Helen comes stealing in the door and says "Boo!"—in my ear.

"You have another pretty new dress on, Helen."

"Yes, I have two new pairs of shoes and a new hat and two new dresses. I didn't want to come upstairs this morning. My brother's down there and I want to stay down. I wanted to bring my brother upstairs, but my daddy wouldn't let me."

"You can go any time you want to, Helen."

"When will *you* go?"

"If you go downstairs, I shall go now."

"I want to go at ten o'clock."

"Very well, you can go any time that you want to."

"Did you expect me this morning?"

"Yes, I did. Why?"

"Well maybe I might not come."

"I think you want to make me feel bad, Helen, by making me think you are not going to come. It would be a nice idea for me to sit and wait and expect you, and then find you were not coming."

She tries the window briefly. Then she says, "Where's the thing that goes up and down?"

"You mean the typewriter?"

"Yes."

"It's over in the other room."

"Why are we in this room?"

"Because the lady downstairs said we were to come here."

She turns to the door that leads into the next room, which she has always tried, but which I have managed to keep

locked. This time she discovers the little catch, and unlocks
the door triumphantly.

Then she rushes over to the window. "Do you want to see
me fall out the window? I am going to fall right down on
my head." I do not even look at her during this perform-
ance, as it is so daring I can't bear to see it. As I pay no
attention she says, "Oh, I ain't going to fall. I am just
kidding you."

"Well, you might kid me once too often."

"I ain't going to do it."

"Well I don't care if you do. I can't help it."

She comes rushing to me and says "Boo!—Did you think
I would do it?"

"I don't know, you might. Anyway, it's your affair." She
runs back to the window and sits on the tip top, and begins
pulling the curtain up and down. "Helen, I guess all you
want to do is to scare me, isn't it?"

"Yes, I want to scare you. I won't do it really."

She then begins to climb around on the chairs, and when
I pay no attention to that, she says, "Do you want to hear
a big noise?" and jumps as heavily as possible. Then she gets
the idea of making me do something, and wants me to draw
a picture. I draw a picture of her which she considers a
present. This idea pleases her greatly and she presents several papers for me to draw upon, but I rebel. "You want
me to do all the work, Helen. I am not going to draw
any more."

"What time is it?" she asks.

"Ten minutes to ten."

"How long can you stay?"

"I can stay until twenty minutes after. But you can go
home any time you want to, Helen. You don't ever have to
come unless you want to."

Instead of going, she reverts to the blackboard and the
chalk.

"Can I take some chalk home?"

"No, you know the chalk doesn't belong to me. You can't take it home."

She begins to get very silly at the board and draws silly things; drops the chalk which breaks. Then she gets the idea of playing teacher, making me be the pupil, and she puts me through various bits of addition. When I make a mistake she is delighted and helps me as the teacher has evidently helped her to find the right answer.

"Helen, you certainly want to make me do all the work this morning. I guess you think you have done enough work, and it is time for me to do it."

"Yes," says Helen. "You write sometimes."

"You don't want me to write, do you, Helen?" Instead of replying she puts me to work again rapidly on the addition. Then she wants me to count while she does various things to surprise me. The play gets very rough and noisy. She begins to draw a Christmas tree, having already drawn a Santa Claus.

"I was going to give this to my brother, but you can have it if you want it."

By this time Helen is getting almost hilarious. She begins singing aloud, looking at me with a great deal of meaning and embarrassment. The song as far as I can make out is something about, "I love you when your hair is silver."

"Want to see me dance? I'm going to be a monkey and dance on the floor." Whereupon she dances in a half shame-faced way to the same tune, singing the words. A little later she is sitting opposite me, trying to get as many drawings as possible finished in the last five minutes. She sings again the refrain about the silver hair.

"Helen, I think you must be singing that to me."

"Yes," she says, "I am."

"We manage to get started in fair time, although she does her best to prolong the end.

"When does your school close, Helen?"

"In two weeks."

"Sometime you will stop coming to see me, won't you?"

"No, I want to come down here."

"Well, you may not want to come always."

"No, not always," says Helen thoughtfully.

She takes me into the waiting-room to see her little brother, who is very attractive and friendly. Shows no signs of jealousy.

From Father's Interview

Comments on Helen's behavior in the neighborhood and at school. She is not being kept in now. She is franker with him and more loving. Helen won't say what happens at Clinic. "It's just play," she says.

June 15, 1931, Monday—Tenth hour

Helen comes in a few moments after I arrive, nearly a half-hour early. She does not express any pleasure at seeing me, and my feeling is that she is not particularly eager to come upstairs. She has on a new red sweater and another dress, the fourth new one since she has been coming here.

She goes downstairs at once to get water. When she comes back I say, "Are you happy this morning, Helen? You don't seem very cheerful." Nothing comes of this question.

"Can I come on Wednesday?"

"No, it is Thursday that we come."

"But I want to come Wednesday. Then I could come the day after, too."

"Sorry, Helen, but we only come Mondays and Thursdays." "How are you this morning?" she asks. I remark that I am quite well, and she gets out the clay. She hits her hand rather hard with the clay and makes a fuss about it. I ask her if she ever gets spanked, but that question elicits nothing of interest. She decides she will make a dish out of the clay and put eggs in it, and then she changes her mind and makes a candle with eggs around the base. She has not done much with the clay before she starts counting and is distracted to the blackboard, where she does nothing but draw lines while she counts. "Santa Claus is going to come to-morrow. He is going to bring something to you. How do you feel this morning?" she says for the second time.

Then she notices that there are screens in the windows and rushes over to examine them. Not finding much she can do there, she turns to the chair with castors and calls it her funny little coach and begins rolling it around on the floor with a great deal of noise. Then she says she saw a coffee-pot on the table downstairs and she is going down to get some water. She soon returns with the pot and the tea-cup and wants me to drink some tea. I tell her the water is too dirty for me to drink. At this moment she notices my writing and says quite explosively, "Stop writing!"

"It makes you mad to have me write, doesn't it, Helen?"

"Yes, it does."

She plays around a little longer with the coffee-pot and then turns her attention to drawing. "I want to see the man doctor." Our relationship is such that I can now joke with her a bit about this subject, so I say in a teasing tone, "Now what do you want to see the man doctor for?" "I ain't saying for real," she says, but never finishes the sentence, nor could I get out of her what she wanted to see him for. I have a feeling she wanted to make me jealous.

She asks for my pencil, as I have been using it a little too much, and wants to know how to spell my name, the first name as well as the last. She puts both on the drawing she makes of a little girl which started out to be herself and ends by being me. By now she is singing, talking to herself, and carrying on quite hilariously.

"You always make me happy," she says.

"What do you mean by that, Helen?"

"Oh, you make me feel nice." Nothing further is elicited on this subject. She begins getting very rough with the water, losing no opportunity to spill a little more, so that the desk blotter is soaked, and she finally begins to get her sweater sleeve wet.

"Helen," I say, "if you ruin your sweater it is absolutely your affair, not mine. It isn't my sweater, and I can't help what you do to yours."

Suddenly she gets interested in her record, which I have had with me every morning, but which she has never mentioned before.

"What's this?" she says, pointing to it.

"Some papers of mine," is my answer.

"What do you do with it?"

"I keep it." She makes no further effort to find out about it, but continues in her wild play with the tea-pot and clay. Suddenly she says, "Do you ever think?" I admit that I sometimes do, and try to find out what she means, but all she can say is, "You think of things I think." I can't get at the meaning of this unless there is something on her mind that she wants me to guess or it may be an expression of her sense of being understood. She returns to the drawing and continues with her scattered singing and talking. "Can you dance?" she says suddenly. I say I can dance ordinary dancing. "Well, dance for me," she says. I have to be very firm to escape. She gets sillier and sillier as the hour goes on.

She begins to talk of a little boy, "a little boy has come," and begins to draw a picture of him. I can't understand, although I ask her repeatedly. I ask her if she is a little boy, but she says, "No, I'm a girl." Then she wants to know if I sing any. I admit I do and ask what she would like to have me sing. "When your hair is turned to silver," acting much more foolish than the last time. I do not know this song, so she has to sing it.

Then she begins to see how much she can get drawn before the end of the hour. I agree to wait five minutes longer. Even in that time her attention is turned to the blackboard and she begins to throw the eraser into the air. She is getting so rough that I tell her it is time to go. She wants to finish one picture, and I agree to that. She tries to sneak in another picture, and I make an issue of the last one. Although she draws on it in spite of me, I do not let her take it home, putting it back in the drawer, telling her it isn't fair. She seems to hold no grudge against me for my firmness—in fact, is rather pleased when I do oppose her in this way. We are perfectly pleasant as we come down the

From Father's Interview

stairs together.

Helen tore her new dress clear across the chest. She talks about vacation, but father thinks he can't afford a camp.

June 18, 1931, Thursday—Eleventh hour

Helen comes in very quietly, seems a bit subdued. She has on the same dress with the red sweater. I suggest that she take her sweater off because it is so warm. She says, as she has said before, that her father told her to keep it on as there are no sleeves in the dress. "But that makes it all the cooler for this morning. Why don't you take it off?" She finally does this. Then she runs to turn off and on the lights, and goes into the next room. As I pay no attention, she returns.

"Did this get all dry?" pointing to the blotter that she had soaked last week.

"It looks to me as if they had put a new blotter in," I say. "I imagine the old one was too bad to use any more."

"I'm going to put a lot of papers on it and cover it up," she says, which she does elaborately. Then she begins to pull out all the drawing paper. "I am going to make these many drawings. Shall I come on Monday?" In an absent-minded moment I reply, "This is Monday."

"No, it isn't," she says, very astonished and shocked. "It

is Thursday." I admit that she is right, and we agree that she is coming Monday.

Then she discovers somebody has filled the inkwell with ink. Without waiting for further developments, I tell her the ink is forbidden, against the rule, and I ask her if she knows what that means. She says, "Oh, yes, the teacher says not to do anything against the rule."

"You don't like that, do you, Helen? It makes you want to do it when it is against the rule." She makes no reply.

"I'm going to work this morning, and I'm not going to play anything, but just see how much I can draw." As she starts to work she notices my writing, and obviously to distract my attention says," "Where's my sweater?" which she knows I have seen her hang on the door. Then, "Did the lady let us come up here this morning?"

"Yes, apparently she did. Why, did you think she wouldn't because we spoiled the blotter last time?"

"Yes," says Helen. "Did it dry?" She seems a little apprehensive about this.

"Well, perhaps it did dry, but anyway they gave us a new blotter. I don't know how often they would be willing to do it. Do you like to be bad, Helen?"

"No," says Helen, and nothing further is forthcoming.

"What time is it?" she asks.

"It is fifteen minutes of ten."

"How long can I stay?"

"Until twenty minutes past, the same as usual."

"But I've just come. Can't I stay a little while?"

I had brought up water for the painting this morning, and, having too much for one vessel, had put a little in another empty dish. Helen discovers the two dishes and begins to pour from one to another. The temptation to spill is beyond resisting. I do not wait for the blotter to be ruined this time, but take one dish away from her. She accepts this calmly.

"School closes this week some time," she says. "I hope I get promoted."

"When school closes, Helen, perhaps you are going to stop coming to see me. You will be having a vacation one of these days."

"No, I'm not, I'm going to keep on coming to see you." She is painting, and I am taking notes again. "If you don't look," says she, "you can't tell what I'm doing. You won't know whether this is a man or a girl. She is painting with the red paint, which gives her a great deal of pleasure. It is a color she hasn't discovered before in the paint-box. After covering one sheet with a great deal of very wet red, she comes around to show me, and presents her hands. "See, I haven't even my hands wet yet. Feel them." She obviously enjoys this process. Just before putting away the paints she starts to paint the doll's face, to which I only remark that it will need washing. Then she deserts the painting and wants me to let her knock at the door and pay me a visit. She goes into the next room and presents herself. I say, "Good morning, Mrs. Brown. How is the baby?" At this moment she has the idea of putting the sweater on the doll, and then she presents herself again. I admire the sweater and she says, "She tore the old sweater and I had to get her a new one. She got whipped, too. See her dress? She got a brand new dress and she didn't tear it yet." I made quite a little effort to find out why she tore her clothes, but all that Helen would say was, "She doesn't tear her clothes any more, but when I take her any place she gets all dirty." "What do you do then? Do you whip her?"

"No, I put her to bed without any dinner, and supper, and breakfast. She wasn't ready to go, and I didn't give her any breakfast."

"She wasn't?" say I. "Is that why she was late?"

"Oh, no, I was ready for real. I was ready this morning. It was the car that was late." Then once more she gets the idea of using the chair with castors for a doll coach, and she goes out and comes in again. "Just see. See her brand new dress, and she never tears her clothes any more," says she, beginning all over again. "I give her pennies and nickels and a new sweater and a dress, and she can wear them all the time and she never tears them."

After this the dialogue is so fast and furious that I cannot take any more notes. I try very hard to find out why the baby tore its dress, and I am not sure that it was not I who suggested that she tore it because she wanted to. At any rate, shortly after that, Helen is asserting that the baby tears her clothes because she wants to. I tell her that it is very strange to me that anybody would want to tear her own clothes. Helen also says, perhaps with some help from me, "I whip her and whip her and don't give her any breakfast, but it doesn't do a bit of good. She goes right on tearing them. They have to get her new clothes, because she tears them all, and they have to give her one hundred dollars." I could not make out what the one hundred dollars was— whether it was a reward for not tearing, or whether it was to buy new clothes because she had torn them. She also produced the idea that the girls at school minded because she tore her clothes.

At this juncture Helen decided that she would be the baby instead of Mrs. Brown. She lay down on the chair, and I had an imaginary conversation with Mrs. Brown, in which I asked about the little girl, and Mrs. Brown told me that she tore her clothes. Then I asked Mrs. Brown what she thought was the best way to treat that, because I had children, too, and they might tear their clothes. Answering for Mrs. Brown, I said that I thought it was a good thing not to pay any attention to it, because the clothes belonged to the little girl, and if she wanted to tear them, why should anybody bother? At this time Helen approaches the table where the doll is beside me, and begins to hit her quite savagely, saying she is going to whip her, slap her eyes. "Are you hitting the doll instead of me?" I say. She is obviously upset at having the play turned upon her in this way, so that she is the bad baby who tears her clothes. She quickly decides to be Mrs. Brown, sits down opposite me and starts a dialogue in which she tells me what to answer.

It is time to go, and Helen makes less fuss about going than usual. She wants to depart in character, she being Mrs. Brown and taking the baby with her. She agrees to come back next Monday with the baby, and we go down on the elevator.

This is the most sustained imaginative play that Helen has tried out here, and the first time there has been any reference to the tearing of clothes. This account is quite inadequate to the material, but it is the best I could do with so few notes.

From Father's Interview

Father mended Helen's torn dress, but she ripped it again yesterday. Wants him not to tell the lady. The worker tells father that we think it would be good for Helen to leave the clinic on her own initiative if possible. A vacation would be a good way, if she likes the idea.

June 22, 1931, Monday—Twelfth hour

As Helen comes in, I recall that she was to come back as Mrs. Brown on Monday morning, so I address her in that way. She has the doll in her arms and calls my attention to the fact that the doll has a new dress and it is all sewed. Someone has sewed the dress on the doll, as Helen had originally wanted to do, but I know it could not have been Helen who has done it. She acts as if it were she and then says, "Not for real," which interests me—I am surprised that she would care to make that discrimination.

I inquire as to the baby's health, and she says she has been a good girl, she has behaved herself. She is much in-

terested in a bracelet she is wearing and wants to take it off
so she won't get it dirty, but we are unable to remove it.

She turns her attention to the chair with the castors and
begins rolling it around. She discovers that there are pencils
and erasers on the table which were not there last time.
Can she take them home? She quickly accepts my negative.
Then she begins writing some figures and makes me add.
She is obviously anxious to get the answer when I cannot,
and exclaims with pleasure, "I got it before you. I am the
teacher."

Then she decides we shall go to sleep and puts the curtains
down and the lights off, and says she is going to sleep in the
next room. She bangs the door and then says, "Boo!"—in
my ear, which is a real surprise, for I thought she had gone
out. This delights her so that she repeats it at intervals
during the interview, though I am not so surprised at the
other occasions. Then she climbs up on the table to get at
the light and gets the idea of playing Billy Goat Gruff and
the Troll. My memory is quite hazy, but she repeats the
story. She is the Billy Goat Gruff, trip trap, trip trap over
the bridge (table) and I am the Troll, and she goes through
this to the very end of the dialogue, when the Troll is
vanquished.

Then she says, changing the subject, "Some day I'm going to summer school."

"You mean you are going on a vacation?"

"No, school is going to be out, and then I'm going to
summer school. I'm going with you, and you are going
with me."

"When is your school out really, Helen?"

"It's out Thursday. What day is this?" she says, looking
at me severely. Remembering my error of last week I think
hard and say, "It is Monday," whereupon she laughs de-
lightedly.

She is very noisy, running around the room and saying, "Boo!"—in my ear, singing at the top of her lungs, drawing the chairs about, and stamping on the floor. Finally she says, "Scratch your head and say a number." I do as requested and say, "Ten." "There are ten bugs in your head," says Helen. This is a delightful game, but she finally tires of it. Then she discovers the phone in the next room, and I think we are going to have trouble. She insists upon taking off the receiver. Finally I impress upon her that it cannot be. She gets noisier and noisier and obviously would like to approach me physically in some way. "I am Mr. Bug," she says, "and I am going to climb all over your head." I manage to avoid the physical contact, and she bethinks herself that she has done no work this morning, she must get some drawing done.

She goes into the other drawer of the desk, which in the meantime has been used by someone else. She finds material there and a personal letter which she hands out and wants me to read. I tell her we do not read other people's letters, and that this drawer evidently belongs to somebody else, but she picks up the letter and pretends to read. She is half singing to herself so the "reading" is very difficult to follow and all I get is the general reference to me. Finally she comes out with "I come to see you and you come to see me."

"You seem very happy this morning. Are you?"

"I'm happy about you," she says promptly. She is full of rhymes and songs and words which do not make very much sense, but the chief part of the song is something like "Down by the river," and "I see you and you see me, and I don't see you and you don't see me."

This goes on for quite a while and then she begins painting, gets paint on her hands to her great delight, and then says "Poppy's going to whip me." I ask her if he ever does, and she says, "No." She starts messing in the paint and water and tries her best to get it all over everything, but I manage to prevent the worst. Then she wants to know if I know a spring song, and she sings me one rather nicely, but she soon goes on with what seems to be her own words, "I love you and you love me."

She has just begun a new picture when I notice it is twenty minutes past ten. Instead of grabbing and snatching as she usually does when the time is announced, she says pleadingly, "Can't you stay until this picture is done?" which of course I am glad to do. There is a little effort to lengthen the time, but not nearly so marked as usual.

From Father's Interview

Worker explains about Deerfield Farm, a summer home for undernourished children, where Helen can go for a month without expense. The father at once objects to a "charity place." They neglect children, abuse them. The worker says she does not know the place herself, but others have found it satisfactory. He can do as he likes. He is very undecided, but finally says to go ahead with the plan.

Worker: Have you discussed the possibility of a vacation with Helen?

Father: Yes, she asked me about it this morning. She said, "How about the place they're going to send me?"

Worker: The clinic is not going to send her. It is for you and Helen to decide and to carry out the plan.

June 25, 1931, Thursday

Father phoned at nine-twenty to say it was the last day of school and that Helen wanted to go. Could they skip until Monday? Helen had told me previously that Thursday would be the last day of school, and that she would probably like to go and get her report. Something was said about arranging for her to come on another day if she wanted to, but I had forgotten it.

June 28, 1931, Monday—Thirteenth hour

Helen is late in arriving this morning, steals in very quietly with the doll in her arms, without the usual "Boo!" Her first remark is "I didn't see you on Tuesday, did I?" (It is interesting that she persistently refuses to recognize Thursday. She has always said she will see me some other day, either Wednesday or Friday, but never the proper day.)

"No, you didn't. Did you get your report at school?"

"Yes, I was promoted into second grade, and I got nine on my report. Were you on the telephone?" she says, and I could not make out what she meant by that—unless she referred to her father's calling the clinic. "What time is it? Do I have plenty of time this morning?"

"It is twenty minutes of ten, Helen, and you have the same time as usual, only you are a little late."

She goes over to the drawer at once and begins to take out her possessions. "There isn't going to be any more school."

"What will you do, Helen, when you don't go to school any more?"

"I'm going to stay home and play with my dolly."

"And are you glad of that?"

"No, I don't be glad because there isn't any more school."

She gets the paints out and has the idea of painting the woodwork in the room. I have some difficulty in discouraging her, she is quite unruly. She begins singing in a loud tone, "The school is broke up, the school is broke up. I'm not going to summer school."

"How is that?"

"It's too far away." She gives the address and proves how far it is.

"Helen, did you know I was here last time and waited for you and you did not come?" She smiles as if pleased at this rehearsal, and says, "I was Mr. Brown so you missed me. Where's the mud? It ain't here."

"Helen, I think you are fooling me again."

Then she begins washing up the paint-box and the doll's face.

"I'm going to play. I'm going to be Mr. Brown."

"Do you really mean Mr. Brown?"

"Oh, Miss Brown."

"I guess you mean Mrs. Brown, don't you?"

"Yes, I'm going to be Mrs. Brown, and I'm going into the next room—I'm going home and wash the baby and then I'm coming to see you." She comes in with the doll, but does not sustain the play particularly well. "When I go home for real, I'm going to play with my doll and my coach and my dishes." This is the first time, as far as I can remember, that she has referred to playing at home as if it were in a class with playing down here.

Then she gets the doll coach, as she calls the rolling chair, and starts all over again.

"What's your name going to be?" she says.

"Whatever you like."

"You can take your own name."

"All right, I'll be Mrs. Taft."

She comes back again with the doll and the coach. I say, "Good morning, Mrs. Brown. Have you brought Helen with you?" But nothing really follows this. She talks about the doll's dress being dirty and nothing more. I talk about my children and she says, "Have you got children for real?" "No," I say.

Then she shuts both the doors and runs from one door to the other when I come to open it. She becomes rough, holds the doll up threateningly as if she meant to throw it on the floor. She seems to feel belligerent.

"Are you mad, Helen? Do you feel like hitting something?" She will not admit it. "I think you are mad at me because you didn't come last time."

"Some day I am going to miss you," she says.

"You mean you are not coming some time, Helen?"

"Yes."

"When will that be?"

"Oh, next year."

"Where are you going?"

"To Atlantic City. I'm going to miss you lots of times." Then she quickly says, as if to comfort me, "But maybe I won't go."

"Little girls get tired coming down to play inside in a hot room when it is vacation time, don't they?"

"Yes," says Helen, "they do." However, she doesn't hold to this point very firmly. She quickly adds, "I'm going to keep right on coming," and takes back all the remarks about going away and missing me.

Her attention is diverted to the ink, and she puts the pencil into it and writes a little. When she shows obvious signs of continuing this process, I remind her that ink is forbidden.

"Doesn't it make you mad, Helen, when I tell you there is something you can't use? I should think it would." She will not admit it. Picks up my watch, wants to know what time it is, tries to put it on her wrist as a bracelet. Finally I am a little nervous about the watch and I say, "Will you please give it to me?" She does this very nicely.

She begins running around the room aimlessly. Notices that the curtains are gone. "Did you take them?"

"No."

"I'm going in the next room and see if the curtains are up in there."

Then she reverts once more to the topic of going away. "I will miss you," she says, "some day."

"How many more times are you coming, Helen?" She is very unsure about this, but repeats that she will miss me.

"Yes," I say, "I think you will miss me, but I think you are a little tired of coming, aren't you? She doesn't like to be pinned down to this. The rest of the hour she plays teacher and makes me do sums. I get the impression it is largely to keep my attention, especially when I try to write —in making me respond, she has me most of the time.

Then she goes at the ink once more, and again I ask her if it doesn't make her mad to be forbidden to use it. She says, "No, I just laugh."

She is reluctant to go this morning, and lingers after I have left the room, finally following me when I am almost at the foot of the stairs.

"Let me know, Helen, before you are going to leave me. Give me some warning."

"I will come next Thursday," she says.

"And will that be the last time?"

Quickly she takes it back and says, "No, I'm coming a lot of times." It is evident that the idea of going has begun to take hold, but she is very guilty about admitting it. Apparently the fact that school is over makes being at home a much more pleasurable way of living than it was when she had to go to school.

From Father's Interview

The father asks if worker has found out any more about vacation. Begins in same breath to talk against charity. Worker asks why he doesn't go to see the place for himself. He says Helen is ready to go right now. After much indecision, he decides to come down for the physical examination required by the Farm the following Monday.

In the Waiting-room

Father: "Do you want to go to the country, Helen?"

Helen: "Sure."

Father: "When?"

Helen: "Saturday."

Father: "How will next Saturday do?"

Helen: "All right."

Worker: "That gives you this Thursday, and next week —Monday and Thursday. Is that long enough?"

Helen (cheerfully): "Sure."

July 2, 1931, Thursday—Fourteenth hour

Helen comes in with her usual "Boo!" and surveys the landscape, taking in all the new objects. On the desk in the next room there are some cylinders that have not been there before. I merely say that they are not to play with, and she desists. She gives the phone the once over, finally abandons it. Calls my attention to a little colored baby who is sunning on the roof of the opposite house. She begins to play with the door and apparently hurts her finger because the tears come to her eyes, something I have not seen before. Then she begins to complain of her physical ailments, shows me a bruise on her ankle. Her father had told her it was sprained. Makes a lot of fuss about it. "I'm always hurting myself."

Then she goes into her own drawer and finds an old drawing which is a great surprise to her. "I never think of it," she says. She investigates the inkwell, and to her astonishment and joy it is almost dry, but there is enough moisture so it can be used on the end of a pencil. She gets a great deal of satisfaction out of being able to do something she has been forbidden to do. As she sees me writing, she says, "Fold your hands, boys and girls." Then she starts me on the figuring, which is certainly her favorite occupation. Pretty soon she reverts to the ink again, seeing how much she can accumulate on the end of the pencil and holding it up with great satisfaction.

"You used the ink in spite of me, didn't you, Helen?"

"Yes," she laughs.

"But," I say, "it isn't wet enough to do any harm."

"If I put water in it, it will be wet enough."

"That's true," I say, "but then you won't be allowed to use it."

She does not attempt to put the water in, to my surprise. She thinks she has a little speck of ink on her dress and says, "I'm not allowed to get this dress dirty. I'm not allowed to use ink. My mother says I mustn't use ink at home, and I don't, because there isn't any ink."

She begins wandering around the room again and discovers the ediphone where I have tried to conceal it back of the door. Luckily she isn't much interested in it. She steals into the room and says, "Boo!" in my ear, but it isn't very entertaining.

"There isn't anything to do to-day," she says.

"Helen, that's the first time you have ever complained of nothing to do down here. I think you must be tired of coming."

She can't admit it. "I'm coming to-morrow," she says. "Will you be here?"

"No, I won't be here to-morrow."

"Where will you be?"

"Somewhere else."

"With other little girls?" anxiously.

"No, not with any other little girls."

She begins singing. "I always laugh when I sing," she says. She begins singing the old song "When your hair is turned to silver."

"Is that your favorite song, Helen?"

"Yes, it's my favorite."

"How is that?"

"Because my hair is going to turn to silver."

"Now I'm going to write a note," she says, and slowly and painfully, with most of the words left out, and with a good deal of help on the spelling from me, she writes, "Helen P. is not going down to Atlantic City."

"Where are you going, Helen?"

"I'm going to a cemetery."

"A cemetery!" I say. "What do you mean by that?"

"To a cemetery where there are lots of children."

"Perhaps you mean a sanatorium. When are you going?"

"Next year."

"Next year?"

"Oh, this week maybe, or next week. Maybe next Saturday. I can't tell. Maybe I might not go."

"Are you going to be here on Monday, Helen?"

"Monday I'll be here, and Thursday, and next Monday and next Thursday maybe, but I can't tell. I might not want to go."

"What do you mean by that, Helen?"

"I might want to come here."

There follows quite a rehearsal of going to a cemetery, to a real cemetery where there are dead people. "The lady next door takes me. There's a lady across the street who has died. She was sick four days."

"Does it make you feel afraid, Helen?"

"I like the lady, but she's gone. They're singing prayers to her."

The next game is whether she shall drink the colored water in the paint dish. She keeps at this quite a while, trying to make me anxious. "Do you want me to drink?" she asks.

"I'm sure I don't care, Helen, if you want to be sick." After a good deal of effort along this line she says, "I wouldn't drink it. I'm only fooling you."

"What color do you like? Do you like pink? Do you want me to give you a pink dress?" holding up a wet, dripping paint brush.

"Do you mean a real dress or just a painting?"

"I mean a real dress."

"Well, I'd rather have it in the picture." hoping to divert her from the white surface of my dress.

Her last game, which she keeps up quite a while, is going around and around the table selling paint-brushes. As I buy a paint-brush, she takes a pencil and crayon and goes around so fast it seems she must drop with dizziness. She calls her wares at huge prices and then gives them away for nothing. I get a distinct feeling that she has in mind, underneath all her activity, the thought that it would be very nice to put paint on my black and white dress. She does not make any gesture in that direction, but there is something in the way she comes around back of me, which makes me think that that is the underlying impulse. If so, she hasn't the courage to carry it out. Instead, she gets paint all over her own face.

I remark that it is nearly time to go, and she says with a sigh, "I have to go home and play with the dolly." She makes one more stab at drinking the water, and when I am not interested, frantically paints one last picture, and we depart. She asks to carry the water down, since we have to take it downstairs to empty it. She goes down very successfully, quietly and carefully until she has reached the first floor. Her interest is diverted to someone in the telephone booth and she walks into the wall, spilling the water all over the floor and the wall. It is amusing to see how disconcerted she is by badness which had not been intended. I say, "It was an accident,—too bad, but get a paper towel and wipe it up." When I say good-by, she is cleaning up the floor busily.

On the whole, this is one of the quietest hours we have had. The general level is distinctly less noisy and rough.

In the Waiting-room

Helen shows her father the note—"Helen P. is not going down to Atlantic City."

Worker: "Where are you going, Helen?"

Helen: "To the country, ain't I, Daddy?" "Yes," says her father.

July 6, 1931, Monday—Fifteenth hour

Helen comes in so quietly that her "Boo!" really does surprise me. "Is it early?" she says.

"I think it is just about the usual time."

"Can I stay until eleven?"

"No, just the regular time."

"But I'm going to see the doctor."

"Oh, yes, you will be able to stay, but I shall have to go as usual."

She wanders around the room. "I don't know what to do this morning. Someone has been in my drawer." Then she examines the ink. "Did you tell the Mister to take the ink away?"

"No."

"Did you get rid of it?"

"No, I think it just dried up, Helen." I have been writing rapidly to get down this bit about the ink, and she quickly starts me adding. It is interesting how annoyed she is at my writing. It is the one thing she can't bear. I can hardly get down a word now without being stopped.

When she has tired of the adding game she says, "Now I think I'll let you draw. Maybe it would be better if you painted." Finally she hands me the crayons and keeps the paint herself. "I want you to paint a hot day,"—I having just complained of the heat.

"But, Helen, I don't know how to do that."

"Oh, yes, you do,—make a little girl sweating." She abandons this idea, however, and says I am to draw a picture of her and a little boy. "Draw a boy and a girl." She busies herself with paints while I am drawing. Finally she says, "Oh, I got my hands all dirty. I'm not allowed to get dirty. I must go and wash my hands."

"In the country you will be able to be dirty."

"But I'm not going to the country."

Then she begins talking about what happened over the week-end. She describes an accident which she and her brother witnessed in the Park. Two automobiles ran into each other, and a little boy got his chin cut, and two men got arrested and they had to get a taxi. And there was something else about a boy who fell down a bank and broke his back.

At this point she decides that she will go downstairs and see if she can find the doll. "Now you draw a mother and father while I'm gone, and you'll have plenty of work to do. I'll be up again soon and you draw the father and all." Soon she scares me again with the "Boo!" and, seeing that I have completed my task, she insists that I shall add a baby. Then she makes me write names under the figures. The little boy is Walter.

She now wanders into the other room where she becomes interested in the ediphone. She thinks it is like a telephone and tries to talk through it. We have a long conversation, with me at the other end of the wire, about her baby, which she insists she left at my house and she hasn't seen it since. When I try to say good-by, she holds me on the wire and finally suggests that I come to see her. This is apparently the consummation of a long desired visit. I agree, and soon I am rapping at her door. She invites me in, gives me a chair, but soon we are diverted again to the telephone conversation, once more on the subject of the lost baby. Then she gets the idea that it would be fun to play hide-and-seek. By this time the play is getting much too active for me, but we do hide in the few available spots, to Helen's intense delight.

It is interesting to see the change in the quality of her play. She really enjoys the play for itself this time, in addition to its value of keeping me out of mischief. She is not rough and there is no showing off. It is much more the attitude she might take toward a playmate. I finally tell her I cannot play hide-and-seek any more, and then I say we have only five minutes left if she is going to see the doctor this morning. She returns to the painting, and colors the pictures that I have drawn. I ask her if she is coming down next Thursday, and if that will be the last time, as she is going to the country. She only says she isn't going now, and says good-by to me very happily.

From Father's Interview

On Sunday Helen said, "You forgot to take me to the cemetery yesterday." She meant the country. Father explained that she would go the following Saturday.

July 9, 1931, Thursday—Sixteenth hour

Helen comes in holding the doll which I had found and put down in the waiting-room, so that she would have it for the last morning. "So you found your baby, did you?"

"Yes, she's come back. She was sitting in the chair."

"I hope she is well."

"I think she's been sick from the way she looks," says Helen. "Where's the lady?"

"What lady do you mean, Helen?"

"The one downstairs in the first room."

"I don't know. Isn't she down there?" I discovered later that she was referring to the young woman who is usually at the phone and who had gone on vacation.

Helen concentrates on the telephone, and this time I show her how to play with it without attracting the operator's attention. It is interesting to see that she carefully observes this, and when she is too busy to hold the receiver down she asks me to do it for her. She enjoys the telephone conversation hugely. She calls me up and says that I am to come up to see her and bring the baby, as she left it in my room. She takes great satisfaction in getting me to come to her. Fully half of the hour I cannot get near the paper to take any notes, as she keeps me so busy doing what she wants me to do. She shuts me in the room, locks the door, and pretends I am a policeman, or that she is a policeman coming to arrest me, and then I am to give the wrong address so we will fool the policeman. This goes on for some time without a great deal of point, just the fun of using the telephone and locking the doors. Finally I say I am so tired I must have a rest, and I go back to my own seat.

Helen was fifteen minutes late this morning and I ask her why. She says it was the cars. This is the regular excuse. "Are you going away, Helen? How about your vacation?"

"Yes," she says; "I'm going on Saturday, and maybe I'm going to stay two Fridays, and then will you be here?" She looks doubtfully at me and finally says, "No, you won't be here." And I say, "No, I am going on my vacation in two or three weeks." "That's how long I'm going to stay," she says.

At this point I have begun to take notes, and Helen is obviously annoyed and tries to find something that will be bad enough to make me stop writing. She goes for the ink and threatens to put the water in it. "Helen, it would be too bad if you should get ink all over your dress on the last day. What would your mother say to me?"

"Oh, I'm only fooling you," she says. "I wouldn't do it really." She begins to get a little rough, however, drags out the clay and begins to bang it around. "This is the last of the mud. I'm going to take it home. Can I take it home?" "If you want to—it is the last of the clay, and the last of the girl," I say laughingly.

Then she gets out her paints and begins playing with her favorite red. She gives the brush a pretty strong flick out of the water so that the water flies. "I was scared," she says.

"Do you mean that you were scared right now, or are you thinking of the time you spilled the water?"

"I was scared then, too."

As she continues with pretty rough use of the paint and flops the clay around, I say, "Helen, you must be a little mad at me this morning. You seem to feel pretty rough." But she denies it.

Presently I tell her it is getting late, and that she has only ten minutes longer.

"Can't I stay until eleven?"

"No, Helen, you know I have to go the same as usual to-day."

"But I have to see the doctor."

"I don't think you have to this morning."

"Can't I stay up here alone after you are gone?"

"I don't know, perhaps you can. But your father will want to go home and go to sleep."

Then she begins to talk a little about the place where she is going on her vacation. She has quite a little apprehension about it. "What do they give you there, and do they feed you?"

"I should think they would, Helen. I never heard of a place like that where they didn't give little girls food."

"Is it nice country? Will I like it?"

"I think it probably is nice country, and I hope the sun will come out."

"Maybe I won't like it, and maybe I won't stay—maybe I'll come down here next Monday."

She puts her painting paper down on the chair, together with the water and the paints. "Now you can hardly see me, can you? I'm going to make some lady." She sings to herself quite gaily and smiles coquettishly at me.

After a while she starts the cut finger game, with the red paint dripping off the end. This she keeps up for fully five minutes, but finally she says, "It really isn't cut. I was just fooling you," and she comes around to show me the scratch that was there before. I announce that the time is up, only two or three minutes more.

"Oh, but we can't go. You haven't done anything. You haven't done your spelling."

"But Helen, I am afraid there isn't time for my spelling."

"If you do it in a hurry there will be time." So I write the alphabet twice over.

Very reluctantly, but sweetly, she parts with each separate object, and puts it back in the drawer. She wants the alphabet which I have done, evidently as a parting present from me, and I take her painting. This morning I am allowed to carry the paint water for safety, and she takes everything else. When she gets downstairs she is a little excited, finds the situation a bit trying. When I finally say good-by to her she holds out the doll and says, "Kiss the baby," which I do. "You kiss it, too," I say, "and good-by. I hope you have a nice vacation."

"Maybe my father will phone," she says, "and let me come in. Have you got your drawing?"

"Yes," I reply, "I have the drawing," and I close the door, while Helen gives a little cry and jumps around excitedly.

In the Waiting-room

As the worker came into the waiting-room, Helen said in an excited voice, "Good-by, I'm going away." Worker answered, "You're going to the country, aren't you, Helen? I hope you will have a good time." Helen answered, "Sure." She turned to her father. "When are you coming for me?" Father turned the question back to her. Helen found it difficult to answer. She was sure she was going on Saturday, the day after to-morrow, and then mentioned that Friday was the day the father was to visit. Father asked which Friday, and Helen counted several times the days of the week, sometimes making it the first Friday, and sometimes taking it beyond the next Saturday and Sunday. "Can you come for me on a Friday, Daddy? If you come early enough, you can bring me down here." Father: "You mean the Friday after next?" Worker suggested she might wait until she saw the farm and then decide when to come home. Helen forgot her paper with the alphabet and lingered at the door, pointing out the "H" that stood for her name. Father said she would have to come along, and she gave the same rather breathless good-by.

About five minutes later father and Helen returned to Clinic. Helen stood quietly by with a confused look on her face, very intent on her father's words. Father was explaining that Helen had told him that she had to go back to the doctor on Thursday. She twisted her thumb behind her,—"The other doctor." Worker said that the doctor had not said anything to her or to her father, and an examination like that was usually over in one time—worker didn't think she had to return. Helen accepted this with no comment. It was clear she did not want to leave. Father: "I forgot to ask what she needed." Worker stated she could go just as she was and not take anything. They had play suits for the children. Helen still stood there, staring a bit blankly. Father drew her toward the door and Helen called, "Good-by." She repeated this when outside the door.

III. THEORETICAL IMPLICATIONS

ANYONE familiar with the Freudian approach either in child or adult analysis will have been struck already by the marked difference of viewpoint and method which this material implies. Perhaps the difference may seem to lie rather in what is absent than what is present. Conspicuously lacking are all the familiar efforts to bring out sex material, developmental history, and parental relationships, nor have I made any attempt, except occasionally when misled by old habits, to force the child into using one content rather than another. As far as I could, I left her free to fashion her hours as she pleased, to fill them with any symbols which suited her purpose and expressed however unconsciously the feeling of the moment. Interpretation, also, is obviously missing as far as Œdipus and castration fears are concerned. In fact there really is no intellectualized interpretation at all (nor would there be with an adult from my point of view) beyond my constant effort to comprehend and respond overtly to the salient feelings and impulses of the hour as present living realities, which a child, like an adult, usually seeks to deny consciously. In fact, from one viewpoint, analysis of the Rankian variety is nothing but an opportunity to feel in the present and gradually to begin to accept responsibility for one's own feelings and impulses in all their ambivalence, with as little denial, rationalization and justification as may be.

Resistance, too, is evident enough here on every page but it is never handled by interpretation nor is any attempt made to break it. Rather it is met, as far as possible, frankly and without denial or counter resistance in feeling, even when its practical execution must be checked, and with a real appreciation of its inevitability and positive value as an expression of the child's will however negatively put.

Perhaps the feature of difference most conspicuously present is the emphasis on time. This came about not so much through my Rankian principles as because the ending was set in advance by practical considerations. Certainly in working with an adult no such arbitrary arrangement would be planned by me although it might happen. But in this case I was really glad of the protection of a predetermined limit which I tried quite consciously with the use of suggestion to put in terms of Helen's vacation rather than my own. However, I am convinced that the suggestion was as acceptable to her as to me and if she had shown genuine unreadiness to take it, I was quite prepared to announce my own vacation well in advance and to work through the more intense resistance and resentment which this would probably have occasioned.

Perhaps the aspect which surprised me as much as it may have surprised the reader is the way in which Helen herself seizes upon every limitation or alteration in time and makes it the bone of contention between us. An adult will react, too, just as promptly, though less openly, to the time elements but one does not expect a child to be so aware. Possibly my own interest in time in this particular case increased her sensitivity to it. Be that as it may, the picture is true in spite of its unusual emphasis. Time,—the time of the individual hour, the number of hours per week, the total number of weeks, all represent, in their different spans, units of experience in which life is accepted, if at all, as it goes, on the painful terms of giving up, of separation, of reluctant admission that it is possible and, if guilt is not too strong, even desirable, to go on to the new experience however precious that which is left behind.

Perhaps just this way of looking at time and the series of endings, of separations of which analysis, like life, is made up, may bring out the difference in the Rankian understanding and use of the transference, so much feared by the lay person. You will find in this material clear evidence of the growing positive feeling, expressed shyly in such phrases as, "I love you and you love me" (note that she will not carry full responsibility for the emotion but makes me share it). My response is first of all to accept her feeling simply, ignoring her reference to mine, and second, to bring out the equally real negative feelings which she is not so ready to admit but which are easier to bear in the presence of the positive and actually strengthen them. If I emphasize the positive at the time she is expressing it, it will throw her back again into the negative. The fact that I can carry the negative side leaves her free to feel the positive to the full. In no case do I try to deny the love emotions or to belittle them but only to balance them with the inevitable opposite which

Helen is expressing in action anyway while denying it consciously.

Transference, like resistance, is accepted for what it is, a stage in the growth process, in the taking over of the own will into the self. It is the point at which the will is yielded up to the other, is worshipped, if you please, in the other and kept in abeyance in the self. Inevitably, as inevitably as life goes on of its own impulse, this transference projection will flow back into the positive will of the patient and be acknowledged as his, unless the vanity of the analyst or his own inability to let himself be abandoned, increases the guilt of the patient so that he cannot admit his own will and the desire to be free. From Rank's point of view, there need be no anxiety about fixation on the analyst, or about breaking up the transference, if one believes in life and growth and individuality. All one need to do is to look to one's own emotions and see that they do not interfere with the struggle of the patient to find himself. The more positive and conscious the emotion he feels for the analysis or the analyst at the end, the more sure one may be, that the actual dependence is over. Conscious feeling measures the degree of the giving up; indicates the abandonment of the effort to possess the other, in favor of the will to be oneself, to go on. One truly loves only what one leaves.

There is something very touching about the fact that life is true to itself even in a child of seven. Despite my experience with adults and my own analysis, somehow I could not believe that a child would be able to bear the leaving of a situation which can take on such meaning as the analytic relationship. My fear expressed itself as it naturally would ambivalently: first, would a child find anything in this type of analysis to compensate for the deprivations, and, second, if it did, could it give up what it had found. In other words, I was afraid either that nothing would happen or that too much would happen, a common enough fear with all of us. Apparently my fear for the child was nothing but my doubt of myself projected, the possibility that I might not be able to bear the child's transference or his withdrawal. It is evident to me now that the child, like the adult, can save himself, can adapt himself to whatever time is at his disposal, can select and use what he needs, go as deep as it is safe to go under the circumstances and no deeper, provided only the analyst is able to see what the child is doing, to bear it, and to be willing to let the child conquer, to have it, finally, his way.

This brings me back to what is after all the only essential in analysis, to speak statically, the bare bones of the process stripped of all content, whether it be drawn from past, present, or future, and this is the meeting of two wills; in this case the actual cash with the child, the living immediately present action and reaction of her will upon mine, which constitutes whatever of reality, therapeutic or otherwise, there may be in the relationship.

Nothing is more obvious than the will conflict which Helen sets up from the first moment of her resistance to going with me to the final leave-taking and her reluctance to say good-by. The initial hesitation and fear which I overcome by direct pressure are followed at once as fast as she gains courage by a great variety of methods of attack, ways of trying out my strength and testing her own negatively; for instance, her persistent efforts from the beginning almost to the bitter end, to find something which she can force me to let her take home. It is not so much a matter of wanting the things she takes, she doubtless destroys or loses them almost at once, but of enjoying the process, the conflict itself. If I gave her everything she asked for, she would only go on to find the forbidden object. She is looking for an external limit, for someone who has the strength to stand up to her but who will not turn upon her destructively. Like all the rest of the world, she longs to find that rock upon which she may safely lean, but to be free also to leave it when she gets ready. It takes a great deal of testing out, many attacks upon me, to get to the point where she feels her own will safe enough from my encroachment to yield it up in the transference emotion of the sixth and seventh hours. Even here aggressiveness is only suspended momentarily, her behavior is still a challenge, now intended more to arouse feeling in me, to make me the one to care rather than to get the better of me externally. The battle continues to the very end as it must but the admission of herself, her own intentions and feelings grows more constant and free. "I won't do it really, I'm only fooling you," "Everything I do is to fool you." This kind of frankness becomes quite the rule. Her dislike of my writing which is present from the beginning but is very indirect at first and apparent only in her increased attempts to gain my attention or prevent me from using the pencil by borrowing it, finally breaks out into an explosive, "Stop that writing" and an admission that it makes her mad. The clash over the ink which comes along in the second half of the relationship has a totally different character from that of earlier encounters. We are now able to be humorous, to assert and accept each other's difference. She allows for my dislike of spilled ink; I enjoy her breaking the letter of the law when the ink dries up enough to make it possible to play with it. A certain tolerance has come into our relationship as well as a mutual understanding. Perhaps this is what she is trying to express in the tenth hour when she says, "You think what I think."

This movement which so obviously takes place as the relationship develops, chiefly in terms of Helen's attitude but secondarily of mine too, results from the nature of the analytic situation, the only situation in life where one is allowed to project to the limit without the interference of counter projection. Because I do not fight Helen back, do not try to conquer her but see and admit the nature even of the negative feelings which naturally arise when her efforts to conquer me come to naught, she is forced for lack of anything to oppose, to fall back upon other aspects of herself, and slowly, with many denials, withdrawals, and negative interludes, she begins to project the positive will, the possessive attitudes. Now she tries to control me through her positive interest instead of the negative. As Santa Claus she gives me the presents I have refused her; she makes me come to see her in play even if I won't in reality; she is the teacher, I am the pupil who is to be corrected. Yet underlying this play world in which she controls me is always the reality of time and place as well as my separateness which continually throws back upon the self of the child even the most positive projection. Gradually, however, so much of herself both positive and negative has been expressed and accepted without interference that now she is somewhat released from the drive to defeat or dominate the other and can take it back partially into herself with new recognition and tenderness for the person who has permitted the projections and a guilt for the dawning impulse to leave the restraining though satisfying conditions under which she has begun to chafe.

It is interesting to see that after the ninth and tenth hours in which she comes to a climax of aggressive possession of me and the situation with wild play and the spilling of water over the blotter, there follows in the eleventh hour just what one would expect, the climax of guilt feeling and the overt expression of anxiety. Repentance and uneasiness regarding her treatment of the blotter are almost the only signs and admissions of fear during the entire time except her reference to being scared in the last hour, while the confession of her sin of clothes tearing in terms of the reformed doll baby is also the only time when the behavior for which she was brought to clinic is spontaneously mentioned.

It is at this point that my traditional morality and pedagogical responsibility for the young overcome the analyst and I am caught in the net of content to the extent of trying to teach her something about the folly of tearing one's own clothes. Analytically, I should realize that she brings up the tearing of clothes as symbolically as she might any tale from her past or dream of the night before to carry her present feeling of guilt which arises not from any actual tearing but from the change in relation to me. She is guilty for what she has done to me, for the freedom of will she has exercised in the situation, for the fact that she has let herself go so far in yielding to another and still more for the realization that underneath she is already feeling the impulse to go. With Helen, clothes tearing is the cardinal sin of the local situation, not lying, stealing or sex as with many children and she brings it in at the moment when she is most aware of guilt to express her present feeling in the analytic situation. That she resents my taking advantage of her to preach is clearly evidenced in her rising from the chair and attacking the doll so viciously. I come to in time to accept this feeling at least, for what it is, an attack upon me, a justifiable resentment for my lack of understanding.

Perhaps what brings the relationship to so sharp a climax at this point, is my deliberate reference in the ninth hour to the close of school, and the fact that she will want to stop coming sometime. This she denies stoutly at first but when I persist, "But you may not always want to come" she says reluctantly as if the truth came out in spite of her, "No, not always." This admission naturally brings about its own denial as a reaction, an aggressive taking possession of the next hour with the simultaneous expression of hate and tenderness, a desire to hurt, to get even, combined with positive emotion, "You always make me happy . . . make me feel nice." The eleventh hour then, naturally produces the full confession of the ambivalent will and the determination to use it constructively at least for that hour; "I'm going to work, not play at all, but see how much I can draw" which expresses as with adults the need for a social justification of will. In this very hour, she herself refers to the closing of school and by the twelfth hour, is almost willing to admit both her love and her readiness to go in one breath.

Guilt, as I have been using it in the Rankian meaning, is an inevitable by-product of self-conscious living, not a symptom of which one may be cured. It arises from the fundamental dualism of life itself as expressed in the ambivalence of will; that human capacity for wanting and not wanting the same thing at the same moment, and the bi-polarity of fear, on the one hand the fear of becoming a separate individual, on the other the fear of dying without having lived.[1] Therapy for guilt and fear conflicts is possible only through an experience in relationship which frees the will from a one-sided expression or repression and leads to a frank admission and utilization of its own contrariness. The emotional, not merely the intellectual acceptance of the ambivalence and the responsibility for it (which is made possible in the analytic experience) can reduce guilt and fear, if anything can, to proportions which are at least compatible with living.

Helen is not the sensitive, self-conscious type that betrays itself so clearly by guilt and fear symptoms. On the contrary she is a creature of impulse, of unrestrained action. She admits of no barrier between herself and the "object" but puts every impulse into immediate execution leaving responsibility to those who

[1] See "Die Analyse des Analytikers," Part 3 of "Technik der Psychoanalyse," by Otto Rank.

so readily assume it, her father and the school. It is for them to check her if they can. She acts and lets them think. Fear which of course underlies her behavior is quite deeply buried under aggression, and guilt too is smothered by activity and the discipline enforced by others. In spite of all the show of emotion and apparent strength, Helen is not on the way to a highly individualized, powerful self. Her will is too unconscious, too impulsive, too negative. It is determined largely by a need to resist someone else rather than a pressure to be itself. It takes no responsibility for itself, finds no planned constructive expression but is content to defeat and destroy in opposition to other wills. What saves her is the comparative absence of strong hatred. With her, negativism as yet is only a game, an exercise of will in the only form she knows, which is full of zest and crowds out fear momentarily. There is nothing genuinely hateful or viciously destructive here but an unfortnate pattern developed to a considerable degree in terms of the father's interest in it. Underlying the obstreperous behavior is a real sweetness which slowly becomes apparent as acquaintance progresses. What she needs is an experience with someone who will not hold her to the negative expression by punishing it, enjoying it, or taking responsibility for it but allow her to satisfy the need for "the other" both positively and negatively sufficiently to permit the will towards individuation, towards separation and growth to come to overt expression.

Such an experience it was my intention to make possible provided she chose to take it and it seems to me quite clear that, however superficial the relationship which is developed here on so slight a basis in time, it is qualitatively a true growth experience, authentic in form and direction. In fact, no matter how prolonged the time, from this viewpoint no analysis is ever completed any more than growth is completed until the final separation of death brings the individual to an apparent ending. Time therefore is always a more or less arbitrary element in analysis and depends largely upon the theoretical conviction of the analyst or upon his sensitivity to the patient's will to leave, his belief in the patient's strength and ability to carry himself and his own willingness to be overcome and deserted. No human being separates from his past in a growth process all at once or completely. Separation experiences are always partial and always repeated at different levels throughout analysis and throughout life. Analysis is merely a concentrated, intensified opportunity for growth under safer and more nearly controlled conditions than life ordinarily affords but only the patient can determine how deep he will go, how far he will separate, or how consciously he will face the emotion of any particular ending.

If Helen had come to me every day over a period of several months, nothing essentially different would have developed as far as general form and movement are concerned. The content, however, the symbols chosen to express the deepening emotional experience, might have taken on a more intimate personal character, might possibly have turned to sex differences, to the various aspects of the physical relation to the mother or social relation to the father, to the details of toilet training or what not, in order to express the growing intensity and gradual acceptance of the fear, guilt, hate, love and jealousy which the analytic situation calls out. However if Helen herself had never brought up such material, it would not have been introduced by me as essential for therapy. From my experience and theoretical belief, the entire gamut of impulse and emotion with the final constructive taking over of the own self and the voluntary giving up of the analytic relationship may well be lived through by certain individuals in non-biological, even non-sociological terms with or without dreams, sometimes with the use of only the most trivial, flimsy content drawn from the local situation and current events. Content is necessary for communication as paint or some other medium is necessary for a picture, but the therapeutic reality is the actual dynamics of the relationship as it develops from hour to hour between the two human beings who enter upon it, the one as patient the other as helper.

From my viewpoint, then, it is not possible to think of one's contacts even with a child as justified by the possibility that he will work out verbally or in action the traumas of his infancy or reproduce and solve either Œdipus or castration complex as related to his parents.[2] He will and can do only one thing; that is, undergo whatever new experience is permitted in the living present in relation to the analyst. If that has depth, significance, and a constructive taking over of will on the part of the child then he will have gained something therapeutic for himself, even though neither

---

[2] See "The Psycho-Analysis of Children," by Melanie Klein (1932), and "The Technic of Child Analysis," by Anna Freud, for two contrasting viewpoints.

parents nor school teachers appear to profit by the results in behavior. Whether such individual treat- ment as this is often advisable where children are con- cerned is for me a very grave question but I think there is no use to deceive ourselves as to what we do when we undertake direct contacts with a child, no use to disguise present realities of which we are a vital part under the veil of intellectual interpretation of the past which after all is gone forever and can never again be utilized for therapy.

Two points remain to be discussed which might be brought against this conception and practical illustra- tion of the analytic relationship. One might easily accuse me of too great activity, of suggesting to the child what she ought to feel. On the other hand, it would be equally possible to convict me of over-pas- sivity, of allowing material to go by without interpreta- tion, of accepting resistance as cheerfully as coöpera- tion. I myself should describe my rôle as highly active but never intentionally suggestive, unless by that is meant making the child more conscious of the nature and meaning of her own feeling and actions. Suggestion, as it is ordinarily used, implies a putting over of something of one's own upon the other, the weaker person, some- thing which one believes the other ought to feel, think, or do, even if he has no impulse of his own in that di- rection. Such use of suggestion in my experience, never gets far because the other, however weak he may seem, always rebels. When I attempt to interpret or to sug- gest as, for instance, I seem to do quite arbitrarily in the third hour with regard to the drawing, it is only because I am convinced of, or better said "feel" immediately the underlying implication of the words or actions and respond on that basis. I am prepared to be wrong—for one may always misunderstand—but if I am, the child will not let me escape. She will block, will resist and resent my failure to see her truly as she did in the eleventh hour (Mrs. Brown and the doll who tore her clothes). The evidence to me of the correctness of my responses lies in the movement, the fact that she is freed to go on to further experience.

It is not so easy as it sounds to learn to ignore content and to go through it to the fundamental attitudes and emotions behind it, but it is possible, if one has no need for the patient to be or feel one thing rather than another and thus is free to perceive and accept what is happening even if it means rejection of the therapeutic goal. The analyst in this view has no goal, has no right to one. He *is* passive in the sense that he tries to keep his own ends out of the situation to the extent of being willing to leave even the "cure" so-called, to the will of the patient. The patient is there to work out his own will and to use the therapist as he can, even to the final overthrow and destroying of the analytic situation. For this is required the most sensitive self-conscious activity of understanding and response plus a readiness to accept and carry to the end the losing rôle. If this be passivity, then as I see it, passivity is essential to the survival of the patient.

That Helen was able to use constructively both my activity and my passivity in this brief experience seems to be evidenced convincingly in the well-balanced organization of attitudes which she presents in the last hour. There is a freedom and an ability to bear the ambivalent emotions of parting which an adult might well envy. She is able to play with real joy even though it is the last time. She combines the old efforts to control and occupy me with a new willingness to accept limitation as in the use of the telephone. She is still annoyed at my writing and expresses in rough play the destructive attitudes which must be present no matter how consciously one accepts the will to go on. These do not shut out either the positive feelings or the inevitable fear of leaving expressed in anxious inquiry about the kind of place she is going to. She signifies her willingness to give as well as take in the parting presents and finally says good-by, courageously and sweetly, in spite of the unaccustomed emotion which sweeps over her as she presents the doll to be kissed.

Reports from the Farm to which Helen went for three weeks indicate no behavior problem [3] but as I see it therapy in the sense of socially desirable behavior can never be the goal of this type of analytic relationship. It is a purely individual affair and can be measured only in terms of its meaning to the person, child or adult; of its value, not for happiness, not for virtue, not for social adjustment but for growth and development in terms of a purely individual norm. The responsible relation which Anna Freud describes in her "Introduction to a Technic of Child Analysis" is a very different affair, much more closely allied to the rôle of parent or teacher. It is a putting over of something, an attempt to reform the child in terms of a

---

[3] As a matter of interest I wish to record the report of a social worker from the Clinic who visited Helen's school a year later (May, 1932). There had been no behavior difficulties at school this year and no visits to the school on the part of the father.

social and moral norm. That it is desirable for a child to overcome antisocial behavior one would not deny but from my point of view to enter into such a relationship with a child is to establish an obligation, a mutuality of aim and interest, a personal claim which I can see no way of carrying out sincerely unless one plans to go on indefinitely as a part of the child's educational background, or to continue to stand in loco parentis, until the child outgrows all need.

On the other hand, children who come for treatment because of antisocial behavior are often highly negative. Their behavior expresses, not so much own will, as resistance to the will of others. To me it seems a very doubtful procedure to subject such a child to the pressure of one more powerful will actually directed upon him and his behavior, however benevolently. I can see no possible escape from increased negativism and guilt unless in actuality, the relationship develops with less pressure than was consciously intended and somehow establishes a new freedom for the child without analyst or child understanding the basis of the experience.

Intention or, too often, determination to help, is from my viewpoint as poor therapy for a child as for an adult. It relieves the other of all responsibility for himself and permits of unlimited negative exercise of the own will. A child who is absorbed in resisting can escape himself and life indefinitely. It seems a pity for the analyst, therefore, even though the axe he seeks to grind be a therapeutic one, to add one more to the number of adults who stand ready to reinforce the negative mechanism.

If the child can undergo any experience which releases him from his negative will to a positive finding of himself, that experience should register ultimately as a positive gain for society; at least if it does not, what will? It may well be that parental relationships active at the moment are too determining for a young child to assert himself positively against them and that no direct analytic experience however therapeutic potentially can counteract sufficiently a damaging environmental situation. I do not know how much change, nor how much socially desirable change can take place in a child through an analytic experience without support and understanding on the part of the parents. Perhaps there are far simpler ways of improving the situation by direct approach to parents and school and a more superficially helpful contact with the child. Perhaps direct analytic treatment of a young child would seldom be indicated if analysts and child guidance clinics were not so interested in working with the child and were willing to leave with the parents the responsibility for relationship to the child and to approach the problem if at all through the parents' willingness to accept and take responsibility.

I have no answer to any of these problems, but I have tried to make clear in this simple case material what it is we really do, when we enter into the helping relationship with child or adult, and to show that therapy must remain with the individual himself, a personally chosen, not a socially dictated, goal.

PART III

THIRTY–ONE TREATMENT CONTACTS WITH
A SEVEN YEAR OLD BOY AS PREPARATION
FOR PLACEMENT IN A FOSTER HOME

I. INTRODUCTORY STATEMENT

THE case of John H. differs from that of Helen P. in many particulars but in general the theoretical implications are equally applicable to both. The chief differences for me are the greater ease and freedom of my own office, the increased confidence which the experience with Helen had engendered, the leeway in time, with the added hour a week, and the absence of a vacation restriction plus the personality of John himself who seems to me better suited to this type of therapy than Helen.

Whether the differences in environmental problem made matters better or worse for the children I do not know. Certainly it was easier for me to separate from Helen with home and family back of her than from John, who had nothing but the fear and uncertainty of a new foster home for the selection of which I had to be partially responsible. A therapist accustomed to dealing with the responsible adult or with the children of responsible parents, may well shrink from the dual rôle which forces him to a practical responsibility for his child patient, a responsibility which has no legitimate place in the therapeutic process and must be divorced from it as far as possible. To have a stake in the practical results either in terms of one's own plan or the expectation of a social agency is to run the risk of being handicapped in carrying through

the therapeutic relationship. Only after a long discipline in bearing results which others may label
"failure" and an assurance of the inherent worth of
every individual hour which requires no external justification, can one afford to take such a chance and even
so, I would not choose it were choice permitted.

Moreover, every other person related to the child
through the social agency has to be considered with reference to the therapeutic situation, since the practical
plan which determines the child's future to a large
extent depends upon the case workers who are immediately responsible for the choice of home and the relation of the agency to the foster parents. Failure to
relate oneself constructively and considerately to the
rest of the agency, to keep workers as well as the
child in mind, or to remember how difficult it is to bear
the therapeutic relationship of which one is not a vital
part, will bring out inevitable resistances and resentments which may vitiate otherwise promising therapeutic results. One can never forget that living comes first
for the child, not the relation to the therapist which
must and should yield to the realities of the practical
situation. I would go even farther and say that one
should be grateful for the practical exigencies which
the child can accept and which help him to release himself from the therapeutic situation without undue guilt.

The child cannot in the nature of things be completely responsible either for coming to the therapist
or for leaving him. He must be helped to come and
helped to go, which is true of the adult also in lesser
degree. Only one can see to it that his coming and
going take place in his own terms, according to his

own pattern as far as possible without violation of his personal freedom and integrity. The child, who cannot control the situation by paying for it as the grown-up does, needs then even more the weapon of environmental claims and obligations. It may annoy us but it also helps to make the therapeutic process possible and constructive. In this case the move to the new home carefully timed with reference to the therapeutic situation and prepared for from the start, puts John in the position of being able to leave me, not entirely in terms of his own desire it is true, but at least in terms of a practical necessity which he recognizes and which controls me also.

Perhaps the reader will note a difference in the therapist in the second relationship. The pedagogic impulse is under better control, the need to interpret or to extract material is practically absent, while the uncertainties which were so evident in the contacts with Helen are greatly reduced. There is at first an underlying nervousness as to the fate of my possessions. I do not know how far a little boy may carry his hostile attitudes. I do not want my office made unfit for use nor do I desire extra expense but this soon passes off as John and I become surer of each other. Little as it is ordinarily recognized, the therapeutic relationship involves a certain amount of fear which is mutual, in the sense that any unknown situation is a source of apprehension, far greater of course for the patient who knows so little what to expect and who has so much more at stake emotionally. Nevertheless, there is for me an appreciable and highly enjoyable difference in my approach to John as contrasted with the uncertainty of my first contacts with Helen. Fear of being inconsistent, of being in the wrong, of giving in at one point and holding out at another irrationally, is lessened to a degree. I find myself able to be almost as free and spontaneous with John, as with an adult. It is a satisfaction to discover that one can trust the moment and one's immediate feeling even in this swiftly moving, confusing impact with an active little boy, who is full of wiles and logical traps for the unwary grown-up.

From this remark it is evident that I do not consider the therapeutic process a rational or intellectualized affair for the therapist any more than it is for the patient. On the contrary, it seems to me, the therapist above all must be able to be, what the patient is not for a long time, spontaneous and aware of his own slightest feeling response. Only if he is swift and sure in regard to his own reactions can he trust them without thought as an index to the nature of the patient's momentary behavior or attitude, which has caused them. The therapist must be a barometer, sensitive to the least change in the therapeutic atmosphere, removed enough from personal necessity for this particular hour to use his more conscious and more reliable feeling reactions to bring the patient to a deeper realization and tolerance of his own. Intellectualized organization of the therapeutic experience must take place after the fact. The therapeutic value of the hour lies in its immediacy and spontaneity, but the spontaneity of the therapist must of necessity be unfailingly oriented and reoriented with reference to the patient, as the central and dominating figure of the relationship, with a prior, never to be forgotten claim. Which is one reason, perhaps *the* reason, why therapy is non-scientific, and the therapeutic relationship not open to research at the moment. If I had followed out my own theoretical interest, I should have pursued some of the biological material introduced by John, his symbolic use of the rug in a birth struggle, his references to toilet functions and breast, his use of the tent, etc. But I am convinced that in so doing I should have lost sight of and interfered with the creative use of a present experience, which I had only to understand and respond to intuitively not to interpret or investigate in terms of my own intellectual curiosity. To pursue the symbol may be science. It is not therapy.

The difference in the type of child presented in the second record is significant in what it can teach us regarding the selection of cases. John who is fearful, self-conscious, cautious, the so-called neurotic in embryo, is far more suited to relationship therapy than an impulsive child like Helen, who, denying her fear and her resentment, rushes into blind action to relieve them regardless of the other person. Relationship therapy is not all-powerful. It has its limitations, not only in what the patient can take, but also in what the therapist can accept, which will differ for every individual but is certainly limited by the necessity, therapeutic as well as personal, not to be actually injured by the patient. Every patient of necessity encroaches as far as he dares, feels his way step by step as he explores the boundaries of the therapeutic situation, comes as close as he can to the border line of the forbidden. But he depends in this process not only on the therapist's apparent immunity to attack and firmness in holding his own, but on his own capacity eventually to become aware of the inherent destructiveness of these impulse projections in their initial stages, and his willingness to inhibit them without denial of their import before they have plunged him into overt behavior which he has not chosen with his total self or which is too extreme for the therapist to accept.

These unassimilated, unorganized impulses of which he has refused to be conscious before but which have influenced his behavior without his will, must necessarily come to expression in the therapeutic situation but this is possible only in terms of speech, physical symptoms confined to his own person or in the relatively slight overstepping and disregard of the therapist which all patients manifest in terms of the hour, use of the office, payment of bill, or the like. The therapist by bringing out unfailingly the aggressive intent which such reactions mask and not allowing these slight unrecognized hostilities to mount to proportions which cannot be handled therapeutically, can usually help the patient to feel them in embryo and to accept them responsibly as part of the self however painful, without the necessity to put them out blindly in a truly injurious form. However, the less able the individual is to bear the pain of his own humanity, the less willing he is to sacrifice a partial unwilled response in favor of a consciousness which permits a choice by the whole self; in other words the less able he is to become emotionally self-conscious, the less suited will he prove for a kind of therapy which depends on the possibility of substituting feeling, emotion, thoughtful voluntary behavior for unconscious irresponsible projection.

The same problem of fitness must arise in the selection of children for individual treatment since children are naturally and necessarily far more impulsive and tend to action rather than to emotion or speech. For the self-conscious inhibited child who is burdened with fear and guilt and for whom action is a problem, the therapeutic relationship despite its restrictions may offer just the release into freer expression which he needs, while the over-impulsive child, especially if he is old enough to be classed as delinquent, may be too unable or too slow to reach the point of feeling and self-inhibition of impulse which is essential to forming a new relation to the object, and will perhaps require a discipline which is incompatible with a strictly therapeutic relationship. With such a child there is always the problem of how far he will have to carry the destructive behavior patterns before he is able to face and bear in himself, the need, pain and fear which they seek to relieve.

I recall an instance where a social worker carried out her theory of allowing the child as free an expression as possible, unprepared for however by any gradual making conscious of the hostile elements in the relationship, to the extent of allowing a nine year old boy to stab her hand repeatedly with a penknife. Very few therapists would be able or willing to bear this type of attack. This particular person apparently was, but it seems to me to indicate an identification with the child which is too great for the patient's good and to permit a degree of hostile projection which is incompatible with professional therapy. It may succeed in one instance, it certainly could not be repeated frequently.

In my first attempt at relationship therapy with a child, a girl of eleven, already a delinquent with a long record of petty stealing, lying, fighting and sex offense, I came up against a similar impasse when she stole my purse, an injury which, although real and never made good in this instance, I could bear easily enough, at least once, but whether from lack of skill or from the child's personality limitations, I was not able to handle the situation therapeutically for her. This did not happen early in the relationship but after a month or two of effort to bring her to an emotional realization of her desire to hurt. I can see now that a freer use of prohibition and a franker defense of myself against her unadmitted slighter attacks, might have broken through her denial before it reached such a pitch, but even so, I question the feasibility of living through so strenuous an experience with a child whose fear is so great, whose capacity to bear it is so slight and whose patterns of antisocial behavior are already so thoroughly established.

If with the best skill the therapist can exercise, the patient cannot or will not accept the limitations of the therapeutic situation, then it seems to me the impossibility of therapy under these conditions should be frankly admitted and the patient helped to go as constructively as possible before he has hurt himself and the therapist by putting his aggressive impulses into execution. Actual injury is a wound to both and can seldom be incorporated into a therapeutic relationship without too great a denial of pain or too extreme identification resulting in a real tie which implies more or less permanent responsibility. The child, like the adult, wants to hurt in order to establish the reality of the therapist's love. If he cannot turn this aggression first into conscious awareness of need and then into anger and pain, he will not be able to reach the point of tenderness where the impulse to injure is taken over and inhibited voluntarily by the whole self for love of the other. Instead, he will remain on the level of action, where a mutual relationship in reality is possible. The best place to deal with this problem of fitness is at the point of selection, unless one's interest is largely experimental. If one must consider budget, time and a practical program, the confirmed delinquent is certainly questionable as a choice for relationship therapy. Technically however, the same kind of problem can become acute with a child of any age or type where the therapist holds to a theory of passivity for himself and complete freedom of expression for the child. The four or five year old may turn his attention to a different form of encroachment, a seeing how far he can go in investigating the person of the therapist, or sharing in intimate functions. Here too it is a question of limits and these are difficult to set up and hard for the child to accept unless they have been maintained frankly and vigorously from the first hour.

Theoretically whether the child stabs, steals, or oversteps with regard to one's person makes little difference. The point which is important for therapy is the necessity for accepting limitation, in the self and in the other. The therapist who cannot bear to re-sist the child, to insist upon his own rights when they are threatened as well as to respect the rights of the child, violates in my opinion the very nature of the therapeutic relationship, which in the last analysis can be used constructively for release only when its limita-tions are upheld. Otherwise it becomes a substitute for, not a gateway to, reality. In the case of John, the barriers I set up are much more naturally and easily maintained than with Helen, partly because Helen is so much more aggressive but also because I am more free to be myself. It might be simpler to work with children in a playroom where there is nothing to be hurt and one's personal possessions are not threat-ened. In that case the struggle would only be shifted to some other limit which might or might not be easier to handle. Since for the child as for the adult, it is no particular goal which is desired but the process of striving and testing one's strength, any set up no matter how carefully guarded will be utilized eventually for the will conflict on which therapy depends.

II. SOCIAL BACKGROUND AND
IMMEDIATE SITUATION

Selection of Case

JOHN is a seven year old boy (born 11–30–23) committed by the court as a dependent child to the Children's Aid Society of Pennsylvania in which I function as supervisor of permanent placement. My contacts are with the case workers, not the children, so that I should never have met John in the ordinary course of events. When the record of this boy was sent to me by the reception worker for suggestions as to a permanent foster home, I was so dubious over the possibility of giving him a satisfactory home in view of the apparently destructive attachment to his own mother, and so impressed with the picture of extreme fearfulness and resistance to growth, that I proposed an experiment in preliminary therapeutic interviews with myself as an outside person unrelated to John as far as Children's Aid authority was concerned. This procedure is entirely impractical for a large child placing agency as a matter of routine and for the most part unnecessary. Very few children need such preliminary attention because very few children fail to respond quite promptly to a home which meets their needs. Special therapy, in our experience, is seldom indicated particularly with younger children if our placements are well chosen.

But there are occasional cases where the attachment to the own parent, usually the mother, seems too strong to break and too destructive to encourage. Sometimes patient case work with the parent and a very wise foster home will handle even this type of problem at least on the level of surface adjustment, but at times we are forced to admit that a particular child is not placeable in any home we can provide. In the picture of John H., as presented to me, I saw a comparatively young child of potential promise likely to prove impossible for placement because of the extreme fear, the excessive fixation on a mother who failed to give any real return in care or feeling, and a number of habits so hard to bear that any foster home placement could easily be broken up by them if John himself were resisting the situation inwardly, while accepting it outwardly.

Why I should have picked out this particular child, and whether he, like many others, might not have adjusted without my intervention I will not attempt to answer. Obviously he appealed to me personally and I was glad of another opportunity to try out therapeutic contacts with a child. Also I was quite aware that this could be no precedent. It was a single case, and John was no more neurotic than many others who had gone and would continue to go, untreated. Another element was the fact that I happened to have some time to give to it. In any case, whatever my rationalization we finally decided to make the experiment for what we might learn and John might gain personally even though we should never be able to afford the time and money to repeat it for any other child. I might add that I had no guilt regarding the child this time, since after the experience with Helen I knew what a child might get from such an experience and that it could do no harm, if controlled not experimentally in the scientific sense, but in the interest of and from the viewpoint of the child.

John as a Placement Problem:

Perhaps the best way to give the picture of John and his background briefly, is to quote from the summary written for my use in selecting a home by the reception worker Mrs. T. who later brings John on his visits to my office.

Reasons for Placement

Mrs. H. requested that care be given John since she could not keep him any longer. She and Mr. H. had separated a year and a half ago after six years of continual quarrelling, drunkenness and fighting. The real difficulty between the two started when Mrs. H. was carrying Jackie. Mr. H. came home drunk night after night and beat her. Mrs. H. and Paul, the older boy, went to live with her mother. Jackie stayed with her sister who had three children. They were living that way when we came into the case. Mrs. H. said that Jackie could not stay with her since he got on her mother's nerves. Jackie was nervous and needed a great deal of medical attention and they could not afford it. Then, too, she had to get a job, and her sister had to get a job, too, so they could not any of them take care of Jackie who was a lot of trouble. Mrs. H. says she wants us to keep him until his health gets better. We feel she might leave him with us for a year, two years, or possibly longer. It is hard to tell at this time.

Relationship to Own Family

Jackie is very attached to his mother. He looks for her to come every week and is continually disappointed by her not appearing. He does not want to go to another home. He wants to go back to his mother. On the other hand Mrs. H. is not so interested in Jackie. She visits him but once a month. She tells him she is coming and then does not appear. She promises him she will phone every day, then does not fulfill her promise. He never cries as a result of these disappointments, but seems crushed and resorts to infantile behavior as bed-wetting, being unable to dress himself, etc. He makes a definite distinction between himself and his brother Paul. Paul does not have to do the things he does because Paul is not sick. He never talks of Paul or mentions his name when speaking of his family, nor does he seem to like his aunt, with whom he lived. He longs for his mother continually and no one can take her place. He will not easily accept a foster home.

Worker's Evaluation of Child

Since he has been in his foster home Jackie has shown several signs of regression and complete inability to face living. His second night at the foster home he threw up his supper. He wets himself continually both during the day and at night. He cannot seem to get dressed completely without having to be told that he has forgotten something, except when his mother is coming. Then he will be the first one up and have all his clothes on, even his glasses. On the other hand, when he has made visits to the clinic or to C.A.S. he has not been a retiring or bashful child. He gives one the impression that he can stand on his own feet and take care of himself. He takes an interest in everything that goes on around, asking questions when he does not understand something. He does not mix with other children very well. He told us of the many things he did! He fought all the boys in the neighborhood. He ran faster than any of them, when playing football, etc. We know from his mother and from his foster mother, however, that he does not play with the children. He sits on his bicycle and watches them playing. He continually wants to be babied and told what to do. His mother, aunt and grandmother always ask how the baby is and treat him like a two year old. His mother, when she visits in the foster home, dresses him, bathes him and even carries him around in her arms. The foster mother is at her wit's end about him. She thinks she has made no progress with Jackie. She feels that she has tried everything to get him to change his behavior but has failed to bring about any good results. We feel she expects too much to want him to change his whole attitude and behavior immediately, but her attitude might be shared by another foster mother. It is necessary that the foster mother be quiet and loving and not aggressive or too interested in working out problems.

Jackie is in the first grade. His I.Q. is 95. He seems to have difficulty in his school work, which is probably due to his emotional instability. He has enuresis and occasional masturbation. He is a small and forlorn looking youngster with glasses. Nevertheless he is a likeable child, but he will find it difficult to adjust in a foster home.

L. T.

The medical examinations show underweight, but aside from teeth, tonsils and internal strabismus, there is no physical problem.

Environmental Background during Treatment:

John was taken from his aunt's home and placed in a temporary agency boarding home on 10–26–31, where he was to remain while going through with the psychological and medical examinations preliminary to permanent placement. In this home he saw his own mother frequently and seemed contented enough but the foster mother was very critical of his baby ways and blamed his mother for them. His bed-wetting and masturbation continued unabated in spite of her efforts to train him. Later, we learned that he was spanked frequently for enuresis. It was soon evident that despite his apparent acceptance of the home, he was resisting strenuously and finally the foster mother became impatient for his removal. Since by this time we had decided to try individual therapy, it seemed better to move John to a second temporary home, so that he might utilize the leaving of the therapist and the temporary home at the end of treatment as a swing away from the old, including his own mother, into the new situation which would be a permanent home selected carefully with John in mind.

The second temporary home was not ideal but on the whole John although disturbed at being moved was freer and happier there partly because he needed the home less while relying on his relation to the therapist. He was placed there 2–19–32 and began to visit me 2–25–32.

John's Relation to the Visits

No explanation was ever made to John as to his coming except the first time when the worker, Mrs. T., brought him in for a visit to medical clinic and told him he was to stay with a friend of hers for an hour until she was ready to go. Since my private office is across the street from the Social Service Building this seemed not unnatural. I used suggestion and the pressure of the worker's assumption that she was to bring him back, to get him to return two or three times.

After that he was free to stop if he so desired and I really meant this. It seems to me that no child has a basis for choice until he has gained some idea of what it is like by coming several times. After that, I believe the relationship should stand or fall absolutely on its own merits, as it would in the case of an adult and for my own part, I know that I should be unable to go on with a relationship which the child could not accept fundamentally, despite the inevitable resistances.

John never knew clearly what was my relation to Children's Aid. While he frequently saw me come into the office and I spoke to him in passing, there was never any conversation except in my private office and I took no practical responsibility as far as he knew, although I was in constant contact with the worker and of course selected the new home and planned very carefully in order to make the time for going to the new home coincide with the time for giving up the visits to me.

The worker, who was a student in training, fitted into a difficult situation and relationship remarkably. She was able to handle her own resistance to this type of treatment for John, and to let him go into the new attachment and to a new home freely, despite the value which this, her first important case, had for her. The fact that it worked so smoothly shows the genuineness of her acceptance and interest in John's progress. Placement of a child is not easy at best and to combine it with the leaving of a therapeutic relationship requires all the skill and foresight which can be brought to bear.

Office Set-up

The office consists of two rooms furnished like a private apartment with a small toilet which is reached by going across the hall at the rear. In preparing for a child I did nothing except to clear the upper part of my desk and the lowest drawer. I bought two fifty-cent dolls, which might pass for a boy and a girl, and a tiny baby doll in a bed, because I had heard that John enjoyed playing with dolls. I added to this a small baby carriage that would hold the little doll, and a few dishes with which to set the table. These were all put away in the lowest drawer together with some boxes that might be utilized in playing. In the top part of the desk there were pencils, crayons, drawing paper and a few little odds and ends that a child might be interested in. I have in the room a small red table and I brought in a little stool that a child could sit on. There were some old *New Yorkers* which could be used for cutting out.

Personal Appearance of Child

It will not do to let the reader go without some idea of John's appearance for it is all a part of the picture. He is a very undersized seven year old, and thin as he is tiny. His clothes always seem to hang loosely as if he had shrunk after getting them. His hair is very pale, almost white, his eyes which are grey-blue but look black because the pupils are so distended, are slightly crossed, behind the big and usually dirty glasses which add to his quaint, little old man quality. He holds himself rather tensely, like one on guard, and darts rapidly—running like a rabbit for shelter when he crosses the street. His face is mobile and sensitive. He is always wrinkling it up and cocking his head on one side as he looks at you with his funny squint and a quizzical expression like a little old gnome. His greatest attraction is his voice and his habit of falling into rhythm and half song as he plays. The record fails completely to give the charm of his arrival in the morning with the "Is she in or is she out"—or something equally balanced and delightfully intoned. He is a child who appeals to adults instantly, a child who is capable of seeing the adult and setting up an intimate personal relationship very quickly.

III. RECORD OF CONTACTS

February 25, 1932, Thursday—First hour

Visitor[1] appears with John a little before nine. I say, "Good morning," very casually, asking whether his name is John or Jack. "Jack," is the answer. He looks around cautiously, but with no obvious sign of fear. He understands that he is going to stay, wants to know just where he is to come afterwards. Visitor takes him to the window and points out the building. Then he inquires carefully just where she will be and how he can find her. Having satisfied himself on this point, he says, "Good-by," calmly, and at my suggestion takes off his wraps.

He makes no motion on his own initiative but is quick to pick up anything I suggest. I first take him out to the toilet, so that he may be familiar with it and free to use it if he needs to. Then I say, "I think you will find some things for children to play with in the top of the desk and in the bottom drawer." He opens the bottom drawer first and looks at every object in it without much interest, carefully returning each to its place. Then he starts in the top of the desk, and I suggest a chair, which he brings over. He is aware of me, looking around occasionally to see if I am watching. But I am absorbed in my writing, as I began taking notes from the start.

Having gone through the desk he says, "Have you any tracers?"

I do not understand at first, but soon realize it is what

[1] "Visitor" is name used for social worker in children's agency.

134

children use for drawing. "You can do your own drawings, can't you, without any tracers?"

He settles down to drawing with considerable purpose. After some silence, "Have you got any little girls or boys?"

"Do you mean around here?"

"Yes."

"No, I don't have any. Do you want them?"

"Yes, I want them to play with."

"Well, I'm sorry, but I haven't anybody."

"I'm satisfied that I have got something to draw with." To himself, "I'll make designs all the way down." He coughs.

"Do you have a cold?"

"Yes, I have to get some medicine. That's why Mrs. T. (visitor) is going to be over there."

He draws busily trying out the pencils and crayons. "What's in that tin box?"—pointing to a wooden box on top of the desk.

"You can look."

He goes through it carefully, finds a miniature pipe which has been broken in two, blows through it, then puts it back and returns to his drawing. His eye lights on an advertising pamphlet in one of the pigeonholes. "I wish I had that book."

"What would you do with it?" I ask.

"I'd try to read it."

"Are you learning to read?"

"Yes, I know a whole book."

"I don't think this book would be very good for reading. There are some books in the bottom drawer. Did you see them?" He returns to the bottom drawer and with great care takes out one of several copies of the *New Yorker*. He returns to the desk again with his book, sits down quietly.

"I wish I had a book just like this one."

"You can play with them here when you come again."

"Will somebody tear them?"

"No, I don't think so, but you can if you want to. They

are old magazines. Do you want to cut out pictures?" He assents, and I get the scissors from the top drawer.

"How many can I cut?"

"As many as you want to." He chooses a lady and has a good deal of difficulty in managing the scissors.

"Have you ever tried to cut out before?"

"Yes, my sister gave me a magazine to cut. I wonder what noise that is."

"I think it is a coal wagon going by."

"The scissors are sticky."

"I will help you cut any time you want me to, if it is too hard." He starts to come over and then thinks better of it.

"I wonder what time it is." He evidently does not understand time, but I try to explain that it is a quarter past nine.

"You can stay half an hour longer if you want to. Do you?" He thinks he does. The scissors seem to be hard to handle and he finally brings them over to me. They need oiling, and I try to fix them with cold cream, which helps a little. People go through the hall. Jack listens with some apprehension. I explain about the noises.

He goes to the front door, evidently intending to go to the toilet and corrects his error. I let him go to the toilet alone. When he returns, I suggest sitting on the floor or using the little table. He finally sits on the floor. After cutting a little, he says triumphantly, "There's one side cut out. I'm glad I didn't cut that suit case in two." More cutting. "Did *you* ever have a blood test when *you* was little? You have to have it three times."

"No, I never had one. Does it hurt?"

"You bet!" He describes in detail just how they put the needle in and—"there's a little needle with a place that holds the blood, and maybe it doesn't hurt! Mrs. T. said she had one. If you go this way," snapping the scissors briskly, "the paper comes right off."

"I guess you are learning to use the scissors, aren't you?"

"I got two things cut good, but I meant to do the other side, not this one. Oh, I cut the man right in two!"

"Sometimes if you take the whole sheet out first it is easier." He looks at me as if to find out whether he has to do what I say, but I do not look at him.

"Did *you* ever ride in the bus by yourself when *you* was little?"

"No, I rode in the street car with horses." He looks skeptical.

"*I* rode in a bus all by myself! It's a good thing I didn't get lost."

"When was this?"

"When I was at Horsham."

"How did you come this morning?"

"Mrs. T. came out to get me. We came in the trolley."

"Can you come by yourself?"

"Yes, if I have the money and the tickets." More cutting.

"Did *you* ever have your teeth out when you was little?"

"Yes."

"Did you have them filled too?"

"Yes. Do you have to have your teeth filled?"

"Yes, I have one more to do."

"Does it hurt?"

"No. I don't mind it. Did it hurt *you?*"

"Yes, it used to hurt me."

"They put a big rubber thing in my mouth. I didn't like that. It goes mm-mm-mm."

Turning the pages of the magazine, "This looks like coloring pictures."

"You can color them if you want to."

"No. I'll cut it. Can I take these home?"

"You can take all that you cut."

"Do you know the names of any of our boys and girls?"

"No, I don't believe I do. What are they?"

"Well, there are lots of Billies."

"Did you like school when you was little?"

"Yes, do you?"

"Yes."

He discovers a picture which interests him greatly. He describes the way the lady looks and finally brings it over to me at my suggestion. I say how silly they look. Then he finds a funny man. "You just ought to see him." He is evidently growing more interested in my response. "I cut that straight line. You ought to see his eyelashes, and his mouth is just like this," pursing his own. "Now he's all cut out." "You seem to be learning, Jackie. This is better than the first one."

"Yes, the first one was all raggedy. Is it time for me to go?"

"Do you want to go?"

"No."

"Well, you have five minutes longer."

"I wish I had more than that." He begins to cut out a lady.

"I didn't cut her toe off. There goes her hand almost. Look at her now. Almost her head went off." He snips the scissors, looking at me provocatively.

"What did you cut off that time?"

"I almost cut her down here," pointing across the body. "It's a good thing the scissors didn't go bang."

"Jack, I almost think you want to cut her." He does not admit this, but the cutting takes on quite an aggressive air. It is now about time to go, so I ask him whether he would like to take his cut-outs home or leave them in a box down here. He thinks he'd like a box, so he goes through all the drawers hunting for one, and finally gets one that is suitable.

It is interesting to see the methodical care with which he cleans up. He puts everything away and in the place where he found it, even to the scissors.

"Would you like to come down on Saturday, Jackie, just as you did this morning?"

"I have company coming on Saturday."

"Oh, you mean your mother?"

"Yes."

"What time does she come usually?" He seems uncertain, and I say, "Mrs. T. can find out about it, and if your mother is coming, of course, you wouldn't want to come. But if she isn't, or if she is coming in the afternoon, perhaps you could come again on Saturday morning and play with me. You will find your things just where you leave them."

His whole attention is now concentrated on where he is going and how he gets to Mrs. T. He wants to know what floor it is, and I tell him it is the same as his age, seven. "I'll take you to the front door this time and watch you across the street, and after this you can go by yourself." He crosses the street like a child engaged in a great adventure, scurrying like a little animal after he has looked carefully in both directions.

From the Visitor's Record

On the way to clinic Jack said that the lady had told him he was not to come to see her if his mother was coming to see him in the morning. We told him that we knew his mother was not coming in the morning. If she came on Saturday it would be in the afternoon. He said we must be very sure, because he would not come if he thought he might miss his mother.

L. T.

February 27, 1932, Saturday—Second hour

Found Jack and Mrs. T. in the hall, waiting for me at quarter of nine. Jack comes in without hesitation, takes off his wraps. His first remark is, "Do you know Miss Y?"

"Yes, I do. Why?"

"She's going to put me on the trolley." He goes to the upper part of the desk first and then quickly to the door that leads to the toilet. When he comes back he gets out the scissors from the top drawer. "Are these the same scissors I had before?"

"Yes, are they still stiff?"

"Yes, they are." I try them and decide that they aren't so bad. "But may be I can get some vaseline some day." He inquires carefully what vaseline is.

He gets out the same magazine, sits in the same place, and begins cutting out pictures.

"What are you thinking about, Jackie?"

"I'm thinking if I get my teeth filled. I don't want to. I'm going with Miss Y."

"Do you like Miss Y. as well as Mrs. T.?"

"I like them both. Mrs. T. has to work this morning."

"Did you want to come this morning?"

"Yes, my mother's coming this afternoon or to-morrow."

There is a noise in the hall and as usual he is startled by it. I explain that there is someone going through the hall.

"We rang your bell this morning and it sounded like upstairs."

"Maybe you didn't ring the right one. Which one was it?" He tried to explain in detail where the bell was. "You'd better go out and try it, Jackie, and then we'll see whether it was my bell." He proceeds to do this with a good deal of interest.

As he is sitting cutting he gives a phone number.

"Is that the number of the place where you live?"

"It's the place where I was last."

"Oh, are you in a new home?"

"I never came here before, did I?"

"You mean right here in this room?"

"Yes."

"No, never except last Thursday."

"Guess who brought us here this morning."

"I don't know."

"Mrs. T.'s husband. If you'd come a little before, you could see him." He pulls out a toy wrist watch.

"I've got a witch watch and a pistol and a badge and a club."

"Where did you get all these?"

"From my mother and my Uncle Al, and the witch watch from some little girl." He has trouble getting it on, and I fasten it for him. He goes into the other room and brings back a coat which he puts on with great joy, showing me how small it is for him. Once more he is on the floor cutting.

"Was you hot last night?"

"Yes, I was. And how about you now? Are you hot?" He admits that he is, and we put the window up.

Talks a good deal about his medicine and how much he has taken of it, and coughs repeatedly. Doesn't seem much interested in his magazine, and yet shows no particular initiative in doing anything else. I ask him if he is tired of that magazine, and remind him that there are two or three others and that he can cut any of them he wants to. He goes to get the others, and I inadvertently suggest that he can throw the one he is through with into the waste-basket. Quickly he seizes his opportunity.

"Then can I take it home if you don't want it?" I am caught and have to admit it.

"Jack, I know it doesn't seem fair to you not to let you take this home if I don't want it myself. I have a reason, but I don't think you would understand it. You can't take any magazine home, even the old one, but you can take home anything you cut out or anything you draw. Is that a bargain?"

"O.K.," he says. He gets another magazine and cuts for a while. Finally, "Is it time for me to get ready yet?"

"No, Jackie, it is only ten minutes past nine. Are you tired? Do you want to go?"

"No, I just wanted to know."

He begins to cut out some horses. "Oh, oh, this man had a head on, and it went zip—right off!" Brings it over to show me.

"You fixed him, didn't you?"

"Now I have cut the horse's face off."

"You treated him pretty mean."

"I guess he didn't like that. I hope I didn't cut his feet off. I'll cut the whole horse. I'll cut him in half." (Obviously a reaction to my refusal to let him take the magazine.)

"You certainly like cutting them up, don't you, Jack? Are you a fierce, bad boy?" He doesn't understand the word fierce, but he gets the idea.

"I didn't hurt that one, but I hurt the man." (With a good deal of feeling.)

"Do you like to hurt men, Jackie?"

"No, but I'd like to kick a man that chased me." (If it were not so early in the relationship, I would accept the reference to me openly here.)

"Just look at all I've cut out. Pretty soon I'll have a box full and I'll have to get a bigger box." He cuts with more and more freedom and energy, and begins to make growling noises. He has a very small picture of a bottle, which he begins to cut with a great deal of zest. "Now here's a big bottle." He slashes along the side of it and sings as he cuts, "I can't help it, I can't help it."

"I am cold now," says Jack. "Do you want me to put the window down?"—which he does.

Suddenly the steam comes on and there is a crackling noise in the corner. He is startled by this and wants to know what it is, and I tell him to try the pipe and see if the heat is coming on. He is afraid of being burned, but very curious. I tell him it won't burn him probably, to try it. Evidently it was hotter than I thought. He jumps back and says it has burned him. I find a cold place on the pipe and let him feel that and feel of the hot place myself. It is pretty hot, but I doubt if he had had his hand on it long enough to be burned. He makes a great deal of fuss about it rather indirectly. Shows me a black spot on the finger that touched the hot pipe. Doesn't know whether it is a splinter. Finally decides it may be that it is where he stuck a needle in it. Describes how it happened. During this period he has come over and sits down on the couch by me. "Jackie, I think you must like a sore place." He goes back to sit on the floor, but holds the finger out as if it were hurt. "That fat old pipe burned me."

"I don't believe you will notice it, Jack. Once you begin to play, you will forget all about it."

"Have I got a long time yet?"

"Fifteen minutes. Do you know how long that is? Are you tired? Do you want to go?"

"No, I just wanted to know how long."

"Well, you can do quite a little in fifteen minutes."

"Could I do something in ten minutes?"

"Yes, quite a little." Once more he is absorbed in the cutting.

"If I went like this,"—snip, snip,—"it cuts it right off."

"You do like cutting, don't you, Jackie?"

"I find more bottles in this book than anything."

Suddenly without any apparent connection he begins, dramatically, "Did *you* ever tie a string to a door with something at the other end of it on Hallowe'en, so when the man opened the door he couldn't get out?"

"No, Jackie, I don't think I ever did that. But what made you think about that when you were talking about bottles?"

"Do you know what a brick step is?" says Jack.

"Yes."

"Well, did you ever throw a bottle on a brick step and smash it?"

"No. I never did"—laughing. "Did you?"

"Yes, I did. It was the milkman's bottle." His eyes are shining and he is full of the joy of the bad things he has done. From that point on, he talks so rapidly and is so demanding of my attention that I am not able to write much. "On chalk night I was out and doing a lot of bad things, and the cops nearly got us and we was scared. We was going to be caught and it was night and we couldn't see, but they didn't catch us. Did you ever stick a pin in a door-bell?"

"No, Jack. What do you do that for?"

"Because then it goes until you take it out. Once we did that, and the lady chased us with a broom, and we hid so we could see her, but she couldn't see us."

"Jackie, if you ever get after me, I'm going to have to run, I can see that. I have a broom too, but it is out in the toilet. So it wouldn't do me much good."

He runs out quickly to see if the broom is there. When he comes back the story has grown. "We took the broom away from her and chased her. She was going to chase us, but we chased her."

"And that's what you'll be doing to me some day. I see I have to look out."

"Did you ever throw a brick at a door?"

"No, Jackie."

"Didn't you ever throw a brick and break a glass?" After a little more of this kind of story, the excitement wanes for a minute and he says, "Is it time to get ready yet?"

"You have about five minutes. I think you must want to go."

"I just want to pick up my stuff."

"Perhaps you might begin doing that."

He moves around the room, putting things in order, and I refer casually to other things in the bottom drawer, that he has not looked at. He makes no response, although there is no doubt that he knows exactly what is in the bottom drawer. "What's in this drawer?" he says, turning to the middle drawer.

"Nothing but curtains and things like that. I don't think you'll be interested in them."

"Can I look in the top drawer?"

"Yes, if you want to." He looks through it, seizing a

hammer with joy and holding it up in a threatening manner, but returning it quickly.

He is now up against the problem of whether he will take home the box with the cut-outs. He has permission to do this, but he can't decide, so he goes through, "eeny-meeny-miny-mo," to settle it. The first time he isn't satisfied with the result, so he starts again the other way around. This time he accepts the decision, which is to leave the box in the office.

"That must mean you are coming back, Jackie."

"Yes, I am."

"Well, when is it going to be?"

"Maybe Monday."

"I think Mrs. T. can come only on Tuesday."

"I could come Saturday."

"That's too far off. How would you like to come three days next week—Tuesday, Thursday and Saturday?" He seems willing to do this, and wants to know just exactly how many times that will be. "Jackie, how would you like to keep on coming to see me for quite a little while, maybe a month or two, until you get tired coming and it's such nice weather that you wouldn't want to stay inside?" He seems to think this a good idea, but has already begun to think of how he is going to get on the street car all by himself. His whole attention is now concentrated on getting himself across the street to meet Miss Y. "Good-by, Jackie. See you Tuesday."

February 29, 1932, Monday—Third hour

I had made a mistake in the day and did not get to my office until nine-fifteen, thinking that John was coming on Tuesday. They had been waiting for at least fifteen minutes. I apologize. As soon as Mrs. T. had gone, I said, "Jackie, I wouldn't blame you for being very cross with me for keeping you waiting."

"I am not mad," he says, but he goes on apparently without connection to say that he lives near his mother, and she can come to see him twice a week and "my uncle can come by and take me, so I don't have to come any more."

"Jackie, I don't quite understand. You mean you don't have to come here any more?"

"Yes, that's what I mean."

"You don't have to come here any longer than you want to, Jack, but I don't see what it has to do with your uncle and your mother." He is not able to clear this up. (Probably they are introduced as a refuge and defense against the control of an arrangement purely mine, to which he is being subjected.)

He gets out a magazine and the scissors, but is not very interested.

"What do you write for?" (I have already begun on my notes.)

"Oh, I just have some things that I want to write while you are playing."

"I thought maybe you was writing letters to somebody. These scissors are gooder than before. Did you do anything to them?"

"No, they are just the same."

"It's hot here."

"All right, open the window. Jackie, I don't believe you wanted to come to-day."

"Why not?" he says.

"Well, you see, you planned to come on Tuesday,—that's to-morrow, and then there was a mistake, and you had to come to-day. You didn't like that, did you?"

"Yes, I did like to come," as he walks around the room looking for something else to do. "To-day is Leap Day."

"What?" surprised, and then I remember it is the twenty-ninth of February.

"Do you know what I done? I leaped down the steps, and the lady didn't know what it was. Do you know any little girls' names?"

"What do you mean? Do you mean a little girl you know?"

"Do you know any name?"

"I don't know any little girls that you know."

"Do you know Jane?"

"No. Who is Jane?"

Jackie begins to look very much embarrassed. "I hate to tell you."

"Why?"

"Because—she's—my—" looking more and more embarrassed.

"Girl? Oh, you mean she is your girl." All smiles and confusion, he assents.

"Where does she live, Jack?" He doesn't seem to know. "Does she live near where you are now? Did you just meet her?"

"No, I've known her a long time."

"Then she lives near your mother."

"Yes." (This reference to "his girl" is probably another weapon against me, to make me know I am not his only resource.) "Did you ever have a blood test?"

"No."

"Did I ever ask you that before?"

"Yes, you asked me the first time you were here."

"I thought I did."

"Did your mother come to see you Sunday?"

"Yes, she came and took me home and brought me back again. Do you know Mrs. W. (foster mother)?"

"No."

"Do you know anybody?"

"I know Mrs. T. and Miss Y. Jackie, I think you wonder what you are coming here for?"

"Yes, I do."

"Why do you think it is?"

"To stay here to visit you." [2]

"Do you ever dream, Jack?"

---

[2] I do not answer this because I believe that any answer I can give will have no meaning for Jack. Nothing but the experience itself, the actual living through it successfully, will be convincing. He is bound to be uneasy and fearful until he proves to himself that he is equal to the situation. Therefore why rationalize?

"Yes, I dream with my eyes open."

"What do you dream?"

"I dream about a house, and you can go in, and there are lights, and you can go upstairs, and there's a bed."

"I am cold."

"Well, fix the window." He goes into the front room to shut the window and sees magazines on the table.

"Are those cutting books in there?"

"Yes, you can have them all if you want them." Puts the books in the lowest drawer.

"You don't seem to like the other things in that drawer, Jack."

"They are dolls. Can I play with them?"

"Of course. I told you you could play with anything in the bottom drawer." Thereupon he falls to playing house with great joy. He begins with the baby and coach, which he rolls around the floor. Then he gets out the two larger dolls and wants to put them to bed, but the baby bed is too little, and so he turns the stool upside down and finds they fit in it very nicely.

"Do you know where any chiclet box is?"

"Do you mean you want the box, Jack, or the chiclets? I don't have any down here."

"Any candy?"

"No, Jack, not a bit. Are you hungry?"

"Uh huh."

"Didn't you have breakfast?"

"Yes, but I'm still hungry."

"I'm sorry, Jackie, but I never have any food down here."

"Do you know what this is going to be?" pointing to the stool used as a bed.

"No."

"It's going to be a coach."

"Maybe you can find something else for a bed." He starts to hunt for something and finds a box of dishes.

"Oh, they have to eat." He uses the top of the box.

"This is going to be a cute little table." He sets it with great enthusiasm. "The mother is going to sit here, and this is going to be the father's place, and the little doll will have to wait."

"Perhaps the little doll has a bottle," I say.

"Where is it?"

"We'll just have to pretend. There doesn't seem to be any."

"She's going on the porch to have her bottle. Guess where my place is." Points to it.

"Where's mine?"

"There." He points again.

"Little ones don't have coffee, do they? There are only two cups."

"What are you eating, Jack?"

"An egg. But I need a coffee-pot."

"See if you can't find something that you can use for a coffee-pot."

He goes all around looking, and finally I suggest the brass pot on the table. This is a little large, but he accepts it cheerfully.

"I hope it isn't time for me to go yet."

"I am going to give you some extra time this morning, Jack, to make up."

"What do you mean by making up?"

"I mean that I was late, so I'm going to let you have some extra time."

"What about Mrs. T.?"

"Will she expect you just exactly at a quarter of ten?"

"I don't know. I think so."

"I think she'll wait for a little while, Jack." He goes on with his playing.

"The dolls are going to eat in bed."

"Then they aren't father and mother, are they, Jack?"

"No,"—looking at me very shyly. "I'm the father"—pause—"and you are the mother, and they are the two babies." He collects enough articles to serve as sugar bowl, creamer, pepper and salt.

"Jack, I am very sorry, but it is time to get ready." He puts the things away carefully, with a little help from me where he can't reach. "I am terribly sorry that I was so late, Jack. I hope I won't do it again, and I wouldn't blame you one bit for being cross."

"I don't feel cross."

"I don't see how you can help it. I would. Would you like to come back Thursday?"

"Couldn't I come to-morrow morning?"

"No, because I have to work to-morrow morning. You see, I planned to work this morning and I thought you were coming to-morrow, but now I have seen you this morning, I will have to work to-morrow morning." He gets back at me quickly.

"Maybe my uncle will come and I can't come on Thursday."

"Don't come if you don't want to. But we'll ask Mrs. T. to find out about your uncle." He is not quite assured about crossing the street, although he mutters to himself, "Seventh floor," as he goes.

From Visitor's Record

When Jack was about to get on the trolley, he said very emphatically, "I'm not going to come down here on Thursday. Miss Taft said I didn't have to, if I didn't want to, and I don't want to. My uncle said he was coming to see me." I asked if he would rather see his uncle than Miss Taft. "Well," he replied, "I've seen Miss Taft lots of times, and I ain't seen my uncle in a long time." We told him he could call us up when he wanted to come, if that was the way he felt about it.

L. T.

From Visitor's Record
March 3, 1932, Thursday

Waited for Jackie half an hour. He did not appear. Worker had left it to him to come himself. She was to meet him at the street corner. He had some fear of this, but in addition to that, he was firm in his statement that he did not want to come on Thursday. When the time came he refused to go, so the foster mother said. It was decided that someone should go to get him on Saturday, and bring him in unless he made real objection.

From Visitor's Record
March 4, 1932

Visited Jack in foster home. Found him playing dolls with Marjorie (foster mother's little girl), very contented and happy. "I didn't want to come down yesterday," was his greeting.

"No, you didn't seem to," I answered. "Do you want to come Saturday?"

"No, I don't," says Jack.

"Didn't you have a good time when you went last?"

He nodded. "I would like to go," he said.

"Very well, Miss I. (the driver of agency car) will be up to get you, as I am going away on Saturday."

"Then will I have to get my teeth pulled out?" anxiously.

"No," I said.

"Will they stick a needle in me?"

"No."

"Will Miss I. take me away to another house? I don't want to go away from here. I won't go with her if she takes me away."

We assured him that he would not be moved, or have to go to clinic without being told beforehand, whereupon he seemed glad to go.

L. T.

Note:

Here we have not only the fear of the therapist and the mysterious unknown situation, but also the association with unpleasant visits to clinic, and moving to new homes, which provide all too realistic material on which to project his anxiety.

March 5, 1932, Saturday—Fourth hour

Jack drives up with Miss I. He looks quite excited as he points out the house to her.

"You will be able to come in all by yourself next time, won't you, Jack?" I remark in greeting. "Yes," says Miss I., "He was the one who knew the house this morning."

Jack takes off his wraps quickly and runs to the drawer where the toys are. I take my writing tablet and sit down in a chair.

"Were you writing before I came?"

"No, I hadn't begun yet. You don't like to have me write, do you?"

"Why do you do it?"

"When you are playing I have to do something, so I write."

"Oh, *you* play writing. Did you hear about Lindbergh's baby?"

"Yes, isn't it too bad?"

"There are cops looking in the cars. Did you see them?"

"Yes, I saw them."

Discovers some new dishes. "You got different dishes."

"So I have. How do you suppose I got them?"

"You bought them, I guess."

"No, I didn't."

"Maybe a lady."

"Yes, that's exactly right. A lady gave them to me. She said she had some she didn't want, and did I know anybody who would like them. So I said I had a little boy who came to see me sometimes, and that he might like to play with them." Jack explores the dishes carefully, exclaiming over each kind. Then to his great delight he discovers a magnet which has been left in the box. "I wish I had this."

"You do have it, Jackie, whenever you come here."

"But I mean I wish I had it at home."

"I don't doubt you do." He begins experimenting with the various things that he can do. The magnet will take the lid off the coffee pot and lift the cups and plates.

This time he uses the big rug for the table and sets it elaborately.

"The babies are going to eat with us," he says. "We are going to have a family here." He lacks some utensil and goes to hunt for it in the drawer. Finds the green bottle. "I forget now. What was in this?"

"It used to have perfume in it." He pretends to put perfume on himself.

"Maybe if I put water in it I could make some."

Eager to discourage the use of water, I remark, "I think it wouldn't smell."

"It's not dinner time. The babies have to take a nap. Here's your place, and here's my place," placing the green cups. "The babies ought to have milk."

He reverts to the magnet again. "Here's what I wish I had home."

"It would be nice, Jackie."

"Is Mrs. T. coming here?"

"I don't know; is she?"

"I don't know how I am going to get home. I've got a note to give her about my clothes." He now uses the big green bottle for a baby's bottle. Puts it in the crib with the baby. "Look at her. She's eating."

"That's a pretty big bottle. She going to get fat."

"She'll be as fat as a pig." He puts the other dolls to bed. Uses a cup for one and top of the bottle as a little bottle for the other. "They are going to eat all the time." He wants something for the cream, and runs into the next room to get one of the ash trays that he used before.

"You wasn't late this morning."

"No, I wasn't. Was it because I had been late that you didn't come Thursday?"

"No, I wasn't mad because you was late."

"But you *were* mad, Jackie. Why was it?" He looks at me in a very meaningful way and cautiously and fearfully, as if it were an important revelation, he says, "Because—you—don't—let—me—take—this—home."

"Oh, you mean the magnet?" "Yes," he answers.

"You are mad at me *this morning* because I won't let you take the magnet home. That's right now, isn't it?"

"Is it time to go?"

"No, you have half an hour yet."

"Gee, I'm glad!" He takes the babies out of the bed. "She's fat."

"Are all those children girls, Jackie?"

"Oh, one baby broke her bottle."

"What are you going to do?"

"I'm going to whip her. Which baby broke it?"

"I don't know."

"I'm going to whip them both," which he does. As he is whipping the green doll, he says in a squeaky little voice, "I didn't do it." We finally agree that the green one is a girl.

"You'd better give them names. We won't know which one is which."

"The green one is Cuppy and the red one is Skippy. Which one said he didn't do it?"

"I think it was the boy, Jack."

"It was Cuppy. She's bad. *She* broke the bottle."

He gets a miniature broken pipe out of a box, puts it in his mouth and struts around.

"You must be the man of the house smoking a pipe, Jack."

"Oh, I've dropped it on the floor. The house is on fire! Fire! Fire! Where is the engine?" He seizes the red stool and rushes it to the spot, shouting fire all the time. Then he gets the idea that the stool will be a good thing for him to slide on, so he tries it on the waxed floor in all possible positions. "Can I have a pillow?" I point out two which can be used roughly. He stuffs them into the stool and sits on it. Tries to make it slide. Then he uses the pillow alone and goes belly-bumping, throwing himself on the floor with great force and abandon. Finally wearying of this, he returns once more to the magnet. "Can I take the magnet home?" This is the first time he has put it directly and he is evidently a little timid about it.

"I am afraid not, Jackie."

"Why? Isn't it yours?"

"Yes, but it's here for children to play with when they come to see me. Sometimes other children come here to play."

"But they haven't seen it. They won't know it was here if I take it."

"No, that's true enough, Jackie, but it's a rule not to take anything home. Do you know what a rule is?"

"No."

"Well, a rule is something you have to mind, and the rule is that you can take home anything you draw or anything you cut out, but no toys."

Jackie, looking discouraged and disgusted, "Shall I go yet?"

"Are you tired? Do you want to go?"

"No."

"You have ten minutes. I'll tell you when it is time."

He goes over to the steam pipes which he has found hot before, and shows extreme caution and fear. Can hardly bring himself to touch the pipe which burned him. Finally does so after much effort, and finds it cold.

"You decided to stay home on Thursday, didn't you, Jack?"

"Yes." No further comment. "It's hot here."

"You can open the window."

"If I bring something down, can I take the magnet home?"

"What do you mean, Jack?"

"If I left one of my toys here, could I take this?"

"What toys would you bring me?"

"Well, I can't just think. I'll have to go home and see. I don't see why I can't take the magnet home. What can I take home?"

"Only what you draw or cut out."

"I don't like that."

"No, Jackie, I'm sure you don't."

"What else can I take? Can I take the little bench?"

"No, nothing else. Just the drawings and the cut-outs. It's the rule."

Jack looks very displeased. "That makes you mad, doesn't it?"

"Yes, it does."

"Well, maybe sometime you'll forgive me."

"But why can't I take it?"

"Because that's the way it is, Jack." He begins to throw himself around the room rather roughly, slamming the toys, and finally lifts the stool in the air as if he were about to throw it violently on the floor.

"You *do* feel like doing something bad, don't you, Jack?" He runs over and begins to throw the pillows. "I think you'd like to shake me that way, Jack."[3] He will not assent to that. He throws himself around the room almost as if he were tempted to have a temper tantrum, but does not quite let go. He lifts the stool in the air, but brings it down fairly gently. "The trouble is, if you broke that stool, you wouldn't have it to play with any more, and you wouldn't like that, either. . . . It's time to go now, Jackie."

Quite in contrast to other mornings, he shows reluctance to put the things away and I help without any comment. He seems to want to go to the toilet and goes at my suggestion. When he comes back he slams his coat around, but is gentle when I come to help him with it. "Jack, are you

---

[3] While no one who is willing to let children be angry with adults could doubt that Jack's anger is directed at me as a thwarting object, the wisdom of pointing it out might be questioned. I do it deliberately to focus the projection on me, where it belongs, more quickly than would happen otherwise.

too mad to want to come to see me again? When are you coming? Next week?"

"How about Saturday?" very tentatively.

"That seems too far off to me."

"I might come to-morrow."

"To-morrow is Sunday. How about Tuesday?"

"I'll come Monday," not willing to accept my day.

"Well, good-by, Jack. I hope you'll forgive me by Monday."

Later, when I go over to the Social Service Building, I find Jack waiting in the outer office. He has never seen me in this building before, and probably will be curious about it.

March 8, 1932, Tuesday—Fifth hour

It is a bad morning, and Mrs. T. is fifteen minutes late. Jack comes in very cheerful and cold. "Feel my ear. See how cold it is."

"You are even with me now. You kept *me* waiting fifteen minutes." [4]

Quick as a flash he answers, "Are you mad at me?"

"Well, maybe a little bit, but not very much. Did you expect to come yesterday, Jack?"

"Yes, but Mrs. T. couldn't get me."

"Then I guess you were mad again."

"Give me your cap, Jack, and I'll see if I can get it sewed to-day. (The binding in the cap is loose, and once before I had suggested that I might mend it.) He runs quickly to the dolls with little cries of greeting. He has with him a toy egg-beater, which he does not use during

[4] Again this is not so much suggestion, as it is a recognition born of long experience, of the meaning which this kind of incident has, or may have for any patient. It is utilized here to carry the negative feelings harmlessly yet successfully. This illustrates the active use of incidental material to bring out the emotional reactions more consciously and focus them in the present and on the therapist, where they can be handled therapeutically.

the hour. Maybe it is intended to be the exchange object for the magnet, although he does not mention it. As he is getting the dolls out, the janitor and his wife talk noisily in the hall outside. He is all attention instantly.

"Is him and her fighting?"

"No, I think it's just that she has a loud voice. She sounds cross even when she isn't!"

"I am going to put the dolls to bed. This box isn't big enough. Can I take this pillow?"—pointing to the one he was allowed to have before. Then he seizes the rubber mat which is used to protect the couch from shoes. "They need this because they wet the bed."

"Do both dolls wet the bed, Jack?"

"No, the boy doesn't. Boys don't wet the bed, do they?" assertively, then overcome by truth he adds reluctantly, "*Little* boys wet the bed."

"Yes, of course, they do." I am taking notes as usual, with the hat and the sewing materials lying beside me, as yet untouched. Jack is probably annoyed at my writing, for he says out of the blue, "Will you get the hat done before I go? I have to go to the play-room this morning. I saw you over at the building," referring to the fact that he had seen me in the waiting-room after the hour last time. "Guess who I went home with! Miss I."

"Jack, are you going to go over to the play-room and leave me after this?"

"No, I'm going to stay here, but I'm going to the play-room afterwards. I'm going to get some clothes too." He discovers a pencil sharpener in the desk, with which he occupies himself off and on for the rest of the hour. "I'd like to take home this pencil sharpener. I don't suppose I can."

"You know what the rule is."

"But why can't I take it home?"

"Jack, what is the rule? You tell me."

He repeats it faithfully. "But I don't see why you can't let me have the pencil sharpener."

"It's like this, Jack. If I began letting you have things

and other children have things, very soon I wouldn't have anything left."

"Oh, I won't beg for that many things."

"You never can tell, Jack, so I guess it has to be the rule, even if you don't like it very well."

He has produced from his own pockets various articles—an old compact, a whistle, and two little yellow chickens. "Have you any candy down here? I'll give you a penny for some."

"No, Jackie, I haven't any candy. That's another one of the rules you don't like—no candy down here."

"Can I take home the pencils I sharpen?"

This, in Jackie's mind, is equivalent to taking home the pictures he draws and the things he cuts out. "No, Jack, you are trying to catch me. You certainly are trying to get the better of me."

"Well, can I?"

"No, you can't."

Someone is sweeping down the stairs outside, and Jack responds, as he always does, to every sound, with interest and perhaps a little fear. "Who is that outside?"

"You might go and look." This he proceeds to do. When he comes back he grows much more playful and noisy, and sings to himself, jumps around, throwing himself on the floor, sliding on the waxed surface. Quite out of the blue, he refers to a time when he was to say "Hello!" to me, and I wasn't there, and I remember that it was arranged that I was to meet him in the play-room before he came to see me the first time, and that I was unable to do it.

"Can I wash my hands?" holding out hands that are not very dirty.

"Yes, if you want to."

He goes to the toilet, and I hear him singing loudly all the time. There is no waste basket in the toilet this morning, as the maid has taken it out in cleaning, so he brings the paper towel back into the room, and finally arranges the waste baskets properly for me. I have explained that the maid has been cleaning this morning, and that's why they are not in order. With some anxiety he says, "Does the maid go into the toilet?"

"Yes, she goes to clean."

"But does she go to the bathroom there?"

"No, Jackie, I don't think so."

He now begins to practise standing on his head, and with my help arranges pillows so that he can turn a somersault without hitting too hard.

"It's time to go now, Jackie. Too bad that we don't have so much time this morning." Previously I had said that we would take a little extra time, and he reminded me that Mrs. T. had to go to school this morning. (She is a student in the School of Social Work.) He puts the toys away rather reluctantly and without the meticulous care which he has shown before, holding the dolls up threateningly as if he were about to throw them, and slamming things around. I say, "Do they both wet the bed?"

"Yes, we have to hang this up to dry," putting the rubber mat on the end of the couch.

I suggest that he has left his whistle and the egg-beater, but he says he prefers to leave them. *"I* don't take anything home."

"Jackie, you are giving me the presents that I won't give to you, aren't you?" He is still quite obstreperous when he finally goes out the door, and when I say, "See you Thursday at nine o'clock," he makes no objection. His whole mood this morning is in direct contrast to the fighting spirit of last time,—is outgoing and possessive.

March 10, 1932, Thursday—Sixth hour

Jackie comes in the door alone. "I can stay as long as you want me this morning. Only Mrs. T. says I am not to stay to lunch." I have to leave the room a moment and I hear him talking and singing to himself. When I come back, he says, "I am going to start on the pillows. I'm going to fight." He seizes two of the pillows and is rolling back and forth on the floor with great violence.

"Whom are you fighting?"

"A man. He can't hardly breathe. Just look! Here's his face." There is more punching and rolling. "This is a man. See me! See me!" He rolls over and over the full length of the room, with more violent punches and contortions. "The man's nearly dead. He's knocked out."

"You do feel pretty good this morning, don't you, Jackie?"

"Yes, I do. But I've got to bathe my head off."

"Because you've been fighting so hard?"

"Yes, I'm hot." He goes to the toilet and I can hear him talking loudly. As soon as he returns he falls to with the pillow once more. "Oh, he's knocked out." He seizes the pillow and bats the floor with it so violently that I sneeze from the dust.

"Do you fight little boys, Jack?"

"Once I punched my brother in the nose."

"Is he older than you?"

"Yes, he's older and bigger. His name's Paul." Paul is the brother of whom he is jealous.

He goes over to the window and for the first time leans out to see what is there. Opens the window very wide. Slides on the rug. Addresses the pillow as "Andy." At this point there is very rapid change of play with the pillow, and the baby talk is so pronounced that I have difficulty in understanding him. "Now I'm going to sleep." Lies down on the pillow. "My toof is out. I banged it with my hand."

"Did it hurt?"

"Yes, it hurt, but I didn't cry." He now has the two pillows on the rug, and cuddles up to them, putting his head first on one and then on the other. "We all kiss each other," kissing the pillows lovingly, addressing one as "Cold Cream," and the other by some name I could not get.[5]

[5] We seem to have here in symbolic activity the overcoming of the rival (father, brother or sister), who stands between him and

"What makes you feel so good, Jackie?"

"I'm happy about being here." He makes loud explosive noises with his mouth.

"What's that, Jack?"

"It's a mouse." In a baby voice, "Oh, ma-ma," wriggles around on the floor like a very little child.

"Are you a little baby?"

"Yes, I'm a little baby, but I can fight. Here's a big boy now. I'm selling cakes."

He cries his wares in what sounds like Italian dialect, but I can't make out the phrase. He gets sillier and sillier. Talks in a squeaky voice, "Mammie is going to give me a licking." Spanks himself.

"Does your mother spank you sometimes?"

"Yes, she does. Only she can't do it now (regretfully) because I am living with another lady. My mother wants me to stay with another lady. Sometime when she gets work she's going to take me home. I come from the Aid. Do you know about that?"

"Yes, I know about that, Jack."

"Mrs. T. comes from the Aid, too. My mother's young."

"She's younger than I am, Jack, isn't she?"

"Yes, but when I get old she won't be young, will she? Will she get married when I get old?"

"I don't know, Jack. Do you think she will? Is there some man whom she's going to marry?"

"I don't know." There's a great deal of talk that I can't follow here, but very soon he has a pillow on the floor, and he is holding it violently, lying across it. "I've got my mother on the floor." I thought he said, "She's cold," but he didn't accept that word, and interpreted it, "She's dead."

"How did she get dead? Did you kill her?"

complete possession of the mother, in this case the therapist. This taking possession seems to me not primarily sexual, but rather human and infantile, true for girl and boy alike, and physical in that it implies the deepest, most complete form of organic union experienced once, and only once by every person in the uterus, and secondarily at the breast. Sexual union is an attempt at restoration of the earlier relation, on another level, less fearful, less complete, but compatible with adulthood.

"No."

"Are you sorry she's dead?"

"Yes, I'm sorry. I'll kill myself." He bangs himself around. Then he cheerfully remarks, "I'll buy medicine." Goes through the motion of opening her mouth and pouring it down her throat, making hissing noises as he does so, which is very suggestive and the motion is equally so. "My mother's alive now. She won't give me no more paddles." [6]

Off and on throughout, there had been reference to being hot, as he has been very active. I had remarked that I would freeze if the windows were open any more. At this point he refers again to how hot he is, and with a good deal of emphasis in my direction wants to open the window.

"Jack, I think you want to freeze me." [7] This amuses him a good deal.

"No, I'm cold. I mean I'm hot," laughing. "Let me open the front window." He gets very foolish. "I go to sleep lying on the floor. I'm falling down the stairs. I'm talking in my sleep. Now I say my prayers. Dod is great, Dod is good, and we thank him for this food," etc. "Oh, the bed is falling down. Somebody's tickling me." He begins tickling himself. "Oh, mom, I have to eat dinner."

"Oh, do you?" I ask.

[6] Here again we have not so much an expression of sexual desire for the mother, as the violence and resentment aroused by fear of his own too deep and painful need of someone who understands and bears his feelings, as the therapist is able to do. He cannot get to the positive, until the negative feelings are expressed and the fear reduced in consequence. Toilet functions furnish good material for insult and attack on the mother, who has trained the child against his will.

[7] This may seem to be unwarranted. In fact it does not matter whether it is true or not, as long as it recognizes, admits, or brings out the mixed character of his feelings toward me at this moment, his desire to hurt, but not to hurt too much; to consume, but in love not hate. The introduction of the food element here is not accidental. The mouth noises may refer to toilet functions, but also they include the sucking, smacking sounds of nursing. His desire to be spanked is not a desire for punishment, but rather an expression of his need for physical contact which he cannot put in positive terms.

He gets out the red table, which he has never used before, and sits on the stool. The rest of the hour is devoted to learning how to fold the table up and put it back again.

"Mom don't give me my dinner. I'm a bad boy."

"What do you do that's bad?"

"Oh, nothing." He's now talking in a high singing tone, which rises as he nears the end of a sentence. "I can have dinner. I can have dinner." Suddenly, "Is it past ten?"

"No, you have fifteen minutes yet."

"How long is fifteen minutes? Is it half an hour?"

"No, it's half of a half-hour. You have time enough to play yet. As much as recess at school."

"Ma says I can't eat anything because we have to move away. Ma, ma, I can't fix the table."

"Am I your ma, Jack?"

"Yes."

"I'm not a very good ma, am I?"

"I have to move away." The baby talk gets so bad I really can't understand him, and he is as silly as he can possibly be. The explosive mouth noises continue. "I want dinner."

"Well, why don't you have it?"

"Mom won't let me."

"Do you want me to get dinner for you, Jackie?"

"No, I'll cook the dinner, mom, but the table is to be fixed." He does it himself.

"There, ma. Oh, me, I can eat dinner now."

"What are you going to have?"

"Fish cakes." Sitting at the table, "You ought to see the way I eat dinner. I push the table right down on me. Oh, the table upset. Do you see the salt and pepper on me? Oh, ma-me, oh, ma-me. Play ma-mee gives me a licking."

"Jack, do you wish I'd lick you?"

"Yes, and then I'd get a broom."

"Well, perhaps I'd better not in that case." Jack approaches the screen which is around the washbasin. He has never investigated this before. Comes back with motions of eating.

"What are you eating?"

"We're going to have soap for dinner. Ain't that nice?" He continues to make the hissing noise.

"Jack, what is that noise you make?"

"It's a cough noise."

"No, it isn't. It doesn't sound like that to me." I suggest that it might be well to shut the windows. He only opens them wider. "You do want me to be cold, don't you, Jack?"

"Is it time for me to get ready?"

"Just about."

"Let me stay a little longer."

"Not much longer, Jack, because I have to work."

"Where do you work?"

"I work over in the building where Mrs. T. does."

"Do you take children away?"

"I teach and talk to grown people."

"But it's school time now."

"It isn't like your school, Jack."

"Let me take a nap." Lies down on the floor.

"Well, it will have to be a quick one. Now it's time to shut the windows, Jack." He opens them wider before he is willing to shut them.

"Next time I come, it's going to be Saturday. Don't forget." He says this with a positive assertion that has never been present before. He approaches the screen again with a cautious look at me.

"Jack, that screen is one thing we aren't going to play with. It's easy to break and it cost a lot of money. Almost everything in the room you can play with, but not the screen." He lingers about the room, obviously unwilling to go. I have to assist in putting things to rights. When I help him put on his wraps, he makes it as hard for me as possible. "You want to make me work, Jack." He says good-by in the friendliest way, calling loudly as he goes down the hall, "Don't forget about Saturday."

"No," I say, "we'll make it Tuesday, Thursday and Saturday." He has to be told just how the days come. As he is going out the outer door, he calls, "See you later down town."

March 12, 1932, Saturday—Seventh hour

Jack arrives before nine, bright and cheerful. "You are a little early this morning, Jackie."

"Did I come before time?"

"Yes, five minutes before time. It's a good thing I was here. Now you have five minutes extra."

"Have you got a glass?"

"You mean you are thirsty?"

"Yes." I get the water for him from the faucet back of the forbidden screen.

Immediately he gets down the two pillows, and one becomes a horse which he rides.

"Oh, ma-mee, look what I got," referring to the red table. "Daddy bought it."

"Do you wish there was a daddy?" [8]

"Yes. Daddy's working." He seems to have forgotten how to manage the table and lets me show him. "There's going to be a picnic. Just see the table. It's going to be fixed fancy. The boy that spills on it is going to get a licking." He begins fighting with the two pillows very strenuously.

"Who are the two people you are fighting, Jackie?"

"Cuppy and Pop Eye. No, I mean Cold Cream and Pop Eye. His face is getting punched," growling and rolling around the floor. "Quit that, Pop Eye. You know who I'd

[8] However jealous the child may be of the father as rival, he needs him in the situation, if only as protection against too close a relationship with the mother. When Jack feels the pressure of his own too powerful need of the mother (the therapist), he tries to bring in a third person to relieve the tension.

like to punch? He's the man that stole the Lindbergh baby."
Sudden change of voice, "Oh, da-da," like a baby. "Here's
a pillow. I'm going to take a nap on it." Begins to make
baby sounds, but quickly goes back to the table and its
manipulation. I tell him how to do it, but he seems to be
persistently stupid.

"Jack, I don't believe you want to do that table right.
You don't want me to tell you how to do it. Well, you do it
just the way you want to." He leaves it unfastened and
sets it up on the floor that way.

"It's going to be a fine dinner. Coffee and oatmeal.
Better not break the table," as the table comes down on
him and he falls over under it.

"Oh, dear, is that window open?"
"Yes, a little."
"I'm hot. Is it really open?" Quickly he is back at the
table again, talking rapidly to himself in dialogue form.
"Oh, ma-mee, my bran' new table's broken." In a changed
voice, "I told you not to do that. I'll hit you. I'll hit you."
He says something about wanting to hit a man he got mad
at. I thought he said that he did want to, but he insisted
he didn't when I asked him to repeat it. "This table is a
nuisance. I bought it to-day and it's broke." He is a little
rough with the table and begins to fight the pillows again.

"What makes you fight so hard, Jackie?"
"I'm only playing." Continues to fight and roll around,
making explosive noises. His stocking is coming down. "I
don't care if my garter comes way up." Talking to the
pillow, "Now, you take a nap you naughty girl. I have to
go to the bathroom," making suggestive noises. When he
comes back into the room, as soon as he is inside the door,
he gets on the floor and creeps up back of the couch where
I am sitting. Pretty soon I feel him tickling my arm.

"I feel somebody."
Jack, running away, "I'd better go away, the lady says she
feels someone tickling her." Gets the glass and starts to go
behind the screen. As he handles the screen very carefully,

I let him do it. "I can manage it." He turns back to the room and rushes at the pillows saying, "Now for liberty! Can I take the blanket?"

"Yes, if you aren't too rough with it."
"Well, can I play with it?"
"Yes, if you don't wipe the floor with it."
"I want to make a bed."
"That's all right."
"Can I do tumblesaults?"
"Yes, you just take it, Jack, and go ahead, and if it gets too rough I'll take it away. That's all."

Lies down, covers himself with blanket. In a second, "Oh, it's morning already."

"Did you dream, Jack?"

"Yes, I dreamed the table fell on me when I got ready to eat. My mother didn't know it was going to fall down, and it spilled all over her and over your cover."

"Well, I guess you did get even with me, Jack, didn't you? You'd be tickled if you spilled something on my cover." He tries to fold the blanket. "It's a little hard, Jack."

"Not for me." Then he struggles with the table again, and seems really not to understand how to manage the wooden button.

"If you bring it over to me, Jack, I'll show you about it." He brings it very sweetly and seems to be willing to learn.

"Can't I have this pillow?" pointing to the pillow against which I am leaning. He had already asked for the pillow on the chair and I had refused.

"No, these pillows don't go on the floor."
"Why?"
"Because I keep them clean for the couch. You have two pillows. You can wipe the floor with those if you want to."

"But can't I have just the purple one like the one on the floor?"

"No, not any of these."

"But I want to turn somersaults."

"If you fix the blanket a little differently, I think you will have all you need." He arranges the blanket and falls flat across the pillows and blanket.

"The lady falls right down. She's dead. But she hurt herself when she fell, and woke up." Lies on the bed for a while. "It's time for me to get up and tee."

"What do you mean, Jack? What are you saying?" He repeats it. "Do you mean you have to go to the toilet?"

"No, I mean eat." Goes over to the red table and pretends to eat, putting the food in with his hands. "I don't use any dishes." Acts like a very little baby, singing in a high voice, "Oh, ma-mee, ma-mee. I fell on the floor." With a sudden change of interest, "Oh, could I get something in your desk?"

"Why not, Jack? I told you you could use anything you found in the top part." Gets out the egg-beater and the blotter. "Why, it's your egg-beater, Jack."

"Could I beat some water?"

"No, but you can pretend."

"Don't say it's time for me to get ready."

"No, it isn't."

"Is it most time?"

"No, you have lots of time." He begins to play with the double door between the two rooms. Wants to open the side which is fastened from above. I try to open it and find it is stuck with paint. "It will take a man and a good strong tool to open that door, Jack."

"Aren't you strong enough?"

"Not unless I have a tool. Here's a screw-driver." I find I can slide the catch and open the door for him. Then he has to understand just how he can lock the double door, and he learns to work the catch himself by climbing on a chair.

While he is playing with the door, he says, "Here comes the devil," and tries very hard to get the door shut and locked.

"Are you afraid of the devil, Jack?"

"Yes, wouldn't you be?" He rushes to the third door in the room which he has never tried before. This goes out into the same hall that the back door opens into. The lock is stiff. In fact, it is almost impossible for him to turn it, but he persists, and with my help he finally manages it. He runs out into the hall, but is quickly frightened and returns. I am interested in his persistence in working with a thing as hard for him as the lock, and he is quite willing to take any suggestion that is given. He now goes to bed again.

"Good night, sleep tight," I say.

He completes the rhyme, "Don't let the bugs bite." Singing in a high, squeaky voice, "Oh, ma-mee."

I say, "Baby isn't sleeping very well." At this suggestion he begins to cry, and the cry grows louder and louder until I can see that there will be no limit to this form of expression. However, he stops of his own accord, jumping up from the bed and playing he is a little boy again. "Play you hear a noise," he says, with an expression of great fear.

"Jack, are you scared?" [9]

A little ashamed, he says, "The husky man is coming."

With a burst of extreme violence he throws the rubber mat against the wall so hard that I dodge and say, "Goodness, Jack!" in real surprise.

"Would you be afraid if a ghost came? I'd pick up a heavy iron thing and throw it at his chest. Would that kill him?"

"I guess it would. But I don't believe in ghosts, Jack. Where is the ghost?"

"Are there any closets in this room?"

"No, there aren't any closets."

"Then there is no place for the ghost." Once more he tries to get pillows for the floor and I refuse.

"You have your own pillows, Jack. Isn't that fair?"

[9] The fear in this hour is probably a projection of the fear of himself, of the unknown impulses which he feels, and the danger of being carried too far beyond the point of ego control.

He now opens the windows wide with a good deal of glee, insisting on the front one, although he has to climb on a chair to open the lock.

"It's just about time to go," I say.

"Is it just about time?" regretfully.

"Yes."

Beginning slowly to put things away, "Are you coming over to-day?"

"I'm coming after a while."

"Do you know what Mrs. T. did? She lit a candle when there wasn't any electric light and she burned her glasses." Gets himself another drink.

"Jack, it really is time to go now."

"Can't I have just one little nap?" Lies down on the couch, but quickly he gets up and runs into the other room. "Now don't you come in here." I stay out till he calls me. I find him sitting in the big chair all dressed in his coat and hat to surprise me.

"Good-by, Jack. When are you coming again? Tuesday?"

"O.K.," as he goes out the front door. "See you later down town."

March 15, 1932, Tuesday—Eighth hour

My bell rings twice at nine-fifteen. A little voice is heard in the hall singing, "Out or in? Out or in? Is she out or is she in?"

"Yes, somebody is home. Come right in." Jack comes in very cold but very cheerful.

"Were the cars late this morning?" I ask.

"They certainly was late, and we missed one, too. Are Cuppy and Cold Cream asleep?"

"I guess they are." He rushes immediately to the couch and produces the two pillows from underneath the rug.

"Oh, you mean the pillows are Cuppy and Cold Cream," I say.

"Yes, what did you think I meant?"

"I thought the dolls were Cuppy and Cold Cream."

"Oh, I ain't going to play with them any more," scornfully. "I didn't come Monday."

"No, Jack, you weren't supposed to. You come Tuesday, Thursday and Saturday."

"I thought I came Monday. Do you come in the trolley?"

"No, I come in an automobile."

"Did you tell me that before?"

"I think I did."

He has the two pillows and the rubber mat on the floor by this time. "Can I take the rug?"

"Yes, you can take it, but you know what I said last time, that if it gets too rough, I'll take it away." (Not a threat, just a statement of fact.)

He takes off his glasses, which are in his way, and gives them to me as usual. "Who do I look like without my glasses?"

"I don't know. Whom *do* you look like?"

"I look like my brother."

"Is your brother at home with your mother?"

"Yes. Do you know his name?"

"You told me his name was Paul, didn't you?"

"Yes, that's right. Have you got a mirror?"

"What do you want a mirror for?"

"I want to see if I look like my brother." I give him one out of my bag. He now turns his attention to the folding doors, runs to them and locks them. Mysteriously, "Here comes Mr. Midnight. He's a robber." We whisper back and forth, with much show of fear, about what the robber is going to do. Jackie holds a dialogue with him. Finally he says, "All right, you may come in," and runs to the door and opens it. Apparently he has frightened himself a little bit with all this play. He turns a little fearfully, "Do you think there's a robber?" [10]

[10] The real robber is Jack who feels his own impulses to take from me not only material gifts, but love and physical response if he can get it,—in other words he wants to dominate and possess.

"I think he is just a play robber, Jack."

He opens the door with a burst. "Oh, there's a Chinese. He's dead. Can I use the rug to put my feet on?"

"I don't think you will hurt it that way." He puts the rubber mat over the rug. "Now I can't hurt it. Did you ask the lady not to make the floor so slippery?"

"Yes, I did."

"But did she do it?"

"I don't think she's done much about it."

"What did she say to you?"

"I don't see her very often, Jack. She cleans when I'm not here."

"But you did see her. You told her not to make the floor slippery."

"Yes, I see her sometimes."

"What is she like?"

"She's a colored lady."

"Do you call her that?"

"No. I don't know her name. She works for the janitor, not for me."

"Who's that?"

"He's the man you saw when you looked out in the hall once."

Jack is now lying on the floor, pretending to go to sleep. "Do you dream much, Jackie?"

"I dream when I'm awake." This is the same reply he made once before. He now attacks the problem of unlocking and locking the folding door from the top. He knows he can do it if he uses the chair, but he prefers to work out some way to use the stool, which isn't high enough. He puts on it two pillows, then, looking askance at me, the rug. It is still not high enough. He needs another pillow.

"You may use the pillow in the chair just this once, Jack." He gets it and puts the rubber mat on top so he won't hurt it. By dint of much stretching, he is now able to unlock the door, but in order to lock it he has to use the chair. He returns the pillow to the chair very obediently. I say, "Thank you," and he says, "What for?"

"For putting the pillow back." He turns his attention to the windows. It is a very cold morning. "Jack, if you open the windows, I shall have to have the rug."

"I'll shut them when *I* freeze."

"But how about me?" He is once more trying to lock the door. "She won't move," obviously wanting to get me excited.

"Jack, I think you are fooling me, and I think you like to freeze me, too."

"No, let the nice air come in." Opens the door wide so that there is free circulation. He can't stand this himself. "Boy, I'm cold! I'm going to shut them."

"Well, I'm glad of that."

Once more he returns to the rug to see if he can find the limit. "Can I fight with this?"

"Go ahead and try. I'll tell you to stop if it's too bad."

"Won't you give me one more chance?" He throws the rug. "Is it rough?" looking at me.

"It's getting pretty rough, Jack."

"I'll go to sleep. Is that O.K.?" In using the rug he manages to have it cover a good deal of the bare floor, which is the thing I have said I didn't want. "Me rough?"

"You seem to be getting rougher all the time, Jack."

"Can I use it for a tent?"

"Go ahead and I'll see what you do with it. If you put it up on the couch, perhaps it won't slip off too much." He doesn't like that, wants it on the floor. "Jack, you are just trying to see how much you can do without my taking the rug away, aren't you?"

"Uh huh," fixing it up elaborately for the tent. "Now is it O.K.?" I give up, since he isn't doing anything very bad with the rug. "Good-night." He goes underneath the tent. He is in and out, and there is a good deal of conversation about the tent. Finally he stands looking at me thoughtfully.

"What are you thinking about, Jack? You look like mischief." He retires.

"Good night." Voice from the tent, "You don't know how I sleep."

"How do you?"

"What is that noise?"

"I don't know what it is, Jack."

"It's a mouse." Jack is rubbing the floor with something. I suspect that he is planning to rub the floor with the rug. "Gee, this is a nifty bed!"

"It's almost time to go, Jack."

"I'll get underneath the tent, where she can't get me. She'll get the broom, and I'll take it off her."

"Do I have to get the broom to get you out?"

"Yes, you get the broom. If I don't come out, stick it under."

"You must want me to do something bad, Jack. You must want me to punish you."

To himself, "*Was* the floor dirty?" I strongly suspect that he is about to scrub the dirty floor with the rug.

"It's time for little boys to get ready to go," I say firmly.

"The little boy wants another nap."

"I guess I will have to get the broom, Jack." I get a little whisk broom and make believe to paddle him, but take pains not to carry this too far. He wants to take the mirror home. "You can't have it, Jack. It belongs to my purse."

"Is a pocketbook the same as a purse? That's a funny word. Sounds like curse."

For the first time he gets interested in the articles on the mantelpiece, which is higher than he, and he sees the box containing my cigarettes. "I would have been glad to stop him, but it's too late. "What's this?" opening it. "Cigarettes?"

"Yes."

"Whose are they?"

"Mine."

"Do you smoke?"

"Yes."

"Really?"

"Yes."

"I'm going to tell the cop. And then won't he lock you up?" [11]

"It's time to go." Jack throws himself on the couch. "I have to take a little nap." In a very baby voice, "I'm the littlest boy in the world." As if he had gone a little too far, himself, he jumps up and prepares to go. Getting his things on,—"When I go out in the hall, I'm going to ring the bell twice, but don't you come out."

"And then when I do come out, Jack, you'll be gone," I say. We do as agreed.

March 17, 1932, Thursday—Ninth hour

Jack comes in cheerful and elated. "You don't know how I came. I came in a car with Mrs. T.'s husband." As he takes off his coat, "It's St. Pattie's Day."

"Why, so it is, Jack. It's St. Patrick's Day."

"No, not that. St. Pattie's. Oh, somebody has to tie my shoes," looking at me to see if I will bite.

"Jack, I don't believe that you can't tie your shoes. I think you were just fooling me last week when you got me to do it." Jack begins slowly working with the laces.

"Am I tying them?"

"I don't know, Jackie. Maybe you are." He fumbles with them a while longer and finally produces a perfectly good bow knot. "Did you tie your own shoes this morning, Jack?"

"No, grandma did."

"So you are fooling her too, are you? She thinks you can't tie them. I'd better tell her."

"It's kinda hot here to-day. I'm going to open the window." Looking at me, "Can I open it?"

---

[11] There is a value in such a discovery of sin or weakness in the therapist, as it can become the symbol of a real difference, which the patient learns however painfully to accept as part of an objective reality, the most therapeutic experience he can have.

"Why do you ask me that? You know you are going to open it anyway. You like to make me cold." He goes to the window and throws it wide open.

"I hope no wind comes in."

"What you mean is that you hope it does come in and freezes me up." He is quite a little amused at this, but will not admit his intention. (This has become a pleasant game, an accepted difference by now.)

"Can I make a tent this morning?" He seizes the rug and throws it violently on the floor.

"You just want me to take that rug away, don't you, Jack?"

"Are you going to?"

"Maybe."

"Maybe and maybe not," rhythmically. I am busy writing and pay very little attention.

"Maybe and maybe not," says Jack over and over, louder and louder, until I respond.

That seems to settle the issue on the rug. And from that moment he uses the rug constructively for his own purpose, without any reference to getting a rise out of me. He plays in and out of the tent for the greater part of the hour. After he has gone to sleep in the tent, he calls out, "It's cold."

"I'm glad. I hope *you* freeze, too."

Jack, crawling out and looking at me in a very silly fashion, "I don't want to freeze you. You can't fool me."

"No, I don't suppose I can. But what *you* are trying to do is to fool me." He goes to the window and shuts it with a bang, stamps around on the floor. "What's that rattle?"

"I don't know." He stamps again. "Let's see." Whenever Jack hears a noise, he has to know what it is. I think that it is a copper vase rattling on the mantelpiece, but when I lift the vase and he stamps, the rattle continues. Jack thinks it is the electric light globe. I hold it and he stamps. The noise ceases. He is triumphant.

For some moments he seems to be a little at a loss as to what to do. He tries on my rubbers and runs around with them. "Oh, it's nice and cool here!" He tries to fix the tent and can't get it to suit him. I suggest another arrangement of the chair, which, to my surprise, he accepts. Finally he decides to work on the door and wants to stand on the little table. The table is frail, and I say no. Jack, teasingly, "Can't I just one time?"

"No, not one single time."

"Oh, bah! bah!"

"Makes you mad, doesn't it, Jack?"

"Uh huh." He gives up apparently, and runs over to the desk. Then he starts in on the "taking home" interest. Finds an old calendar. "Can I take this home?"

"I don't see why you want it, Jack, but you can have it if you want it. I have no use for it."

"And can I have that little book?" The book is only an advertising book, and I decide to give in and let him have it. This is a terrific victory, and he kicks up his heels and stamps around at a great rate, throwing the window open.

"*You* had your way that time, didn't you, Jack?" He grabs a pillow and begins fighting. "Listen here, you shut up. Here comes a man. I'll lock the tent so he can't come in." (Begins to feel the fear of success.)

He retreats to the tent. "Peek-a-boo, I see you." Suddenly he rushes out with his hand to his mouth, running to the door.

"Are you sick, Jack?" He nods, and I take him out to the toilet, where he spits a little phlegm. "Were you sick at your stomach?"

"A little bit, not very much. There is something on the floor. It came out of my mouth."

"All right. We'll clean it up." I look under the tent and find a small particle of phlegm. Jack seems filled with disgust. "I don't like it. It smells. Can't you smell it?" There is a slight sour odor, which one can detect with a little effort.

Jack, sitting down on the couch beside me, "Have you
a penny?" [12]

"Why? Do you want one?"

"Yes; will you give me one?"

"No, Jack, I can't give you pennies."

"I'll vomit again," threateningly.

"I guess you'll have to, if that's the way you feel."

"I'll open your pocketbook and see."

"No. No pennies, Jack."

He goes to the drawer and gets out the hammer. I rather
expect him to use it, but he does not. He finds my powder
compacts and brings them over to me. "What are they
for?"

"They have powder in them."

"Show me." I open one of them and show him.

"Do you want it?"

"Yes. If they were empty, would you give them to me?"

"What do you want them for, Jack?" At this point he is
rummaging around in the drawer and has found the needle
case.

"Can I sew?"

"Yes, if you want to." From that moment to the end of
the hour, which is about fifteen minutes, he is completely absorbed in trying to thread a needle and sew a straight line.
His coördinations are not very good. He cannot thread as
small a needle as I have, and I tell him that I will bring him
a large one next time if he wants me to. He does manage to
put the needle in and out and pull the thread through, but
is very awkward. He is fascinated by it and persists, allowing me to thread the needle when it comes unthreaded,
until he has finished one side of the bag he proposes to

[12] Asking for money is perhaps the height of boldness—the symbol for feeling, the request for love, and he uses a powerful infantile weapon, vomiting, not unlike the enuresis at home, to en-
force it. Begging for something to take home is at first merely a
game, a way of trying to win out, but gradually it becomes the painful admission of a need which seeks a material gift as a symbol of
love and physical response from the therapist.

make. The interesting thing about this child is his willingness to learn, to take help from the other person, combined with a good deal of determination to do it himself independently.

"Jack, it's time to go now."

"Can I come to-morrow?"

"No. You come on Saturday. To-morrow is Friday."

"But I want to come to-morrow. Why can't I?"

"Because I work. I can only see you the three days."

"Can't I stay a little later?"

"No. I have to go now and so do you."

"Can I take this sewing home? I'll do it there."

"No, you leave it here, and then you can do it when you come again."

"Can I have a penny?"

"No. No pennies. I don't give little boys any candy or any pennies."

"Why?"

"Because if I gave away my pennies I wouldn't have any." He throws himself on the couch. "I'll just stay here. I won't go."

"Well, Jack, then you'll have to stay here alone, because I'm going."

"I'll mess the room up."

"If you do that, you won't have it to play in when you come next time." At this he goes into the other room and begins to put on his coat.

"Are you very mad at me, Jack?"

"No. Will you get me the book?"

"It's where you left it, Jack."

"Well, will you get it for me?"

"All right, I'll get it and the calendar too." (It is my turn to yield.)

He is now intent upon what he is going to do when he leaves. "I'm going to go outside the door and put them through the hole just like a letter." This he proceeds to do and then comes back in to get them. "Now, don't forget to say good-by when I ring the bell." He rings the bell.

I call, "Good-by," and as I open the door he is at the entrance saying, "See you later down town."

"See you Saturday, Jack."

March 19, 1932, Saturday—Tenth hour

Jack comes in rather more quietly than usual. Sings out as he comes down the hall, "Anybody home?"

"Good morning, Jack. Why, where are your glasses?"

"I broke them. It's a good thing they didn't go into my eyes. I'm going to sew this morning."

"All right. But I forgot to get your big needle. I'm very sorry." No apparent reaction from Jackie. He gets out the sewing things and settles down beside me on the couch. "Jack, you don't seem like yourself this morning. Are you tired?"

"I didn't sleep very well."

"Why?"

"We got a little baby at home and he wakes me up." The needle is threaded and the knots tied and Jackie starts on the second side of his bag, which is a little rumpled and hard to hold in place. He stops to get a drink, which he does very carefully, putting the glass back on the high mantel. Then he goes to the bathroom. When he comes back and picks up his sewing he seems rather uninterested.

"Maybe you don't want to sew, Jackie."

"Yes, I do." He makes much more use of me than before. Asks me at every turn what he shall do next.[13] He has learned how to get the needle in and out without its coming unthreaded, but finds it very difficult to keep the stitches close together and in a straight line. Finally he sews the remaining side of the bag with long, crooked stitches. "Gee, that's a swell bag! Look at that edge," pointing to the one he did last time, which is much better.

"If you turn it inside out, you'll have the seam on the in-

---

[13] This is the acting out of dependence, which goes beyond mere desire or the aggressive attitude of domination. He has accepted his use of me.

side." He is much interested in this, but finds that there are large gaps in the side that has just been sewed.

"How can I fix that?" I turn the bag again and show him how to fill in. Sings to himself, "I'll just go in and out, in and out, in and out." Very soon he is discouraged. "*You* do it."

"But, Jack, if I do it, it won't be the same as if you do it. Why don't you wait till next time when you feel more like it?"

"I want the bag. I want to take it home. *You* finish it."

"I think you must be tired, Jack, but if you want me to, I will do it for you."

"Is me bothering you?"

"No. What do you mean?"

"Don't you want to write?"

"No, I don't have to write." Evidently he had more than one reason for making me help him.[14]

"Is it time for me to get ready yet?"

"Would you like to go, Jackie?"

"No."

"I think perhaps you would. You sound to me as if you were a little tired."

"I go to the play-room when I go from here."

"Would you like to go there now?"

"You might be mad."

"No, I wouldn't be mad, Jack. Go ahead if you want to."

"I'll stay here till the time's up."

"Jack, if you really want to go, you run right along."

"No, I'll wait till it's my time. Are you sure I can stay?"

"Yes, of course, you can."

"I wish they'd find the Lindbergh baby, don't you? What do you suppose has happened to him? Don't you think maybe he'll be dead when they find him?"

---

[14] I think the real emotion here is guilt, not for wanting to absorb or dominate me, but because he is expressing so much of his own will to yield, that he feels the independent ego in danger of being overwhelmed by the love emotion and begins to experience fear for it. (Note reference to Lindbergh baby and feeling sick.)

"Jack, are you afraid that somebody will kidnap you?"

"My mother hasn't got any money."

"That's a good thing, isn't it?"

"Will they take me?"

"I shouldn't think so, Jack, if you haven't any money." He seems very listless and without purpose. "How do you feel, Jack? You don't seem quite like yourself."

"I feel a little sick," lying on the pillow.

"Do you feel sick at your stomach?"

"No, I feel sick here," pointing to his throat. "I need air." He goes over to the window and soon is playing cheerfully with the ball out the window.

"Jack, if you lose that ball out in the court, I can't get it for you, because the back door is locked."

"Who has the key?"

"The janitor. I don't think he is here this morning." He quickly desists. Lies on the floor aimlessly. Coughs violently. "Did you wish you weren't coming this morning, Jack?"

"No, I wanted to come. When can I come again? Monday?"

"No, Tuesday."

"Why can't I come Sunday?"

"Because I'm not here on Sunday."

"Can I come Monday?"

"No, the next day, Tuesday."

"Does Tuesday come after Monday? Are you sure I can come?" He goes on trying to make me tell him which day follows which, as if he did not know the days of the week. Pretty soon I turn the tables on him and ask him what the next day is and before he knows what he has done, he has betrayed his knowledge.

"You were fooling me, Jack. You are trying to make me think you don't know the days."

"Next Sunday will be Easter. I'm going to have a rabbit."

"Who will give it to you?"

"My mother." He begins throwing his ball against the

wall. I have wondered whether it will make a mark, but so far as I can see it does not. After a good many violent throws, looking at me anxiously, "Do you think the ball makes a spot?"

"I don't think so, Jack." He tries it out thoroughly, finally almost rubbing the ball against the wall. "It doesn't seem to, does it? I guess you wish it would, don't you?" (The old will conflict is a relief from the inside pressure.)

"No, I don't want to dirty the pretty wall."

"Is it time for me to go?"

"Not quite. But you can go any time you feel like it. Don't you want to go now?"

"No. Why can't I stay longer?"

"You don't really want to this morning, Jack."

"Yes, I do." He carries out a long argument. "If I could stay longer the morning that you was late and the morning I was late, why can't I stay longer this morning? Can't I stay after ten?"

"No, Jack. I don't stay after ten. I didn't even the morning that you were late. But there's fifteen minutes that I can use to stay a little longer if I have to."

"Who owns this place?"

"I do."

"Well, why don't you stay in it?"

"I do stay here sometimes, but I work over at the other building, too."

"Do you take kids away?"

"No, I sit in an office and talk to grown people and work at a desk."

Restlessly, "I think I'd better get ready and put my things away."

"All right, Jack. I think maybe you are a little tired of coming."

"No, I'm not."

"Well, some day you will be." [15]

"How do you know?"

"Because people do get tired of doing things after a while, and they want to do something else. And after a while you will be tired of playing here."

"I'll tell my bunny rabbit that you won't let me play."

"I didn't say that, Jack."

"What did you say?"

"I said that you would be tired and not want to play here any more."

"My bunny rabbit will come." He now puts on his coat and hat quickly and is ready to go. "When I ring, you say good-by." As usual, "See you later down town at——" (something I could not understand).

"What did you say, Jack?"

"It means 'down at Gimbel's,'" as he runs quite excitedly down the steps.

March 22, 1932, Tuesday—Eleventh hour

When I arrive at five minutes of nine I find the maid cleaning and Jackie already there, sitting quietly on the couch. "I didn't know whether you was coming or not." (Note the absence of fear.)

"I would come all right, Jack, but you are a little early this morning, that's all."

"What have you got in those bags?" (I am carrying two suit cases.) "Clothes?"

"Yes."

"Are they for somebody else?"

"No. I have something for myself." He asks me a good many questions about where I come from and what I am going to do. Finally he says, "Are you a doctor?"

[15] This is an effort to recognize and pave the way for the natural impulse to withdraw from a too entangling situation, which begins to make itself felt as the contrary impulse toward union with the "other," the giving up of self in yielding and dependence approaches a climax.

"No, not really."

"Are you half a doctor?"

"Just about that."

"What do you do to children?"

"Play with them."

"You don't play with me."

"Well, I let you play here."

"Yes, you always do that," with feeling.

Jack is full of questions this morning. He runs to the steamer rug. "I haven't played this for a long time." Begins to arrange a tent. "I am going to get an Easter bunny and I'm going to bring it down here. Maybe I'll get two. I have to go to the bathroom. I wonder if she's out there?" meaning the maid.

"Even if she is, it's all right to go. You go ahead and ask her to let you come in."

I can hear him making his request. When he comes back he opens the window and breathes out so that his breath makes frost. "The cop will catch me."

"What for?"

"Smoking." (Identification with me.) He plays for a time with the tent, arranging a shade which goes up and down quite cleverly. Out of the blue he remarks, "Did you think I wasn't here?"

There is a lot of desultory play—sliding on the floor, opening the double door, talking to himself about his engine. Finally he addresses me, "Are you mad because I bring stuff here?"

"What do you mean, Jackie?"

"I mean the egg-beater and the watch."

"But why should I be mad?"

"Because I bring stuff here."

"You mean because you thought that I would give you something in place of your toys?"

"No."

"Jack, you remember that you told me you would bring

a toy if I would give you one. And then I didn't do it, and weren't you mad at me?"

"Almost, not quite." (The reply I had made to him.)

"Well, Jack, you remember you didn't tell me to give you anything for those toys. You just left them here." .

"Are you mad at me?" he asks.

"No."

"Well, it feels as if you are. Are you cold?"

"No. Do you wish I was?"

"I want the window open and you told me to shut it maybe." He becomes very joyful, retires to the tent and sings with a marked baby lisp, "When it's pingtime in the Wockies, and I'm far away from you, I'll come back and say I'm lonesome—" There's a great deal of byplay with this singing. He sticks his head out of his tent window and looks at me languishingly as he sings. "Jackie, I think you must like me this morning." [16]

"Yes, I do. I like you every morning."

"No. Sometimes you don't. Sometimes you are mad at me."

" What time is it?"

"Do you want to go?"

"No. How much time do I have?"

"You have lots of time yet."

"Look at my tent. Will you fix it?"

"Do you really want me to, Jack? You can fix it yourself. You fix it better than I do."

"You fix it," coaxingly.

"All right, I will." I pause to add to my notes.

"When are you going to fix it? Next week?" I do my best to arrange the tent but am not very successful. "I think you do it better than I do, Jack." He begins questioning

[16] This is the emotional climax, the confession of love. The reference to the toys he had brought down for exchange is part of his sense of the situation as demanding a response in kind—the real exchange is to be in feeling terms.

me about why he can't stay after ten. I do my best to explain about the fifteen minutes leeway. But it does not satisfy him. His garter is too tight. He says he can't untie the knot. Wants me to fix it, which I do. "Jackie, I wouldn't be surprised if you could untie this better than I can. I think you like to fool me."

"What makes you think that?"

"You remember how you made me tie your shoes and you could do it all the time."

"What'll you do at ten if this garter isn't right?" It seems to be still a little tight. "Suppose it's ten o'clock. Would you fix it?"

"No. If it's ten o'clock, it will have to wait until next time." There is more desultory play in which he instructs me as to what to say. "You say the baby is crying.—You say the shed's coming down.—Mammy's going to lick me." Then he turns to the drawer. "Let's see what's in this drawer." He finds the hammer and the screw-driver. "Have you got any old pieces of wood?"

"You mean something that you can pound? I'm afraid not."

"Have you got any nails? Why do you have a hammer if you don't have any nails?"

"Maybe I can find you a piece of wood to bring down next time, Jack, but I don't believe there is any now."

"I'm going to smash my watch and fix it." (This is a defiance in terms of his own property, where I have no right to object but where adults frequently do.)

"I'm afraid if you open that watch with the hammer, Jack, you won't be able to fix it. I think that's going to be the end of the watch." He looks at me to see what I am going to do and begins working with the watch. "Good-by, watch." He pounds on the watch and uses the screw-driver comparatively skilfully, considering what a small object he is working on, and manages to open it without destroying it completely.

"You did get it open, didn't you, Jack?"

"I might know how to fix it back and I might not." He works with it the rest of the hour. "Are you mad because I broke it?"

"No. Why should I be? It's your watch. If it were my watch, I should be mad."

"Would you give me a scolding?"

"Well, I don't think I would give you a chance to break the watch."

Singing to himself, "I don't know if this goes backwards or frontwards, or frontwards or backwards. Nobody knows, but I do know how to fix the watch. I get this upside down." Finally, after much manipulation, "I'm going to break the whole works." Pounds at it vigorously with the hammer, but does not seem to have any anger. It is just a pleasant experience.[17] He still is wondering a little whether I am going to object, but I do not.

"It's time to go, Jack."

"In a minute." I begin to put the room to rights while he still works with the pieces of the watch. "It's all smashed."

"Are you glad you did it, Jack?"

"No, I'm sorry," in an unreal voice.

"Since you have done it, it's too bad you're sorry. You'd better be glad." Jackie puts up the most prolonged resistance to going that he ever has. I pick up everything and throw the pieces of the watch in the wastebasket. Jackie still does not get ready. He retreats to the tent. Lying on the floor, "You've got to get the big broom this time. I won't go for the little broom."

"I haven't time to get the broom this morning, Jackie; you'll have to go without it."

I leave the room for a few minutes, and when I come back he is still lying on the floor, unwilling to go. I produce

[17] Note the vigorous ego reaction following his overcoming of fear to the point of declaring the love emotions. This is a more courageous, less defensive, expression of self, because he now has more self to express.

his sweater, firmly but cheerfully. "Here's your sweater, Jackie. Put it on. Time to go."

"Oh, gee! Well, I suppose I have to."

"I know you're mad, Jackie, but it can't be helped. You do have to go." He now puts on the rest of his garments cheerfully and goes down the hall. "Oh, I forgot to ring the bell." Comes back and rings the bell vigorously. His usual, "See you later," is missing.

March 24, 1932, Thursday—Twelfth hour [18]

Someone is moving out of the apartment house this morning, so that Jack has to go past several men when he comes in. I notice that he waits until they are all out of the hall, then I hear his voice, "Is there anybody here?" He always inquires before he opens the door. Almost the moment he comes in he says, "I'm going to take a nap."

"Why, Jackie, are you tired?"

"Yes." He has on a new spring suit which I admire. "It's for Easter. Easter is coming soon." Apparently he means to take a nap in the tent, because he begins at once to arrange it. Is a little impatient with it because the rug falls off so many times, and I finally help him. "They were moving stuff out when I came in. Two mans. Were they moving any of your furniture?"

"No. Did you think maybe they were?"

"Uh huh."

"And were you scared?"

"No. I just opened the door and came right in."

"Did you feel bad when you thought I was moving?" (I ask this because I know beforehand the effect of this kind of incident and want him to know that I understand how he feels.)

"Uh huh."

"I wouldn't move without telling you first." He is going

---

[18] This hour illustrates the new sense of balance in the relationship—less fear, more freedom to express his own will positively, not merely in resistance.

on with his arrangements for the tent, fixing the little curtain that he can pull up and down. "Are you going to school after Easter, Jack?"

"I think so."

"Maybe that's why you have your new suit—for school."

"No. It's for Easter."

"Perhaps you will be wearing it to school afterwards." He is now in the tent, with only one little peep hole. I smile at him as he looks through it. "What are you laughing at?"

"I'm not laughing. I am just smiling."

"Then what are you smiling at?"

"At you. I feel pleasant."

"What makes you feel pleasant?"

"Because it's a nice morning."

"Springtime, like in the Rockies. Could you see if the light was out?"

"Yes, put it out if you want to." He does so, and opens the window as wide as he can. He is arranging a bed for himself in the tent, using the little rug folded up, at my suggestion.

"Did you ever go to a shoemaker?"

"Yes. Why? Have you been to the shoemaker?"

"Once I went to a shoemaker and he said, 'I'll break your neck,' and he said a bad word. I wouldn't say it."

"What was the word, Jackie?"

"It's a bad word. I don't want to say it. Do you want me to?"

"No, not unless you want to. Do just as you like."

"Well, I won't. Do you ever say bad words?"

"Yes, sometimes."

"Do you say them to yourself?"

"Yes."

"Well, that's what I do sometimes, too." (Identification even in badness.) By this time he has remembered the hammer and the screw-driver and has discovered two pieces of wood in the table drawer in the front room. He starts jabbing viciously with the screw-driver, and trying to pound the wood with the hammer. "Did any of the boys ever do this here?"

"I don't believe so, Jack. I think that wood is pretty hard. There are some tacks that I found in the drawer that you can use if you want to." He finds half a dozen thumb tacks stuck in a piece of soft wood. I have to give him a good many suggestions because I do not want the floor mutilated. Also, it is so slippery that he can't pound a piece of wood on it safely. He learns to use a little mat to pound on, and to hold on to the wood so that it will not strike him in the face. It is interesting to see how much inhibition he has to exercise in order to keep from hurting himself, which is the only thing that protects the furniture. It is evident that he is aching to pound as hard as he possibly can, but realizes that it isn't quite safe to do.

"Can I take these home?"

Assuming that he refers only to the little block with the tacks, I say, "I have no objection, but I think you might like to have them down here next time."

"Do you care if I take them home?"

"No, I don't care, but I don't think it's a very good idea. You wouldn't have any hammer at home, and you wouldn't have any place to put the tacks. Somebody would get mad at you if you stuck them into things." He gives that up without any apparent resistance.

"Is it ten o'clock?"

"No, not yet." He begins to pound quite freely on the little piece of wood that held the tacks, which is soft, and pieces of it break off, to his joy. "Boy, that flew apart!" Pounding more viciously, "I'll get this!" Then he takes the heavy piece of wood, which has some screw holes in it, and begins to dig into the holes with the screw-driver. "She's going to get broken in a minute!"

"What do you want to break her for, Jack?"

"To see what she does. Is these Jimmy's tools? I mean the janitor's."

"No, they are mine."

"I call the janitor 'Jimmy.' " He is digging with all his might with the screw-driver, puffing and panting with the effort.

"Jack, I think you want to make a hole right through it."

"I'd better put it on this," putting it over a second piece of wood, "It might make a hole in the rug." He works until he is breathless, and then has to go to the toilet. I was interested to see that while there may have been a reaction toward me in this attack on the wood, he was able to keep it fairly constructive and never merely an expression of rage. He stayed so long in the toilet that I wondered what he was doing, and went into the hall to find out. I finally opened the toilet door. "What's the matter, Jack?"

"I'm just cleaning my knee off. It was dirty." He was sitting on the toilet seat, scrubbing one knee. I produced a paper towel and left him, remarking that he stayed so long I thought he was lost. After a few minutes he comes back. "Where did you think I was? Did you think I was with the janitor?"

"I thought maybe you might feel sick."

"I hope it ain't time to go."

"It is, Jack. I'm sorry. It's just about time to put your things away."

At my suggestion he puts his tools and his tacks in the front table drawer.

"I wish I hadn't said that."

"What do you mean, Jack? Said what?"

"I wish I hadn't said, 'What time is it?' "

"I would have known anyway."

"Do you watch the clock all the time?"

"No, but I have to keep track of the time because I have to do something else."

Although he expresses his resistance to going, it is a very sweet expression. There is no fight in it, just a little delay. He stops to examine the lock on the front door, and then, "Now, say good-by when I ring," and the usual,—"See you later down town."

March 26, 1932, Saturday—Thirteenth hour [19]

I arrived at a quarter of nine, but Jack was already there, although not able to get in.

"Did you think I wasn't coming?"

"I didn't know." He is apparently not upset. His first spontaneous remark is, "To-morrow is Easter." He is full of a sense of holiday. Points out that he has his glasses fixed, gives them to me to keep, and starts in to build his tent, as usual.

"I was in the hall this morning and I was saying, 'Is anybody there?' Then I was going to ask the janitor lady where you was." Continues to arrange the tent. Without any connection, a little later, he continues, "I came in and I rang the doorbell twice and when nobody answered I went right out." He starts to take off his sweater, and his shirt comes with it.

"You are about to lose all of your clothes, Jack." He has some interest in this fact. Begins sliding violently.

"Those ain't my Easter pants."

"It's a good thing they aren't, isn't it?"

He wants more space to slide in, and is going to open the folding door. Looking at my chair with his face all twisted up, "Can I take that only wunst?"

"But why not take the chair in the front room, Jack?"

He goes in and gets the wooden chair.

"I guess it's too heavy, isn't it?"

"No, it's not too heavy for me." A good part of this hour he is making explosive noises with his mouth. He wants to use the big rug in the back room, which is my best rug. He has never tackled this before. I am very firm in my refusal. "I'm not going to do anything with it—just going to put it away." So I allow him to roll it up and put it to

[19] In this hour we see a breaking up of the unity attained, the initiation of a fresh and deeper conflict, a renewed effort to dominate me and to see how far he can go. Note the elation engendered by the increased self-confidence.

one side. Then he slides the full length of the floor. Tiring of that, he goes to bed in his tent and begins peeking out at me through various holes.

"What are you up to, Jackie?"

"Do you know what I am doing? I broke the chair. What are you going to do?"

"What can I do?"

"I broke just one round."

"I don't see that I can do anything about it, Jack."

He comes out of the tent with a bounce and begins to rush around.

"You are full of prunes this morning, Jack."

"Do you know what I am happy about?"

"No. What is it?"

"It's Easter, Easter, Easter, Easter, and I'm going to get bunny rabbits and jelly beans and eat them." He begins throwing the pillow violently into the air and hits the light.

"It's a good thing you didn't break that, Jack." Evidently he has no regrets, and continues to throw the pillow. "Jack, are you afraid you will hit it, or do you wish you would hit it?"

"I'm afraid *you* will hit *me*, if I hit it. What would you do if I broke it? Would you let me come any more?"

"If you kept on breaking my lights, Jack, I don't see how I could let you come. I have to have lights."

"If I broke it just once, would you keep me?"

"I don't know, Jack. I wouldn't like to have the light broken."

He now turns his attention to the back window and works with it violently, trying to get it as high as it will go. Occasionally I get up to help him. He leans out the window, calling, "Jimmy! Jimmy!" Spits out the window. Turning suddenly from the window, "Have I got time yet?"

"Yes, lots of time."

"Ha, Ha! Ha, Ha!" Begins sliding again, and turns his attention to the rugs in the front room. "Can I take those up?"

"If you want to take the trouble."

"Hot dog!" talking to the rug. "You're hard to manage."

"You will have a job getting those rugs down again, Jack."

"Who cares?" He slides the full length of the two rooms. With some disappointment, "It's sticky."

"Yes, there is a place under the rug where it isn't shiny." I leave the room at this point, and when I come back Jack has vanished. "I think there is a robber under the bed. I guess I had better get the gun." Jack has brought a toy pistol this morning. At this point Jack sticks his head out and I say, "Hands up!" He is a little overpowered by my taking this rôle and submits at once. His revenge is to begin to put his dirty hands on my clean pillows. "I think you had better wash your hands. Won't the lady where you live scold you if you get your white shirt all dirty?"

"She just scolds. She don't lick. Suppose I push your pillows."

"I'm not going to let you do it with those dirty hands, so you had better go wash them."

He complies, and when he comes back, goes out into the front hall and gets himself locked out both ways.

"Suppose I wouldn't let you in, Jack?"

"I'd holler 'Help' and 'Murder,' and I'd go out the front door, or else I'd climb in that window." He begins sliding on the forbidden steamer rug.

"Jack, no sliding on that rug." He is making many explosive hissing noises. "What kind of noise is that you are making, Jack?"

"What kind of noise do you think it is?"

"It sounds to me like a going-to-the-bathroom noise. Is that what you mean it to be?"

And with something I could not catch about ". . . coming from the back," he gets more and more noisy. Throws himself around on the floor.

"My belly flew off—I mean the pillow." Turns somersaults. "Miss Taft ain't home to-day. Is this a bed?"—
looking under the couch.

"Yes, it has a mattress." He is fooling about the couch
and suddenly rolls over and begins to cry, apparently.

"I hurt my eye,"—more and more crying sounds.

"I think you're just fooling me, Jack."

"No, I ain't, Miss Taft."

"I think you are." He looks up, laughing, and begins to
throw himself about. Sits down very hard on the floor.
"You hurt your own sit-down that time."

Jack kicks himself in the trousers and is very silly. Repeats a phrase which I cannot make out, excepting the
first part of it, "Itchy, Itchy,"—scratching himself on the
buttocks. This is repeated with a very suggestive pointing
to the anus. Begins sliding on my steamer rug.

"Jack, no sliding on that rug."

"No more nice rides," sadly. He desists from the sliding, puts his feet on the couch (which he has not done
before), lying with his head on the floor. He stands on
his head, makes noises, and finally goes and looks out
of the window. "Is that man colored?" meaning the
janitor.

"No, he is white. Are you afraid of colored men, Jack?"

"Yes, are you?"

"Not if they are good. Not any more than I am of white
men."

"Are you afraid of white men?"

"If they are bad, I am, aren't you?"

"I'd pick up this (putting his hand around my ankle)
and hit them. I'll show you a good trick. Can you see
now?"—(referring to my writing) as he pulls down the
curtain. "Yes, I can still see, Jack, so it doesn't do me
any harm."

He now throws himself upon the forbidden steamer rug
and slides across the floor on it.

"Jack, this is too much. I am going to have to take the rug away." He resists, but finally gives in and throws the rug upon the couch in a temper. Then he throws himself face down on the floor and appears to be crying. "Jack, I don't doubt that you are mad at me." He will not admit it. "But I guess you will just have to be." He takes some shredded paper out of his pocket and wipes his nose and ears and plays foolishly with it. Then he points to the screen.

"Can I play with this?"

"No."

"Can I play with it at all?"

"Absolutely no, Jack."

"Then what can I do? Can I turn the chair upside down?"

"No."

"Won't you let me? Oh, It's no good. It's no good. It's no good,"—in a despairing tone of voice.

"I think you are trying to find out what it is I won't let you do,.aren't you?"

"No, I just want to play with the chair and you won't let me."

"It's time to get ready anyway, Jack."

He runs around and cries loudly, "Will you let me put the rugs down?"

"Yes, you took them up, so I think you had better put them back."

"Wait until I have one sticky ride, then I'll put them down and you be waiting."

I can see that he would like to take the sticky ride for the rest of the morning to keep me waiting, so I begin to clean up the room.

"You let *me* put the rugs down. You do your work, I'll do mine," says Jack.

"They are quite hard rugs to manage. I think you will have a hard job."

"I can manage them." He tugs away at the rugs and gets them back after a fashion, but I have to help.

"Jack, I have something to tell you. I am not going to be here next Saturday. I'm going away." [20]

"Will you be here Monday?"

"No, Jack. You don't come on Monday. But I will be here Tuesday. That is the day you come. Then I will be here Thursday, but on Saturday I won't be here."

"That's next Saturday."

"Yes, Jack, next Saturday, and then the Saturday after that I can't come either, I'm very sorry."

Jack is somewhat sobered by this time and goes out the door, stopping, however, to fool with the lock, put his pistol through the mail chute, and ring the bell. He leaves with his usual "See you later down town."

Just before he left, I said, "Jack, I hope you will be able to forgive me. I know you are mad at me. I was a little bad and you were a little bad, too. Perhaps we can forgive each other." He seems to accept this as being a correct version of the situation.

From Visitor's Record
March 29, 1932

Jack had been disappointed in his Easter visit from his mother. She had come too late for the bunnies. He talked about moving from Aunt May's (present foster mother), hoped it would not be soon. Wondered where he would go if his mother didn't want him to come home. Hoped it wouldn't be like the last home, where they licked him with the hairbrush. I suggested that he stay with Aunt May for six more Saturdays. How would that be? He thought that would be O.K.

At this time foster mother gets discouraged over enuresis and asks for removal, but Jack is entered in school, and

[20] The therapist's absence is always an injury to the patient, has the weight of a desertion by the mother or the beloved and is very difficult to accept because it is imposed from the outside, is not the result of choice. A counter reaction is inevitable.

after she gets a little rest from him, she consents to keep him until he goes to permanent home.

L. T.

March 29, 1932, Tuesday—Fourteenth hour

Jack comes in the door without ringing or calling. "What time is it?"

"It's about ten minutes past nine, Jack. You are a little bit late."

"Mrs. T. says to tell you that there was a flat tire and they had to fix it before they could come for me."

"Then it's not your fault, is it?"

"It wasn't anybody's fault."

"No, so it wasn't."

"What did you get for Easter?" he asks.

"Not very much. What did *you* get?"

"Oh, I got some jelly beans, and some easter eggs, and four bunnies."

"That was quite a lot."

"What did *you* get?"

"I got a box of salted nuts and a victrola record." He now devotes his entire attention to the matter of the heat and the window. He has an interest that has to be satisfied by accurate information. He keeps at it until I show him exactly how the heat is turned off and on, and how I know which is which. He tugs away at the window, climbing up to open the lock, until he succeeds in raising it. What Jack lacks in aggressiveness he makes up in persistence. "Can I take the rugs up? Does she take the rugs up? In there too? Does she clean under them?"

"I hope so, Jack."

"It's a little stuck. I wonder if she put wax on the floor to-day. I hope she did."

He slides awhile on the floor.

"It's a good thing your trousers are short. You would get them good and dirty." He has on his new ones.

"Who cares?"

"I should think *you* would. They are your trousers."

"Can you see without the light?" Puts it out. "I want it to be cool," lying down underneath the open window. "I lay my head on the pillow, and let some nice fresh air in. Do you want the heat off or on?"

"I don't care, Jack."

"Hee-hee. I turned it off. Do you care?"

"No, I don't. What are you trying to do—freeze me?"

"No. I just want to know how it goes off and on."

"When do you start to school?"

"To-morrow morning or next week. I think it's to-morrow morning." He is quiet awhile.

"What are you thinking?"

"I want to sew." The rest of the time is spent in his efforts to sew a long seam on a piece of white cloth.

"I hope it ain't time yet."

"Not quite."

"Now I'm going to cut this, so I can have half of it for the doll's coach."

"If you do, the hem will come out."

"The time is up." He is not as resistant as usual but suddenly begins, "Is there anything I can take home? Can't I have this?" (The rubber mat.)

"No, I use that."

"Can't I have this?" pointing to the brass pot.

"I use that, too."

"What for?"

"For flowers."

"Well, you can't use that for flowers."

"No, it's an ash tray. Jack, I think you must have wanted me to give you an Easter present."

"Uh huh."

"I'm sorry, but I don't give presents to little boys and girls."

"What do you do?" [21]

"I just let them play here if they like to. But that isn't very nice, and I think probably you don't like it—that you are a little mad at me." As he goes out the door, I explain to him once more about Saturday, and he says it over after me carefully two or three times to make sure about the second Saturday. He lingers in the hall to examine the mail boxes for the other apartments, and the speaking tubes. When I have satisfied his curiosity, he takes a regretful departure, without the usual "See you later."

From Visitor's Record
March 31, 1932

Jackie very dilatory. Delays over dressing. On the way home after visit to Dr. Taft he had in his hand a red envelope which he said Dr. Taft had given him. He carried also his new shoes and a token. He decided that he had too much in his hands and thought he would throw the envelope away. I said, "Do as you like,"—whereupon he threw it on the ground and stamped on it saying, "Good riddance to bad rubbish."

Mrs. T.

March 31, 1932, Thursday—Fifteenth hour

"Is anybody home to-day?"

"Somebody is. Good morning."

"Am I late this morning?"

"About ten minutes. What's the matter?" (Worker says he wasted time.)

"They couldn't get my trousers fixed. There was something wrong with the buttons."

He is full of spirits, singing, talking to himself all the time. Rushes into the other room, begins to take up the

---

[21] It is as if my intention to stay away had brought on an acute feeling of deprivation which demands a material giving.

rugs, singing to himself loudly, "I fold my rugs, I fold my rugs." (Indicates a don't-care-if-you-are-going-away feeling.)

"I go to school this afternoon."

"Oh, did you go to school yesterday?"

"Yes, I did."

He jingles some coins in his pocket, looking at me teasingly. "What have you got, Jackie?" He produces five pennies proudly. "Where did you get those?"

"In my bank. My bank's only an old tin can."

"How did you get them?"

"I saved them. My mommie and my father and my uncle Tommy gave them to me." Begins sliding wildly on the floor. "These old rubbers stop me from sliding." Throws them violently, then a little apologetically to me "I'll pick them up." He is full of explosive noises and rough behavior. Looking at his trousers, "Oh, I thought those trousers were down to here."

"It's a good thing they are the short ones, isn't it?" He lies flat on his back so that he can slide on the seat of his trousers. "I'm sliding on them just the same," provocatively.

"I can't help that. They're your trousers."

"I can't help it, either," sliding away and then getting up to show me the seat.

"Now are they dirty?" anxiously.

"I can't tell, Jackie, but they certainly will be. I know the floor is dirty."

Slides some more and shows me again, "Now can you see any dirt?"

"Evidently you want to get them dirty. You do just as you like, they are yours." He gets a drink with a great deal of fuss and ceremony, coughing, choking, and coming dangerously near to throwing the water around. "Jack, why do you want to get dirty? Is it to make me mad?" He will not admit this. "You see, Jack, it's no use, because they are not my trousers, so I don't care if you do get them dirty. It's your own affair."

He seizes the steamer rug and puts it on the floor. "Now don't take this away from me. If I do something bad, will you take it away?"

"Yes, I will. You seem to be looking for trouble, Jack." He grows louder and noisier and has quite an air of defiance. Turns tumblesaults violently on the pillow. "Watch the brave man. Don't take this away," as he slides the rug a little.

"Why should I, Jack? You aren't hurting it." Slides it a little further on the floor.

"Me hurting it now? I almost done it, didn't I? I'm going to see if it's dirty. Yes, it's kinda dirty."

He now turns his attention to the little table, is going to put his full weight on it.

"You don't want to break that table, do you?"

"Who cares if it breaks?"

"I do. I think you are mad at me. You are just trying to be as bad as you possibly can." He mumbles something about me so that I cannot understand it. Finally says, "Are you going crazy?"

"I don't know. I hope not."

"I'm going crazy. Want to go with me?"

"No, thank you." He rolls around on the floor violently and makes noises through his nose, very near the steamer rug. "I blew my nose. It went right there on the floor between the pillow and the steamer rug."

"I don't want any nose blown on that steamer rug." He rubs the steamer rug over the place where he is supposed to have blown his nose. "I am just fooling you." The noises and the foolishness increase. Tumbles around wildly. "Do I come to-morrow?"

"No."

"Will you be here?"

"No, I won't be here."

He now finds my umbrella and begins to see what use he can make of it, but is comparatively careful with it. "Can I take this home? Why can't I take this home?"

"Because I need it."

"I need it, too."

"You'll have to get one of your own."

Takes down the cigarette box and finds a key in it. "What's this key?"

"I'm not sure. Perhaps it's the desk key." The rest of the hour is spent in trying this key out on every possible keyhole. To his delight, he finds he can lock the back door with it, but he can't unlock it. "It's a dirty gyp. It won't open. It's a dirty gyp. Can I take this key home and see if it will open our front door?"

"I don't think it will, Jack."

"But let me take it home. I promise to bring it back."

"All right, you can take it home if you will bring it back. It's time to go now."

He hates to stop, and delays as usual.

"You won't see me for a long time, Jack."

"I'll still be happy."

"You won't care a bit? Well, that's good. You let me be the one to care. I'll have to be sorry. Let's see when you are coming again, Jack. Next Tuesday, isn't it?" He looks a little doubtful. "Maybe you are tired of coming?"

"Yes, I am tired," he says.[22]

"Well, you don't have to come any longer than you want to, but I think you'd better come once more anyway, so you come on Tuesday and bring the key back, and then we'll see if you want to come any more." He looks a little startled with himself for having said this. Perhaps the key was taken to insure return.

April 5, 1932, Tuesday—Sixteenth hour

I find Jackie already waiting for me, as the maid is there and I am a little later than usual. He is behind the door

[22] Here we get the full negative compensatory reaction to my desertion.

when I come in. He makes no spontaneous references to the Saturday absence, and is apparently quite calm and friendly. "I am going to be a locker." At first I do not understand, but I soon realize it has to do with the key which he took home last time, and which he has brought back with him. He plays with the locking of the desk a good part of the time. He comes across the pencil-sharpener again. "Can I take this home?"

"No, Jack."

"I'll bring it back like I did the key."

"Well, if you want to do that, you may."

"What's this?"

"An ink-well." He finds a solitary jack. "Could I take this?"

"I'll give you that, if you want it, Jack. You can have it to keep." He comes across an old Red Cross button. "Yes, you can have that too." [23] Pins it on his shirt. Inquires what the Red Cross is. He is very docile this morning. Gets the wastebasket and puts it in the proper place before he sharpens the pencil. Does everything he is asked to do. Comes across the egg-beater. "Oh, that's your egg-beater, Jack. You left it here."

"Yes, but I ain't going to leave the fire engine here," referring to a toy engine in his pocket. Goes to the desk, talking to himself, "What can I have now?"

Turning to me plaintively and appealingly, "If I give you something, can I keep this?" (The pencil-sharpener.)

"Can you pay for the pencil-sharpener?"

"I don't know."

"Find out what the pencil-sharpener costs, and I'll let you have it for half price."

"I'll give you a penny for it."

"But I don't know what it cost, Jack. You'll have to find out."

[23] This is plain inconsistency on my part. I can't bear to say "no" any more for the moment.

"There isn't any store where I can get a pencil-sharpener."

"I can't help that, you will have to find out."

"Is it time for me to go?"

"Do you want to?"

"No."

"You have plenty of time yet. What did you do Saturday?"

"I forget. Oh, I played with my bike and all."

"Did you miss me Saturday?" He only nods. (I bring this up, not for vanity, but to help him admit his own feeling instead of denying it.)

"Jack, where do you live? Do you live in the country?"

"No, I live in the city."

"Did you ever live in the country, on a farm?"

"I've seen a farm," says Jack. "There was cows and bulls, and the bulls chased red. There was a bull that had sticks around him. Once I saw a great big cow and it was dead. I kicked it to see if it would come alive."

"Had it been killed for meat?"

"Yes. That's where we get our beef."

"Meat?" says Jack in astonishment. "Does meat come from a cow?"

"Does ham and liverwurst and scrapple come from there?" He is overcome with the surprise of this discovery.

"Where did you think meat came from, Jack?"

"From the butcher." There is a good deal of conversation about the origin of meat, which I am not able to repeat.

"Did you see your mother Saturday?"

"No," says Jack without further comment. He seems to become listless.

"Are you tired?"

"Yes, I'm going to close my eyes." Gets the pillows and lies down on the floor.

"Is it time to go?"

"No, not yet."

Then he begins on a long list of questions. "Where does tobacco come from? Where does paper come from?" Unlike most children who ask questions, he listens to the answers. Is much interested in the idea of paper. "Do you think we could make it?"

"I don't believe we could, Jack, but you could learn when you grow up."

"Could you be a cab driver?"

"Yes, if you wanted to."

"Who tells you to be a cab driver? Do we go up to God and see if we can drive a cab or not?"

"Not that I know of, Jack."

"Do you know how to get up there?"

"No, I don't believe I do. Do you?"

"Yes. You could get there by airplane or Zeppelin." He seems to grow a little uncertain. "Could you get to God by an airplane?"

"I never heard of anybody who did, Jack."

"Well, do you think we could?"

"I don't know, Jack."

"You think half 'yes' and half 'no.' I know where chairs come from," with a little relief.

"It's very hard to tell where things come from, Jack, isn't it?"

"Do you know where fur comes from?"

"I think *you* know that."

"Yes. I just wanted to see if you knew." So he goes on through iron, glass and tin. The tin reminds him of nanny goats. "Do you know where nanny goats come from?"

"They come from their mothers. Just like kittens."

"From big mothers like you?"

"Yes. Only not nanny goats, but little babies."

"Well, how do they get out?"

"They come out of a hole."

"Does the mother die?"

"No. Why should she?"

"Because the nanny goat comes out of her."

"But that doesn't kill her," getting a little mixed myself.

"Is she sick?"

"Yes, she is sick."

"How sick?"

"She goes to the hospital sometimes."

"Does the mother goat go to the hospital?"

"No, just people go to hospitals."

"What do they do with the nanny goats when they are sick?"

"There's no hospital for goats, Jack." [24]

"What time is it?"

"It's not quite time to go. You have about three minutes."

"How long is a minute?"

"If you can count to sixty, you can tell how long a minute is." He can't count by himself, so we count together. "Now, Jack, it's really time to get ready."

"You put the things away," plaintively.

"I see you are a very tired boy. If you are so tired, I'll do all the work."

"Get my coat and hat."

"I think you are trying to make me your servant. If you'd ask me more politely, maybe I would."

"Please get my coat and hat."

"Seeing that you are such a very tired boy this morning, I will do it." He has to put the coat on in a fancy way, lying on the floor with his arms in the air, taking a great pleasure in making me do just what he wants me to. He peeks through the letter slot as he goes out the door. Rings the bell vigorously. "So long. See you next Thursday."

(Note) A little boy of about two years, ward of Children's Aid, was removed from Jack's boarding home to a permanent home to-day April 5, 1932.

[24] This interest in origins seems to me the child's way of expressing his anxiety over separation, which, as with adults, is likely to come in terms of curiosity or fear about birth.

April 7, 1932, Thursday—Seventeenth hour

Jack is ten minutes late. Mrs. T. talks to me through the window from the street as Jack is coming in the door. Says he is not feeling well and that they have been delayed by engine trouble. Jack comes in without any of his usual greeting. "You seem sober this morning, Jack."

"I'm sick. I dreamed last night there was a robber and I vomited." He wants a drink at once. "I think I'll lay down."

"Where do I lay down?" (He asks me if I want to write. I always sit on the couch.) "Do you want to lie on the couch?" This is evidently his desire, so I arrange the pillow with some protection in case he should be sick again. He settles himself with great satisfaction and remains there the rest of the hour. Most of the time has his fingers in his mouth, like a little baby.[25] "Tell me what you dreamed last night, Jack."

"I didn't really dream it. I thought there was a robber coming through the screen at the window, and there was one under the bed, too, but I couldn't see, and I wanted my flash light, and it hasn't any battery. I'm going to get a new one to-day. I felt awfully sick. The little screen at the window—it just kept rattling, and I could hardly turn my head."

"You seem to have had kind of a bad time. Did anything go wrong yesterday? Are you worried about something?"

"No, nothing, but last night about the robber."

"Do you worry about your mother, Jack?"

"Yes, sometimes. Sometimes I cry." He coughs violently, and I hastily produce a paper towel, but he does not throw up. "I've got a bad headache. My sister had an earache, and the cop came for her. I knew she had an earache before the cop came."

---

[25] Here we have his capitulation to the pain and fear of the coming absence, which he threw off with a denial of feeling the week before. The fear comes out in the dream, the pain in physical symptoms. The vomiting is a rejection of the whole painful situation and also an admission of weakness and need for help.

"Why did the cop come, Jack?"

"Oh, he came to see why she wasn't in school."

"Do you want to stay home from school, too, Jack?"

"Yes."

"Then you don't like school?"

"No. You have to read and write."

"You feel a little bit afraid of everything to-day, don't you, Jack?"

"I think it was the ghost that made me dream. Don't you remember how I closed that double door quick one day and there was a ghost outside? I think he made me dream."

"Maybe you are a little afraid about coming down here, Jack. Maybe you think I might go away and leave you the way I did last Saturday. And then you know I am not coming this Saturday either." He inquires carefully about which Saturday I mean, and says, "When do I come again?"

"Next Tuesday, Jack."

"I was afraid to go to the bathroom," once more referring to the experience of the night.

"What happens when you are afraid to go to the bathroom, Jack?"

"I wet the bed."

"Do they punish you when you wet the bed?"

"Not this lady, but, gee, maybe the other lady didn't spank me with the hairbrush! Right on my bare skin."

"Can you help wetting the bed, Jack? Do you ever have a dry night?"

"Yes, sometimes I don't wet the bed if they take me up. Why did you close the door?" I had closed the door between the back and front rooms to keep the sun out of his eyes, and I explained this. "Do you want it open? All right, we'll open it." He is lying very quietly, his fingers in his mouth, looking very young and helpless. "Jack, do you feel just like a baby?" He will not admit it.

"I felt sick in the car, and I thought I'd vomit, but I did it outside. Sometimes when I close my eyes when the sun's in 'em, the tears come down." He inquires carefully again about dreams and daydreams. It seems to puzzle him. "How can you tell when you dream? How do you know it isn't a daydream? Once I thought it was a ghost pushing the bed up."

"That was pretty scary, Jack."

"There is no such thing as a ghost, is there?"

"I never saw one."

"Is a bunny rabbit real?" He answers this himself. "It is a real rabbit, but he doesn't give you eggs. Your mother buys them."

"Eggs come from chickens, Jack, not rabbits."

"Do they lay hard-boiled eggs? Maybe the rabbit gives you hard-boiled eggs. Maybe he gives them even if he doesn't lay them. I get sick from eggs. I ate a lot a long time ago."

"Jack, are you going to stay in the home where you are now?"

"I have to go somewhere else if my mother doesn't take me."

"Who told you that?"

"Mrs. T."

"Do you think your mother will take you?"

"I don't know. I hope she does."

After some seconds, he asks what time it is.

"It's nearly time to go, Jack, but not quite."

"How many minutes do I have?"

"Ten minutes. That's long enough to take a nap."

"Have you any birds?"

"No. Do you?"

"Yes, we have one."

"Would you like to live where there are chickens and ducks and pigs and cows, Jack?"

"I know where there are cows. On the way to school. Now I'm going to take a nap. Only, I want to know first how many minutes I've got."

"You have eight now."

"I thought I had ten."

"We have used up two of them talking." He is still for a second, with his face turned from me. Then quickly he turns over, "I want to talk. You tell me about something. You make something up." (It is as if he were admitting his need of me, while at the same time he is willing to let me be myself, have a share in the situation.)

"What did Mrs. T. say to you at the window?" I repeated her words. "Yes, the car kept popping, and they had to take it to the garage, and we went on the trolley car, but I had to vomit, so we got off. I'm glad I vomited, because I feel better."

"Jack, I wonder if maybe you were upset about coming here because you thought maybe I'd leave you again."

"I didn't even think about that."

"No, I don't suppose you did. Did anybody say something that upset you yesterday or this morning?"

"My brother scared me a long time ago. He said, 'Look out, Jack, there's a ghost back of you.' But I still like him and he still likes me. My cousin cries. He wants me home. Martha and Buddy. Buddy is the boy and Martha is the girl."

"Now it is time to go." And again he wants me to wait upon him, bringing him his coat and hat. He lies down with his hands up back of him, putting the coat on as before. "Jack, I think you are trying to make me do all the work. I think you are trying to boss me." He admits this with some pleasure. "I think you are feeling a little better." He must have one more minute for a nap before he will go. Finally says good-by without the usual ceremony.

From Visitor's Record

When I went to get him after he had been to see Dr. Taft, he wanted to know immediately if I had his flash light, and could we go right away and get the batteries? I gave the light to him and he clutched it as if he would never be able to part with it. "My mother gave it to me a long time ago. I've had it for years and years, all the time at Grandmom's and Aunt Ethel's and Aunt May's. The batteries have lasted a long time, and I hope these new ones will, too." Looked extremely forlorn and wistful. Said he didn't like ghosts.

L. T.

April 12, 1932, Tuesday—Eighteenth hour [26]

Jackie comes down the hall in his old way, calling, "Anybody home?" Gives the mail slot a flip as he goes by. Seems to be in the best of spirits. "I got a 'waash,'" pointing to his cheek.

"Jackie, can you say 'rash'?" He repeats it perfectly. "You can do it, can't you? You just fool us. What have you got? The measles?"

"What do *you* think it is?"

"I don't know. Do you have a sore throat?" He coughs violently at this. "You seem to feel pretty well. I don't believe it is anything." He hauls out the pillows and the rug and begins tumbling.

He goes rummaging through the desk. Comes across the Porteus mazes which have been left from previous examinations. Wants to know just what they are. "This is a game Jack. Do you want to play it?" He does, so I show him what to do and give him the various years in order. It is interesting to see how differently a child behaves when not aware of taking a test. He is highly amused and makes no effort to do them properly, just enjoys himself. Makes a noise all the time he is working at them and is not nearly as serious as he is when wrestling with a problem of his own. Is impulsive and shows very poor motor coördination.

---

[26] He is quite restored and able to express his resentment over my absence vigorously during this hour.

Does not do very well because it is apparent that he would as soon make a mistake as not. In fact, I think he resists a little the change in my attitude, which is associated with my old use of the mazes and wishing a child to do well. In the middle of the mazes he asks what time it is, as if he rather resented using up his time this way. As soon as he finds they are a little hard, he is no longer interested and gives up, which is not at all characteristic of him. Again inquires the time.

"You have plenty of time, Jack." Seems at a loss what to do. Begins on the middle drawer of the desk, where I keep my supplies. "There's nothing in that drawer for you. Please don't disturb things." He has to inquire about every separate thing in the drawer, but finally closes it. "There is nothing to play with." He begins locking the drawer. Looks in the bottom drawer again, but wants nothing in it. "Can I take these books home?"

"No."

"Oh dear," in a disgusted tone. "There's nothing here I want." Goes through the top of the desk once more. "Oh, gee, only pen points."

"Jack, I think perhaps you are tired coming. There isn't anything you want to do."

"Yes, but I don't know what I want to find." He plays around aimlessly.

"What did you do Saturday, Jack?"

"Played. Do you know when I'm going to come again?"

"Thursday, aren't you?"

"I'm going to come Monday."

"I won't be here on Monday."

"Then, Tuesday."

"Yes, that's all right."

"Well, I'll come next Tuesday."

"Then you don't want to come Thursday and Saturday?"

"No. Oh, yes, I do, too. Does Saturday come before Tuesday?" I explain the order of the days. "Yes, I'll come

Thursday and Saturday. To-morrow I have an old school day," in a most disgusted tone.

"What do you do at school?"

"Oh, write and read and all that." He's tumbling on the pillows once more and wants an extra one, so he turns to the forbidden pillow on my chair, and takes it in his arms. "Put it back, Jack, you can't have it." He looks at me, full of resistance. "Put it back," firmly.

"Oh, dear. What can I take?" He leaves the pillows and turns his attention to the mantels in the two rooms. There is nothing on the mantels that he can play with. Is tempted to take my purse and my hat, but desists when told to. He runs into the other room and comes back with a valuable vase, which he is about to fill with water. He nearly tips the screen over, and I jump to catch it with a cry of alarm. "Jack, you must not play with the screen or the vase. They are both valuable, and I can't afford to have them broken." This is the sharpest I have ever been with him, because I am startled out of my composure. He now runs to the front room and drags out the drawer of the little table, where he has left the wood and the hammer. He brings drawer and all to the back room, and is about to use the drawer as a bed for himself. It is rather a frail object, and I decide he'd better not begin to play with it. He is very restive, and begins to pound a tack in the bottom of the drawer. "Jack, will you put the drawer back, or do you want me to do it?" He still resists, and I get up to take it from him.

"Let *me* put it back," he begs.

"I don't believe you can. It is hard to get in."

"I can," and he does it successfully. He now turns his attention to the tools and begins pounding viciously in a way that is very dangerous to my steamer rug. I remove it and give him a rug he cannot hurt. The rest of the morning he pounds with greater freedom and violence than he has ever shown in any activity. He pounds the screw-driver into a small hole in the hard wood so viciously that it comes out the other side. For once he hits as hard as he possibly can. "Jack, I think you'd like to hit me as hard as that, you are so mad at me." [27]

"Whoever thinks that is a dumb-bell." He pounds and pounds until I tremble for the effect on the other inhabitants of the house. "Well, Jack, have you got it out of your system?"

"What?"

"The madness." He seems to assent to this.

"What time is it? Is it time to go?"

"Yes."

"Just wait." We spend a few minutes getting the screwdriver out of the hard wood and it takes all his strength and mine to do it. He wants me to put the tools back, but I insist that it is his job. Then he gets his coat, and I remark that the rug has to go back. "You do that," he says.

"I think it's your job, Jack. You are getting to be a lazy boy." He has his coat almost on, but slips it off again and insists that I help him. "You put your coat on yourself, Jack. You're just lazy." I see that we have quite a long struggle ahead of us, so I say, "I'll help you with the coat, and you put the rug back." "All right." But as soon as the coat is on, he looks at me wickedly and says, "Now you do the rug." "Jack, I thought you were a man of your word. That isn't fair." Whereupon he puts the rug back.

"When I go out and flip the mail box and ring the bell, you say good-by twice."

There is much flipping and ringing and many good-bys. He yells with zest as he goes down the hall, and when he is out the door, calls through the window, "Hoohoo."

[27] The point of this kind of interpretation is not to catch the child in something he does not know or will not admit, but to help him to feel and accept his own will, as well as his emotion. This has nothing in common with suggestion which imposes the will of the therapist upon the patient. The danger in such a statement lies in the possibility of being mistaken, but the comeback on a misunderstanding is usually swift, and long experience builds up a very sure sensitivity on the part of the therapist to the feelings and impulses underlying the obvious content of the moment.

April 14, 1932, Thursday—Nineteenth hour

I hear a French horn on an automobile sounding outside, and soon Jackie's steps in the hall. Instead of calling "hello" as usual, he rings the bell loudly. "Did you hear the horn?"

"Yes. Was that you?"

"That was Mrs. T.'s husband's horn. Where did you get those?"—looking at some flowers on the mantelpiece.

"I bought them on the street."

"They are pretty."

There follows an uneventful hour of very friendly play and conversation. At the end of the period he says, "Can I come to-morrow?"

"To-morrow's Friday."

"Well, can't I come?"

"I won't be here."

"Oh, gee! Where will you be?"

"I work somewhere else."

"Well, can I come the next day?"

"Yes, it's Saturday. What did you want to come to-morrow for?"

In a disgusted voice, "Because I thought I could come and have a good time."

"I'm sorry, Jack, but it's time to go now." He has a hard time putting the tools back into the drawer as the drawer falls out. All he needs to encourage him to a task is to doubt his ability to do it. He comes back riding on the little stool. "Now you can ride on the little rug, Jack, and put it back where it belongs." Which he does cheerfully. He gets on his suit coat, and then instead of continuing to put on his wraps he flings himself on the couch. "I'm going to leave my glasses here. Mrs. T. can come get them."

"Not at all! You're going to put the glasses on."

"No, I'm not."

"You are a lazy boy, Jack. You want everybody else to do the work."

"Yes, I'm like that at home too," cheerfully.

"Put on your coat."

"You get the coat. I put on the other one."

"Well, I'll tell you what I'll do. I'll get the coat, and you put on the glasses." He puts his hands back of him, lying on the couch. "You put the glasses on first, Jack."

"No, you put the coat on."

"It's a bargain. I'll put the coat on, and you put the glasses on."

"What's a bargain?"

"It's a promise. You do something, and I do something else." He has found a new ceremony for going out. "I'm going out the back door. You must leave it open, then when I get around front you can close it, and when I lift the thing (meaning the mail chute) you say good-by twice," which ceremony we carry out with pains.

From Visitor's Record

April 16, 1932

Jack said Uncle Billy told him his step-mother went around with boy friends. I asked who his step-mother was and he said, "Oh, I mean my mother, and Uncle Bill knows because he's in the government. That's why she doesn't come to see me." I told him one reason why she didn't come was that she had gone to New York to stay with his sick uncle. Jack asked many questions about this, also had I seen his grandma. I said I had, and that she was not well either. " 'Most everybody's getting sick," said Jack, "but, just the same, Uncle Bill said she runs around with boy friends, and I know she does, too. You tell her I was asking about her, won't you, and ask her to write to me?"

He wanted me to be sure to sound the horn in front of Dr. Taft's house so *he* would know he was there. Several times he called Dr. Taft "he," and once I corrected him, but he continues to do it.

L. T.

April 16, 1932, Saturday—Twentieth hour

The French horn is heard outside the window and Jackie is in the hall. "Is anybody home?" He is all excitement. Discovers he can wave to Mr. T. out the window. "I have some money," he says, proudly displaying five pennies. "I'm going to put them on the table."

"Be careful I don't take them, Jackie." Goes out to the toilet and comes back by the front door.

"You've got another bunch of pretty flowers. You are always getting new ones." When he has taken off his wraps, he settles himself by me on the couch. "Have you got five pennies?"

"I don't think so, Jack. What do you want them for?"

"I have to get a balloon for my sister."

"Why do you want to do that?"

"She wants one."

"But you seem to have some money."

"Yes, but it's her money."

"Oh, you mean that you are getting the balloon with your sister's money for her?"

"Yes, and I want one for myself."

"Then what you want is for me to give you five pennies so that you can buy one for yourself."

"Yes, will you do that?"

"No, Jack."

"Why not?"

"Because I can't give away money all the time or I won't have any."

"I wouldn't keep on asking you."

"I don't think there would be any way to stop that if we started it."

"Can't you give it to me just like you did the key?"

"But, Jack, you brought the key back."

"I'll bring the five pennies back."

"All right, if you want me to lend you five cents, I'll do that."

"I'll give it back to you. I'll get it from my mother."

"All right, Jack." He gets my purse, and I give him a nickel. He is very much delighted with the transaction and assures me that he will not forget.

"There are lots of other things in the ten-cent store I'd like to have, too."

"Why don't you earn some money, so you can get them?"

"What does 'earn' mean?"

"You do something like washing the dishes or sweeping the floor, and somebody gives you a penny or a nickel for doing the work. That's better than having to ask for it."

"Sometimes a man sends me for cigarettes and I get a penny."

He now devotes his attention to the steamer rug, of which he first makes a tent by putting it over another chair, and then he seems to go into a sort of ecstasy with the rug, like a cat with catnip, going over and over, and then struggling to get out like a butterfly from a cocoon. Once as he is lying on his back with his knees up to his chest he says, "I'll put my didie on."

"Do you wear didies, Jack?"

"Oh, I'm only playing," disgustedly. He struggles cut from the rug.

"Are you being born, Jack?" No answer. He is now rolling around over the floor at a great rate, probably enjoying this uninterrupted chance to use the rug. It is the end of the season and I have to have it cleaned, so I have given up, but he does not know that. "Are you playing baby, Jack?"

"No, I'm playing getting born. I don't get hurt. I have a little wagon," as he trundles over the floor. Suddenly coming out as if confused, "Where are you?"

"I'm here on the couch."

"It's hot. I'm going to open the window wide." He squirms all over the floor in the rug, playing horsy. Then he suddenly decides to make a robe of the steamer rug and comes marching down the floor, singing, "Here comes the bride, all step aside." He lisps exaggeratedly and talks baby talk.

"You certainly are feeling funny this morning, Jack."

"Do you know when I'm coming?"
"No. When are you, Jack?"
"I'm coming on Monday."
"Oh, you are coming without me, then."
"Won't you be here Monday?"
"No."
"Will you be here Sunday?"
"No."
"Well, will you be here Tuesday?"
"The same as always, Jack."

He has been wiping the floor with his hands, trying to get them as dirty as possible. "Are my hands dirty?"

"They certainly are."

"I'm going to wash them in here."

"No, Jack, you wash them out in the toilet."

"No, I'm going to wash them here. That's the rule. Now are they dirty?" trying to get them a little dirtier.

"They are, Jack, and you will wash them outside, if you are going to do it." He gives up and goes out to the toilet. I can hear him singing as he washes them, "Gee, that's dirty, dirty, dirty." He comes back by the front door, clasping a dead iris, which was outside in the wastebasket. "Me cook it." Begins to strip the leaves off. He has left the back door open and I close it because I am cold.

"Why did you shut that door? So people can't hear such silly things?"

"So you know it's silly, do you, Jack?"

"Oh, me boke the cabbage."

"Jack, you like to talk like a baby, don't you?"

"If you call me a baby I'll lick you."

"I didn't call you a baby. I just said that you like to

talk like a baby. When you say, 'me boke,' that's the way a baby talks."

"I am breaking up the stem," says Jack.

"Yes. That's grown up when you say 'I.' "

Meantime he is diverted to my watch. Wants to understand a little bit more about the time. I tell him it is five minutes before he has to go, and he sits down, holding the watch, to see just how long five minutes is. "How much did this watch cost?"

"Fifty dollars."

"Oh, gee!"

"That's a good deal of money, Jack."

"Suppose I would break it. What would you do?"

"What could I do, Jack? The watch would be broken. I couldn't help myself, could I?"

"Would you scold me?"

"That wouldn't help me, would it? The watch would still be broken."

"Would you lick me?"

"It wouldn't be any use to lick you. That wouldn't mend the watch. I would just feel very bad because you had broken my watch. But I don't see what I could do about it."

"You could lick me."

"But you see that really wouldn't help, Jack. If you break my watch, you hurt me and I can't do anything about it."

"The five minutes are up. Now we have five more minutes to clean up. You have all your cooking things to pick up." He is not the least interested in helping to clear up the room.

"You put down the rugs," he says.

"Yes, I will, but you do your share. You pick up the cooking stuff that's on the floor." He finally does pick up the bits of the flower, but is not very helpful about anything else. He wants to take the tape measure home, and I will not let him. He pretends to strike at me with the string. "You would like to hit me, Jack, but I don't believe it would be a very good idea to do it, because you do like me even if you are mad at me." [28] He is now putting on his coat, but will not take his glasses.

"Miss Y. can get them."

"No, she cannot, Jack, for I will not be here. If you don't take your glasses now, you can go without them until you come again. I'm going to wash them all nice and clean for you." He finally decides to take them.

From Visitor's Record
April 19, 1932

When I came up the street I saw Jackie standing in the window, watching, even though I was much earlier than usual. When I called "Good morning" he said, "My grandmother's here and said I could go home with her a couple of days."

At this point Mr. W. (foster father) came from the back room and said, "Mrs. T., you'll have to find a new home for this boy right away. We can't stand him any longer. My wife is sick all because of him, and he won't go to the bathroom when I tell him. Says he won't go, and then does it in the middle of the room. He won't go to school either."

Mrs. W. soon explained that her husband was unduly irritated over having the housework to do. Jack obeys her, but when Mr. W. gets stern and says, "Do this," Jack refuses and talks back, because Mr. W. is really too easy. Jackie says his mother likes Paul (older brother) better than him. She just doesn't want to be bothered with him.

On the way to Dr. Taft's, Jackie begged with every conceivable argument to go to grandmother's, but was refused. I reminded him that he was staying with Mrs. W. only four

---

[28] The point here is to accept the feeling and intention but discourage action, which is hard to retrieve.

more Saturdays, maybe only three, and asked if he minded leaving. No, but he wanted to be in the city, nearer his mother, where he could get to her on just one car. I said I hoped he might do that, but maybe we couldn't find such a home. Would he mind very much? Yes, he did not want to go to the country. He was anxious to get to Dr. Taft's, and kept asking if we were near and then became reluctant, lagging behind. Teased for a meal in a restaurant or an ice-cream cone.

L. T.

April 19, 1932, Tuesday—Twenty-first hour

Jack comes in quietly, without any greeting from the hall. He seems a little subdued, in some way not his usual self. His first remark is about the money. "I don't have the nickel. My grandma didn't give it to me. Maybe I'll get it next Saturday." Seems quite doubtful and not too responsible.

"I'm sure I hope you can, Jack."

"I hope I'll get it before I go."

"What do you mean?"

"I'm going to move in four more Saturdays."

"Oh, are you?"

"But I'll still come here," hastily.

"When you are in your new home, perhaps you won't want to come here."

"Oh, yes, I will. Mrs. T. will still bring me. When I go home for good, then I won't come any more." (This shows the rôle the therapist plays at this point as the child's most important relationship, but one he won't need once he is at home.)

By this time I have seated myself on the couch and taken up my pencil and paper. "Let's see. Four more Saturdays, you say, Jack? How long is that going to be?"

He goes over it carefully. "Are you writing that down? What are you writing?"

"Oh, just some things that I want to write." I divert him by asking whether he can write, and whether he is learning to read.

"You won't see me very long, so can I do this?" He points to my big chair.

"You mean turn it upside down? You can do that if you take the cushions out. Put the cushions on the couch, then you can play with it." He makes a grand house out of the wicker chair, plus another chair, with the steamer rug thrown over it. He spends a good part of the hour playing in and out of this house. He produces a lollypop which is almost finished and has paper wrapped around it. I soak off the paper, because Jack wants to go to bed in his tent and have his dinner. "Here you are, Jack. Now you can be the baby with the bottle." He accepts this complacently. He begins creeping out from under the tent. "Is this a baby creeping out?" I ask.

"Yes. He is going to the bathroom."

"Are you scared because you are going to move?"

"No. I like to move, 'cause you go in machines a lot."

"Would you like to stay where you are?"

"No, I want to go into the country. I want to be nearer my mother."

"But your mother is not in the country, is she? Do you mean you want to go where there are cows and chickens?"

"No, I mean I want to go further into the city, to be nearer my mother." He begins to talk about "baby," and goes to the drawer to get out the little doll-baby. "The baby stayed out a long time."

"You mean that you haven't played with the doll-baby for a long time?"

"No. It's me."

"Oh, you mean you have been out of the bed for a long time?"

"Yes." He now goes back to his tent and is very quiet. Finishes the candy, sings to himself a little, and after this period of rest says, "I'm going to be a lion." We play back and forth on this subject. I implore him to be a little baby lion, or a nice little kitten, and not to eat me up. He is really quite gentle and changes from a lion to a dog, to a baby, and to a cat with perfect freedom. I suggest a change in the arrangement of his tent. He cannot accept it and pulls the rug down again the way it was.

"Do you care if I put the tent down?"

"No, Jack. Why should I? It is your tent." A few minutes after, he is playing with the little doll and pulls the cap off.

"Do you care if I take the cap off?"

"No."

He begins playing with a mahogany chair, using it for a machine, sitting on the rungs and rocking it back and forth. This is a little doubtful, but I do not want to stop it if I can help it. I am sitting looking rather vacantly into space, waiting to see how long this can go on.

"What are you thinking about? You never laugh. When you look like that, I think you are mad at me."

"Do you think I should be mad, Jack?"

"No. Do you?"

"Well, I don't see any reason for being mad."

"I'm a bus driver," Jack announces, and begins to roll the chair roughly.

"Jack, I think that is getting a little too rough for the chair. You know ordinarily people do not like their furniture played with this way. I've let you do it as long as I can, but I don't want the chair broken."

"You won't lick me, will you?"

"No, I won't lick you. I can't do that."

"You wouldn't be allowed, would you?"

"Yes, I would be allowed, but I wouldn't do it."

Jack's interest in the use of the chair has now become pretty destructive from my point of view. At last I am forced to take it from him. He is rather disgusted and retreats to his tent. "Don't you do any tricks?"

"You are the one who does the tricks, Jack."

He gets a little anxious because he cannot see what I am doing. "What are *you* doing?" he asks.

"I am playing with the little doll."

"Are you kissing her?"

"No. Why don't you do it, if you want her kissed, Jack?"

"She ain't my girl friend."

"Who is?"

"A girl named Jane."

"It's about time to go, Jack." He comes out to look at the watch,—is quite full of resistance. He makes a game of it—seizes the rug and wraps himself up in it, so that I have to untangle him to get it folded. He is going to leave his cap and overcoat, but I tell him that if he does, he will have to get along without them until the next time he comes. He finally puts them on. He wants to come tomorrow. Will come Thursday, but thinks maybe he will go somewhere else on Saturday. Goes out with the usual ceremony, shouting and yelling.

From Visitor's Record
April 21, 1932,

The W.'s feel much better about Jack, now they know he is to go to a new home. Are pleased that he does not want to leave.

He told of a dream last night. "It was about ghosts, but I wasn't scared this time. Me and another boy was sleeping in a bed, and a colored man came and peeped in at the window. I didn't see him, but the other boy did, so I called for help. Uncle Bill heard him and ran in and scared the colored man away. Told him he'd shoot him if he ever came again." [29]

[29] Note the absence of fear and the successful outcome of this dream which in content resembles the one he reacted to so strongly with fear and nausea.

He wanted to know if he could stay for five Saturdays at Aunt May's (foster mother). I suggested that he would rather have a definite time, so he could plan and his new Aunt could plan for him, too. He agreed, but hoped it wouldn't be like Aunt Ethel's (first home). I assured him it would not. He asked if it would be in the city, and I said we were trying to do that.

L. T.

April 21, 1932, Thursday—Twenty-second hour

I find Jack waiting in front of my door, sitting in the car. He seems to enjoy very much coming in with Mr. and Mrs. T., says good-by to them with ceremony. "There's something different in the room, Jack. Can you tell what it is?"

"Yes, it's curtains. They are pretty."

"They are not new. They are just clean curtains." He begins at once on the big wicker chair. Puts the cushions on the couch and turns it over. "I wonder if I could sit on the back of it like this, without breaking it."

"I think perhaps you could."

"I guess I'll pretend that it's my car." Tries to put the little red stool on it to make a seat, and I interfere. This time I take a good deal of pains to show him the difference between his weight spread out over the wicker and concentrated on the legs of the stool, which hit a single strand. It's a pretty complicated idea, but he seems to have some notion of it. At any rate, he makes no further effort to try to use the stool. His next idea is to see if he can slide the big chair along the floor. "Will you let me do this?"

"If it doesn't hurt the floor, you can."

"It doesn't seem to." He tries various things, each time asking me if I think it is going to be all right, which is very different from the way he has been doing before.

"Jack, I'm curious. Will you tell me something? Do you want to use the chair or do you just want to find out what you can't do?"

"I want to see if you will let me do it." He tries various things with the chair, remarking at intervals, "Will this break it?" But he is very cautious and gentle on the whole. Seems anxious to find something that is wrong with the chair. Pointing to a gap in the reed, "See, it's broken."

"No, that isn't broken. But here's a place where it is broken."

"Did me break it?"

"No. It was that way before."

He begins to put the rug over the chair and make a tent. "I wish there was some other little boy here."

"That's one of the things that isn't so good about coming here, Jack."

"Well, it's good to play with the furniture, anyway." Creeping into the tent. "I'm going to be a pussy cat." I pat him on the head and say, "Nice pussy." Very quickly he changes, "I'm going to be a bus driver. Would this do any damage if I laid on it?" referring to the back of the chair.

"I don't think so." He turns over the mahogany chair and begins to see what he can do. "Could I do that?"

"Sure." It's interesting that although he tries a variety of things with the mahogany chair, he does not rock it back and forth, which was the thing I objected to last time. He tried various feats of lifting it with one arm. "You are pretty strong, aren't you, Jack? Do you ever wrestle?"

"Do I wrestle? Just you watch me." He grabs the pillow and the rug and winds himself up in them, fighting an imaginary foe with vehemence. Rolling on the floor and talking. "Here's the way I do with some kids. I put 'em down and sit on them. I'm good at fighting." Takes the pillow and begins to punch it.

"But supposing it's a big boy, Jack."

"I'd kick him, but then they'd call me a coward."

"Why? Isn't kicking fair?"

"No."

"Are you getting hurt, Jack?"

"No, it's the other fellow." He gives a howl. "It's that kid. Shut up, shut up, you silly kid! I got him between my legs now. Gosh, you shrimp! He turned me on my back. Ow, you dirty gyp! You shrimp, you quit!"

"Who is beating, Jack?"

"I am. He's dead. Gosh, I have to take this guy to a hospital. Oh, now I got you! Can't I wrestle?" triumphantly. "How would you like to wrestle?" turning to me.

"I don't think I'd like it at all."

"You'd get batted around. You'd be dead." Once more he attacks the pillow.

"I hope you won't have to wrestle with me, Jack."

"Everything of yours would be torn up and dirty. I'd bite, too." He suddenly turns to a football player and begins kicking the pillows. This is his occupation the rest of the morning—to find out how many things he can almost hit without really doing it. "Gee, it almost went through the window. Oh, it's gone out," hiding the pillow and pretending.

"You hope it will go out, don't you, Jack?" He throws violently, kicking the pillow as hard as he can. "I can throw it high." Suddenly it does go out the window. He is in a great conflict between joy and doubt as to what I will do. Rushes to the window and looks out excitedly. "What are you going to do, Jack?"

"Get a spanking maybe."

"I don't see any use in that. It's your pillow, and you threw it out."

"He went to the hospital, didn't he?"—his delight overcoming his fears. "Are you mad?"

"No, why should I be mad? It's your pillow. If you want to throw them out, it's your affair. I told you you could use them any way you wanted to."

"I didn't want to throw it out. I hope I don't do it accidentally." He now goes at the other pillow with all his strength, hitting so hard that he knocks himself down in the effort. "Oh, it almost went out! Oh, I'm hitting your coat."

"That won't hurt it." Goes over to the window and holds the pillow out, tempted to let it fall. "It went down," hiding it. "It slipped."

"Well, perhaps you can climb out the window and get your pillow, if you want it."

"Let's see." It is evident that the climb is too difficult for a little boy.

"The only way I know, Jack, is for you to go down to the cellar and see if Mr. F. can let you out the back window." Jack practises on Mr. F.'s name. Is very nervous about going, but gets as far as the front door. He comes back.

"The door is shut," he says.

"Yes, it would be. Did you knock?"

"No, I just looked from above. Would anybody hurt me down there?"

"No. Mr. F. is a nice man. He's just deaf, that's all."

"How loud do you have to speak to him?"

"Well, pretty loud and very distinctly."

"I'll call him out the window."

"I don't think he will hear you." Jack calls repeatedly. Then he is overcome by the joy of throwing something else out the window, and before he can be stopped the waste-basket is emptied. Happily it is not full. "Jack, I don't think you will be in a very good position with Mr. F. You want him to do something for you, don't you? And then you have done something that he won't like! What are you going to do about it?"

"I'll say that somebody else did it."

"But that would be a lie."

"Well, I don't know what I can say." Once more he is kicking the remaining pillow. It comes very near the light. Anxiously and eagerly, "Did that hit the light? That one pretty near did." Very soon he throws quite deliberately and hits it. The light is not in much danger, so I do very little about it. Mr. F.'s step is heard in the hall, but before we can open the door he has disappeared. It seems almost as if he had gone into my toilet, which is private. No one has a right there, but it opens into the hall. "Is he in there?" says Jackie under his breath.

"I don't know, Jackie. I hardly think so." We wait quite a while and nobody comes out. "Supposing you go and knock on the door, Jack." He does so. Nobody answers. Then he cautiously opens it. There is nobody there. "I guess he went into his own house, Jack."

"What are you going to do? Are you going to knock on their door?"

"I think I'll have to." It is my idea to let Jack do the work of getting the pillow, but when I speak to Mrs. F. about it, she simply disappears and finally Mr. F. comes up with the pillow. "I guess we'll close the window, Jack, so it won't go out any more."

"Supposing I broke your window, what would you do? Would you let me play here any more?"

"Yes, I'd let you play here, but not with the pillow. It's time to go now, Jack." He winds himself in the rug and resists, but disentangles himself and finally turns his endeavors into helping me to fold the rug. He delays each step of the going in every way he can. I wash his glasses, which are as dirty as possible. Apparently he never cleans them. Finally he goes out the back door reluctantly with the usual good-bys.

"Jack, will you try to come early on Saturday?"

"What time shall I come?"

"A quarter of nine."

"All right. I'll ask Mrs. T." [30]

April 23, 1932, Saturday—Twenty-third hour

I had arranged to see Jackie earlier this morning, and when I drove up at twenty-five minutes of nine he was

---

[30] There is a noticeable difference in Jack's relation to me at this point. We have much more of an understanding. I am less fearful of what he will do next, and while he seems to be trying

already there, waiting in the car with Mr. and Mrs. T. He is much interested to see me arrive, and comes over to look at the car. Wants to know if it is my car, or the lady's who is driving it. Can I drive? He comes in, however, very cheerfully, pretending to shut me out. No sooner are we in the room that he begins on the problem of how he is to get a nickel. Will I lend him a nickel?

"I'll pay you back ten cents when I move. I'm going to get a quarter, or a whole half-dollar, and I'm coming here just the same, so I'll pay you back."

"But, Jack, if you move and it's far away, you may not be able to come so often."

"But, I'm not going to move so far away. I'm going to stay in the city."

"You might not."

"Well, can I have a nickel?"

"I don't see why I should lend you a nickel when I have already given you one, and you haven't returned it. I don't see how I know that you will return another nickel."

"Yes, I will. Please let me have it."

"I'm fishing around in my pocketbook for a pencil and I come upon a piece of a broken watch bracelet. "Here's something you can play with. You can have this." This diverts him for a moment. He doesn't quite understand the difference between the watch bracelet and the watch. Thinks I have a new watch, too. Very soon, however, he is back at the old problem of a nickel.

"I want a nickel to get a battery."

"You'll have to earn it."

"Well, give me the nickel, and if I don't give it back, I'll get a licking off my mom."

"But that won't give me a nickel back."

"My mom will give it to me."

"She isn't here."

"Can I have it?"

me out, he is not doing it nearly so much; is accepting some of the limitations, and has less aggression toward me, combined with more courage to do the things that he wants to do.

"No, Jack, I can't give you any more money."

"My aunt owes me a nickel, and I'll give it to you."

"When are you going to move, Jack?"

"Four more Saturdays."

"But you told me that some time ago. It isn't so many as that now, is it?"

"Are you going to give me a nickel?"

"No."

"Why?"

"You know why."

"Do I have to give you a nickel back? Then will you give me one?"

"Yes, when you pay me back, I will trust you again. But I don't think it's a very good idea to keep on lending money when you don't get any of it back. You remember that I told you I thought it wasn't a very good idea to give anybody money because they would keep on asking, and you see you are doing just that."

"I just want to borrow it like I did before. If I give you the flash light, will you give me a nickel?"

"I don't want a flash light. What do you want a nickel for?"

"I want to get a shovel, and my sister wants one, too, so we can dig in the dirt this afternoon."

"Why don't you use the kitchen spoon? That's good for digging."

"My uncle won't let me."

"Maybe where you move, there will be a spoon you can dig with."

"Will there be any dirt?"

"I should think so. Do you have dirt where you live now?"

"Yes, lots of it under the porch."

"Why don't you ask Mrs. T.? Maybe she will get you a shovel."

"She won't do it. She says she won't."

"Then I guess you will have to earn the money for it."

"Can I earn it down here?"

"The trouble is, there isn't anything I want done."

"If you took one of my things, the other child could play with it."

"Oh, you mean I should pay you for a toy, so that it could be here to play with?"

"Yes."

Trying to divert him, I remark, "Jack, your stocking is on wrong side out." This absorbs him for the moment.

"Would you care if I take it off?"

"No."

"It's all dirty. I better get the wastepaper basket." He proceeds to take the stocking off over the basket. "Hear that noise. That's the dirt dropping in the basket."

"You have been digging, haven't you?"

"Yes, under the porch. And there's a lot of dirt in it."

"Can I take one of your spoons home?"

"I don't have any."

"Yes, you do. Those little ones."

"They are too little. They wouldn't do you any good."

"Oh, please. They *would* do me some good," pleadingly. He now turns to the bottom drawer and gets out the tin dishes. "Can't I take home this tin cup? It would be fine to put dirt in."

"No."

"Can I have the fork?"

"No. Jack, you are just begging this morning. What's the matter?"

"I've got nothing home to play with. Can't I have this horseshoe?"

"No. I'm not going to give you anything."

"You let me take the book home."

"Yes, but I didn't want the book. It wasn't any use to me."

Holding up the tin cup. "There's more of these. Let me take one home, just one. I won't ask for any more."

"It's no use, Jack, you can't."

"Not any?"

"No."

"Oh, gee!"

"You will just have to be mad at me, Jack. I don't see anything else for it."

"You got plenty more of these."

"Jack, if you want to play here, you can, but if you want things to take away with you, it's no use to come here."

"But there's no dirt here."

"No, but you can stay home. You don't have to come here." He is counting out the tin cups carefully.

"There are four for the other children to play with, and some other little dishes. If I just took this one, wouldn't it be all right?"

"It's no use to tease, Jack."

"This is all I will ask for, honest it is. Can't I have this?" turning to the magnet.

"No."

"You gave me the book."

"Jack, I don't think you want to come here unless I will give you things, and I won't do that, so perhaps you don't want to come any more."

"You still got some other dishes. Why won't you give me any?"

"Because I'm mean, Jack. I don't want to."

"You ain't mean, but I want one. You ain't mean to me."

"I think I must seem bad to you, Jack, if I don't give it to you."

"Only one thing. Just a little thing. You won't be bad if you give it to me, and you won't be bad if you don't give it to me, either.[31] The little fork isn't much."

[31] This is not unlike the effort of the adult patient to get some physical response from the therapist, which would release him from the burden of realizing his own need emotionally and becoming responsible for it.

"No, but I'm not going to give it to you, Jack. I don't like to be teased. If there were something I wanted to give to you, I would do it without your teasing me." He keeps on teasing. Wants me to give him the little broken pipe, but now it has become a matter of principle, and I have to stick to my guns. "Jack, you are just trying to have your way. You are trying to boss me. I don't try to make you do things, and I don't like it when you try to make me." He desists for the moment and begins playing reluctantly with the magnet and the plates.

With a new consideration, he says, "Do you want the window shut? Are you cold?"

"Perhaps a little, Jack. Do you want to shut it?" He proceeds to do so.

"Remember the time I was playing football and it went out the window? I told Mrs. T. She said, did you give me a licking, and I said 'No.' You didn't give me any, either."

"Did you want me to?"

"No. Can I have just this?" pointing to the broken pipe.

"No."

"Please."

"No."

"Why not?"

"Because I don't like the way you are treating me, Jack. I like to give things away when I want to. I don't like somebody to try to make me do it." Suddenly his face flushes and before I know it he is crying. "Did I hurt your feelings, Jack? Are you mad at me?" He nods his head. "I am very sorry."

"You won't give me the cup. Can't you give me that pipe?" He continues to cry.

"Very sorry, Jack, but I can't do it."

"Why? Aren't they yours?"

"Yes, they are mine, but you are trying to make me, and I don't want to when you do that. I don't like it. If I were trying to make you, would you like it?"

"If I said 'Please,' would you?"

"No. Because I want you to let me do what I want to

do. You can come down here to play if you want to, and you can stay away if you want to. I don't make you, and I don't like it when you try to make me do something."

"Can I stay home next Saturday and come Tuesday?"
"Yes, if you want to. Would you rather do that?"
"Well, I'd like to play on Saturday, when there isn't any school."
"Did you think you had to come on Saturday, Jack?"
"Would it hurt your feelings if I didn't come Saturday?"
"No, Jack. I want you to do what you want to do."

"Can I get a handkerchief?"
"Yes."
"Do I look as if I was crying?"
"No, it doesn't show."

"Is it time to go?"
"It is, Jack, just time. Shall I clean your glasses for you?" This is the only gift I am able to give him. He still makes one more try, finding the green bottle in the bottom drawer. Sadly but firmly I reply, "I don't like it when you ask for things, Jack."
"But if I don't ask next time, will you give it to me?"
"That depends on the way I feel." Jack is very much subdued, but not so subdued that he cannot stop to look at a picture on the wall, which he has never noticed before.
"Is that water?"
"Yes. If you stand here you can see it better. It's inside of a room looking out on the ocean."
"I could go right out that door and down the steps, couldn't I?"
"Jack, do you think we are mad at each other?" He shakes his head. "I was bad to you and you were a little bad to me. Perhaps we can forgive each other." He goes out of the door quite subdued, and on the verge of tears again, but flaps the mail box twice and rings twice, as usual.

From Visitor's Record
April 26, 1932

I told him I had a disappointment for him—something he wouldn't like was going to happen. "Am I going to have a tooth pulled, or the needle stuck in?" "No, it is about the new home." I told him that the only one we thought he would like was in the country. If he didn't like it he could move at the end of the summer. He had many objections, and he begged and begged to come to see Dr. T. just the same. I told him he could come back a few times if he would like to, but I thought probably he wouldn't want to, once he got out there.

After a few more objections he said, "Well, can I be sure to take my bicycle right out there in the car with me?" I promised, and later on the trolley he said, "Say, when am I going to the country anyhow?" I told him after two more Saturdays. He asked for new clothes, and I refused. I asked if he would like to dig in the dirt. He nodded. Would he like a shovel to dig with? "But I haven't any money," he replied. "Supposing," I said, "the Children's Aid gave you a present of one." "Would there be any dirt?" "Yes, plenty of it, and a chance to have a garden." I explained how the country was different from the suburbs. He was all eagerness for a shovel and pail, but consented to wait.

L. T.

April 26, 1932, Tuesday—Twenty-fourth hour

Jackie is supposed to have been told this morning that he is going to move to the country in two weeks. He makes no reference to it, and as I have not had a chance to see Mrs. T., I do not know whether something has prevented his being told, or whether he simply ignores it. He begins shouting when he is still on the street, and makes loud noises all the way down the hall. "Where did you come from, Jack?"

"From the rain. Me all wet. Mrs. T. is soaked, too."

"That's too bad." He produces some marbles. As he is taking off his wraps, he remarks reminiscently, "Sometimes I leave these here." I am lured by the marbles into sitting on the floor and playing jacks with them. As soon as Jack comes he wants to play boy's marbles, which is very different so I have to get up to give him room. He has no interest in my playing with him. He is soon diverted by the sight of the open desk. "I'm going to play school. Who was here?"

"No one, Jack. I was just looking for something in the desk." Seizes the drawing paper.

"Oh, I'm going to make an airplane flier. Do you think this will fly? Now I'm going to make one with a point. My cousin learned me the other way, but I make it this way. Now I'm going to make an air hole and see how it goes. Boy! it sailed!" From this moment to the very end of the hour, Jack is occupied with making and trying out new paper airplanes. He varies the air holes. Puts in what he calls a "back winger," by tearing a hole in the rear. His play is quite delightful and extremely persistent, and he shows no signs of fatigue. The paper is not heavy enough to hurt anything, so he has perfect freedom. The airplanes land in all kinds of impossible places, and this creates much amusement. At one point I become the object of attack. We have continuous conversation, devoted entirely to comment on how this one sailed or that one didn't. We both make loud exclamations at frequent intervals. Jackie remarks, "You make the same noises I do." He calls one of his airplanes "Abie Fifty-four."

"Jack, I think you must mean 'Navy.' Isn't it 'Navy'?" After that, he tries to say "Navy," but frequently reverts to "Abie."

"Gee, the pointy ones are good! Now, I'm going to try this little shrimp." The little shrimp is his favorite. It is one that I have made, and he admits that I made it better than he can. As he is always tearing out air holes, the floor

is covered with little bits of paper. I remark that we will
have a lot to pick up. "Oh, let's leave them there," says
Jack. "Don't do anything about it now. I'll pick it up
afterwards. Here comes the Navy gooder and gooder!
Here comes Hot Doggie! I'm going to make another pointed
one, ain't you? Oh, I'm saying 'ain't you'! Oh, I'd like to
go up in one of those! Whoops-a-daisie! Gee, those pointy
ones are good! I know why Navy always hits you. Because you are the one that made him. Here goes Flossie!
That's the boy," under his breath. "We go flying and flying. Here goes Fatsie! Boy, this is a little shrimp. He's
a funny little shrimp." He sends the smallest one from
the back room into the front room and lands it on the
mantel. This is a remarkable feat which fills us with joy.

It is finally time to pick up the scraps. "You clear up,"
says Jack, "and I'll get a few more chances to fly before
I go."

"Jack, I can't pick up those little scraps. I am too old.
My joints are too stiff. You'll have to do it. I'll pick up
the big things." Jackie succumbs gracefully and picks up
every single bit. When I have collected the airplanes, he
feels he must fly each one before he goes. He decides to take
only one with him, puts the rest in the desk for safe-keeping.
He is putting on his rubbers, having rather a hard time.
I come to the rescue with one. He calls me "Mom." He is
a little shy about it. "I think I am more like your grandmom,
Jack." He evidently does not feel that way.

"Have you any boy cousins?" says Jack.
"No."
"Have you any brother?"
"No. Jack, do you want to know if you are the only
little boy?"
"Yes. Are there any other little boys who come here?"
"You are the only one who is coming now."
"Will another one come when I go?"

"Not that I know of. I don't see very many little boys. Sometimes I see big boys."

"What do they do?"

"Oh, they just talk to me."

"Is that all?"

"Yes, that's all." As he is going out the door, he looks quite scornfully at the mail chute. "I ain't going to do that. It's a waste of time."

"See you Thursday, Jack."

"All right. Good-by."

From Visitor's Record
April 28, 1932

Mrs. W. reports two dry nights. Jack wanted to know if I would take him to the farm, but I explained that Miss H. would drive him. He had met her once in the office. Would I come out and bring him in to see Dr. Taft just the same? I said that wouldn't be possible. In the playroom he met Miss H. and asked when she would take him to the country. She explained that it would be after two more Saturdays. Could Mrs. T. come too? "If I have time," was the answer. I said I might arrange it, if he really wanted me to come.

L. T.

April 28, 1932, Thursday—Twenty-fifth hour

The French horn calls me to the window, and for the first time we exchange greetings before Jackie gets out of the car. He is delighted at the situation and hurries in, so that he, too, can wave good-by from the window. The entire time is spent in flying the airplanes. A good deal of the time they are directed toward me, and he enjoys it the most when they hit me in the eye or elsewhere. The second best game is when we bet on where they are going to land.

I am more a part of the game this time. As I do not have to write much, Jack gets all of my attention. It is interesting to see how quickly he becomes accustomed to this monopoly, and at the close of the hour, when I try to put down a note, he cannot bear to have me look the other way for a minute.

Once during the hour I ask if he is still going to school. "Yes," says Jack, "to-day is a school day, but I told the teacher."

"That's one reason why you like to come here, isn't it, Jack?" He laughs and admits it.

When I announce that it is time to go, he reverts to the wanting-to-take-home attitude.

"Can I take all this paper home?"

"No."

"Can I take just one piece?"

"If you want to make it into an airplane, you can take it." He makes it hurriedly, but when the time comes, takes only a few, leaving most of the airplanes in the desk as before.

"Are you coming on Saturday, Jack? You know you thought you might stay home and play in the dirt."

"I decided that I would come."

"How many more Saturdays have you, Jack?"

"Two. This Saturday and the one after that. That's why I decided to come, because I got only two more."

"Where are you moving, Jack?"

"To the country."

"Perhaps you won't be able to come so often after you get out there."

"I'm coming just the same, in a gray car."

"But maybe it will be too far."

He will not hear to this and says to me impatiently, "Well, I'll tell you," as if to indicate that he would manage it, and for me to keep out. He is now trying out all of the airplanes, trying to decide which one he will take with him. I am trying to take notes. In getting my attention, he puts both hands on my waist, a kind of physical contact which he has never ventured before. I have quite a struggle to get him out. Have to count ten and threaten to throw away the airplanes before he finally leaves without any of the usual ceremony. It is interesting that while Jack insists that he is coming just the same, he recognizes the two Saturdays as the last two.

April 30, 1932, Saturday—Twenty-sixth hour

When I arrive, Jack is not waiting, although I am a little late. I go out of the room for a few minutes. When I come back, Jack is there, hanging out the window, yelling to someone, "She's here. I came early and you wasn't here, and I had to go over to the Clinic with Miss I., and then come back. I've got a nickel," proudly.

"Oh, have you? Whose is it?" I ask.

"Mine. I'm going to the ten-cent store." I say nothing. "Are you hurt because I don't give it to you?" he inquires.

"Well, Jackie, you owe me a nickel."

"I'm going to give you the next one, or maybe the one after that."

"How do I know you will? You don't give me this one."

"Well, I'm going to give it to you. My Aunt May is going to give me a nickel, or when I go to my new home, maybe I'll get a nickel." I am silent for a few minutes. "Are you mad?" he asks again.

"I'm not mad, Jack, but I don't see much chance of getting the nickel."

He begins on the airplanes, but can't quite forget about the nickel and remarks, "Do you feel bad because I don't give it to you?"

"I don't feel bad, Jack, but I just wonder if I will ever get it."

"Yes, you will get it sometime," a little doubtfully.

"It is certainly a bad idea to lend people money." He is now working on the airplanes and talking, wanting my attention every minute. It is interesting that now he cannot bear to have me write. Although he says nothing about it, he interrupts me the second I turn my attention from him.

"When I first came here you looked fat."

"Do you mean this morning, Jack, or when you came first of all?"

"I mean the very first time I came. Do *I* look fat? Was I fatter when I first came?"

"No, Jack, I don't think you look any fatter than you did." This is perhaps his way of expressing a sense of change. I'm different. He is different.

"Do you care if I use all this paper?"

"No, use all you want of it."

He now begins on a story of suicide. "Did you hear about the man who killed himself? He was a friend of my Uncle Billy. He made a fire in his auto and burned himself and his dog. He didn't have any father and mother. The funeral is going to be Monday." [32] No other indication of feeling or interest was given. "You make me a plane just like the Shrimp. Who makes the best?" says Jack.

"I guess perhaps you do," I reply.

"No, I think *you* do. Well, perhaps we both can make them best."

He wants me to do all the airplane-making this morning. But suddenly he says, "Do you know why I think they go so good? It's the way I throw them."

"Yes, Jack, I think you have learned to throw much better."

"But it's your help, too, because you made them."

An airplane falls on me, and I throw it back.

"You can throw good, can't you?"

[32] While the relation of this story to the situation is certainly not evident, the fact remains that I have never known a patient to fail to bring in reference to death, at the point where the ending of the analysis is being faced.

"Not so good as you." I try once more with much encouragement from Jack, but not very successfully.

"Boy, you can make them good!"

He jangles his marbles.

"You still have the marbles, Jack."

"Yes, I think I will leave them here."

"Why? Don't you want them?"

"Oh, they are not much good to me."

"Can't you play with them?"

"Yes, I know how to play, but I don't know who to play with." He puts the marbles in the little box on top of the desk, and does leave them there. He seems a little exhausted with his violent exertions.

"Are you tired of sailing your airplanes, Jack?"

"That's what mother says sometimes, 'Are you tired with your airplane, hon?'"

"Does your mother say that to you, Jack?"

"Well, that's what some mothers say." (It is his first expression of tenderness.)

He is having great difficulty distinguishing his airplanes. "I think this is Shrimp-Shrimp and this is Baby-Baby."

"Why don't you use the crayon and make some marks on them, so you can tell the difference?" He has to settle it to his own satisfaction, and then he follows my suggestions and gets the crayons. He begins drawing on the rubber mat at the foot of the couch. "That isn't a very good place. Why don't you use the desk?"

"Yes, it is. It's a good place. It will take a long time to do this, so you might as well do your work," offering me a chance to remove my attention for a few minutes. "I do think this is a poor place," says Jack, and transfers his work to the desk. He draws a picture of himself with his name spelled beside it. Continues drawing on the other plane. "This is some boy's girl friend." Brings it to me.

"It's a lady. I guess it must be I." Now we have the idea of racing the planes. We see which of four can go the farthest. "Time is up, Jack." He addresses the planes, which are all in the other room. "I have to go home, Sonny. Too bad, ain't it? I must get my coat and hat."

"You'd better collect your planes first, Jack."

"Can't I take this paper home?"

"No, leave it for next time."

"Just one sheet."

"If you want it made into a plane, you can."

"No, I'm going to fold it and take it home." At this point I leave the room. "I'm going to run away with it," he says. I hear the door shut. When I come back he is not in sight.

"I guess Jack has gone. He has run away and left me." He is hiding behind the door, very much delighted with my surprise. He has capitulated on the one sheet of paper, making a crude airplane of it. The rest he leaves in the desk.

"I must take my nickel."

"It's a pity that I can't take it, Jack."

"You might not see your nickel until I go to the new house, but you might see it while I'm in this house. I'm coming to-morrow."

"But Jack, to-morrow's Sunday."

"Why can't I come to-morrow?"

"But I'm not here on Sunday."

"Where are you?"

"I'm at home."

"Oh, you don't work on Sunday?"

"No, I stay out in the country where I live."

"I'm going to the country, too." At this point I am writing notes with a good deal of absorption. Jack is impatient. "Good-by, I'm going." I do not answer at once. "Good-by," he yells, flaps the mail box violently, and rings repeatedly. "Why don't you say good-by?"

"Good-by, Jack. See you Tuesday.".

"No, to-morrow," this from the hall.

"Tuesday."

"All right, Tuesday." He has no sooner gotten out than he comes rushing back for his nickel. "I'm afraid you'll take my nickel."

"It's a good thing I didn't."

May 3, 1932, Tuesday—Twenty-seventh hour

Jackie comes in singing cheerfully. "Did you tee me?"

"I saw you, Jack, if that's what you mean. Can you say 'see'?" He repeats it perfectly. "You *do* fool people, don't you, Jack? They think you can't talk plainly." He begins talking gibberish. "That's Jewish talk." He starts at once for the desk and the airplanes. He says something which turns out to be an exclamation—"Oh, God!" I don't get it the first time, and he repeats it explicitly so that I shall be sure to understand. Evidently he expects me to be shocked.

"Here is a marble, Jack. I found it in the yard when I was digging last night. Would you like it?"

"I had one just like this, but it isn't the same one, because this one has dirt on it." He puts it with the others which he has left in my box. Notices a pot of plants. "Oh, those are beautiful flowers. I know what this one is. It's a violet."

"Yes, so it is. In the country there will be lots of them."

"And there are lots of dandelions, too." He is now flying the airplanes. "You make two Shrimps," approaching me with paper. "Me bothering you?"

"No."

"Let me see your pencil." Examines it and then produces an eraser from his pocket. "Here's a rubber, in case you need it." My pencil has no eraser on it.

"I'll give it back to you at the end of the hour." He is not so happy in flying the planes this morning. Finds fault with planes I make. They do not seem to go so well, although he is perfectly cheerful.

Suddenly and without any connection he remarks, "When I move, you come back here, because I'm coming to see you. You be sure to come back here, and you make it Tuesday and Wednesday and Thursday and all like that."

"When you get into the country, I think you will have such a good time that you won't want to come so often."

"But, gee, I'll have to go to school!"

"School stops earlier in the country."

"What do you mean by earlier?"

"I mean it doesn't last so long into the summer. It stops before it does in the city."

He is going at the airplanes again with a reckless burst, "I'll make them go flying. I'll tear an air hole in this. That's going in the waste-paper basket." He is singing at the top of his lungs and throwing the planes around wildly.

"I think you are getting a little tired of airplanes, Jack."

"No, I'm not." We vary the process by racing the planes, but even this is not very successful. The air holes become a matter of conflict between us. Finally I make one and put my initials on it. "This is my plane, Jack. Don't put any holes in it, and then see how it flies compared with the ones that have the holes." He plays this way for a little while, but he cannot bear it—he has to tear an air hole in my plane.

He begins to see how many planes he can get me to make, just using up the paper and keeping me busy. Finally I rebel. "I'm tired, Jack. I'm not going to make any more airplanes. You make your own, if you want them."

"Is it time to go?"

"Just about."

"Oh, no! Oh! Wah! Wah! I'm going to write something before I go, so I can take a piece of paper home. If I write on it, I can take it home, can't I?" He sits at the desk and tries to write. Paper has no value for him, it is obvious.

"Time to collect your airplanes, Jack. If you don't pick them up, I'm going to throw them out." He has very little interest in the airplanes by this time, but puts a few back in the desk, and the rest in the waste-paper basket. He finds his whistle, which has been in the desk ever since he came, and takes it with him. "Don't you want your egg-beater, Jack?"

"No, I'm going to leave those things here forever."

"For somebody else to play with? Well, that's good of you." He goes out whistling unconcernedly, without any ceremony. "See you Thursday, Jack."

"To-morrow."

"No, Thursday."

"The next day?"

"Yes."

From Visitor's Record
May 5, 1932

Mrs. T. informs me that Jack's mother has returned from New York, where she has been for several weeks. She went out to see him, and he told her all about the plans for the country. She is delighted to have him in the country for the summer. Beyond this she had not gone. Jack does not seem to be in the least upset.

May 5, 1932, Thursday—Twenty-eighth hour

"Anybody home?" Jack comes in whistling loudly on his whistle. At once he wants to know if I will pin his cuff for him. Baby talk is extreme. Before I can get myself settled, he has begun to fly the airplane. "Look! Watch me!"

"I can't, Jack. I am not ready yet."

He is impatient. He talks loudly and excitedly. "Me fly this airplane. Watch me! Me do it!"

"Why do you say 'me' so much, instead of 'I'?"

"The lady where I live, she wants me to say 'I.'"

"So that's why you say 'me,'" laughing.

"Uh huh. You make me four Shrimps," bringing the paper.

"You make one yourself, Jack. You are making me do all the work."

"I'll do one and you do one," says Jack. "Now you make another." The excitement increases. He flies the planes vigorously and far better than he has ever done before. They go the full length of both rooms frequently. There is one continuous flow of language and appeal to me to watch. Frequently the airplanes hit me, and this is a cause of great delight.

"I think you throw much better than usual, Jack."

"Me throw good. Can't I throw good?"

"You certainly can."

"Look at these racing! Boy! Ooh!" As he gets louder and louder, "Boys, I'm going crazy!"

"Mrs. F. will say that we are making too much noise if we keep this up."

"Here comes Jack H.," at the top of his lungs. "Watch him sail! I can sail a million miles. This was a bad one, and I made it turn good."

"Are all the planes 'Jack'?"

"Yes, and I drive them. Look at this boy. That's a Hot Doggie."

"It certainly is, isn't it?"

"Oh, you said, 'It's a Hot Doggie,'" laughing.

"Jack, I feel as if there were an army loose in this room."

He is going violently back and forth from one room to the other, shouting battle cries and sending the planes to fight, "Here are two planes. I'm in both of them."

"Jack, I don't know what to make of you. One minute you are talking baby talk, and the next minute you are a big man fighting in the airplanes."

"Here comes one right after another. Here comes one with all his might. Here comes one who says he's the best guy in the world and he ain't. Here comes the Jew. Look at this Jew fly. Here comes Jack. He is the grandest flier in the world. Here comes the boy with all his might." [33]

---

[33] Here we have a burst of ego power and enjoyment as a legitimate reaction to leaving. He feels his own strength acutely

At this point he falls over backward in his efforts, and we both laugh loudly. One plane now hits a vase of violets on the mantel and tips it over. To our intense amusement, not a drop of water is spilled because it empties itself into the ash-tray which is next to it.

He plays a little more with the airplanes, and then suddenly turns to the stool and the table, bringing them up beside the couch. Is very silly, talking baby so that I cannot understand him.

"Is this a baby or is it a fighting man?" I ask.

"Me mad. Me going to fight." Grabs one of the old pillows and rolls around the floor. "Me fighting gooder than before? Gooder than when I first came?" Hauls out the steamer rug, which he has not had for days. Wraps himself in it, rolls on the floor, yelling wildly, "Me getting smothered. Oh, shut up! Oh, come here, you bum!" His legs are sticking out of the blanket and are in dangerous proximity to my head.

"Jack, I don't want to be hit in the eye. You might like to do it, but I wouldn't want you to."

Jack peers out from the blanket, enthralled with the idea. "No, I don't want to hit you in the eye," but continues to throw his legs about and yell, "Shut up!" Suddenly he rises, seizes the table, and holds it in the air over my head threateningly.

"Look out, Jack, I don't want to be killed." There is some conversation about the people who live upstairs, and when they are home and when I am here.

"Suppose you were my mother. What would you do? Would you lick me?"

"Not often."

"Would you at all?"

"I might." He now goes absolutely foolish. Hides his head and in tones I can hardly understand says, "Say you

as he gives up the too dependent relationship. There is some denial, but on the whole it is really an outcome of the development to be hoped for in a truly therapeutic experience.

love me truly," looking at me with much embarrassment but considerable emotion.[34]

"Well, how about you, Jack?"

"I don't want to kiss *you.*"

"You don't? Jack, I think you must be fond of me."

"What does that mean?"

"I think you like me because you are going away. You always like people when you are going away from them."

"But I'm coming to see you just the same. Tuesday and Thursday and Saturday."

"But if you are going far into the country, you may not be able to come so often."

He refuses to consider this. He is now all over the emotion and rapidly goes from one thing to the other.

"You have five minutes, Jack. What are you going to do with them?"

"I'm going to keep them."

"Let's put the things away."

"You pick up that chair," commanding me.

"Why not do it yourself, Jack?" He starts putting away the rug and knocks the table over violently and with pleasure.

"Me upsetting everything." I help him with the rug at his command. "Pick that chair up!"

"Better say please, Jack."

"Please."

"All right." I do it. He sits heavily on the little table, which is one of the things we have avoided. "I think you are trying to be bad, Jack."

A man is calling strawberries. "They are always calling strawberries around our house, but we never buy them. Once we did."

"There will be strawberries in the country, perhaps."

"I'll pick them."

[34] The courage to refer to my feeling for him comes from his increased sense of his own value, his growing independence.

"When are you going to the country? Saturday or Monday?"

"I'm going Monday, and I'm glad, because I don't have to go to school." He slams the desk as hard as he possibly can, runs into the other room, and begins to cry loudly.

"What's the matter, Jack?" His face is hidden in his hands.

"I hurt myself."

"What were you doing?" He laughs suddenly in my face, runs out the door, flaps the mail box violently, and rings repeatedly. "Good-by. Good-by. See you Saturday." His head appears in the front window, "Be sure," with great feeling.

From the Worker's Record

Jack was extremely vivacious. When I came to get him from the play-room I told him that I would not be able to go out with him on Monday to his new home. I had to go to school, after all. "Oh," he said, "I don't mind at all." We went to a store to get his garden tools. Finally selected a rake, hoe, and shovel. He did not understand about the first two. I told him he could plant seeds in the country and would use the tools then.

L. T.

May 7, 1932, Saturday—Twenty-ninth hour

Jack comes in rather quietly.

"It's a nice morning. How are you?" I ask.

"Monday we move."

"Yes, so you do."

"But I'm coming to see you."

"When are you coming?"

"When I come out to my new house. Tuesday and Thursday." I have begun to write. "Are you going to watch me sail my airplanes?"

"Yes." He begins at once. "Watch me, watch me! Look at this!"

He now devotes himself to the flying, but he is not nearly so violent as he was on Thursday, nor so insistent on my doing the work. He sometimes modifies his enthusiasm for his own flying. Such as, "Here comes a good one, I think. Don't you?"

"Dr. T., you make two more Shrimpies and copy off of this one. I won't bother you because you are making something." This refers to his wanting me to look at him constantly, even when I am trying to make him an airplane. There is a feeling for power. "I fly with all my might." He also says he is mad with all his might. There is frequent use of the word might.

Suddenly out of the blue, "Do you think I've got toys at home?"

"I don't know. Have you?"

"Yes, I have a bike. My mama's getting me one."

"Have you anything else?"

"Sure, a little engine."

"Anything else? Did you get anything last Thursday?" He makes no connection, though I know that he was given some garden tools and a pail and shovel for the country.

He now reverts to the planes again. Gets mad at one and destroys it. "This don't go good. I'm going to make a plane for myself." As he tries it, "Does this go good?"

"It goes pretty well."

"Yours goes pretty well, too. Don't that go good?" referring to mine.

"Try yours again, Jack. That's a peach!"

"Yours is a peach, too." But it does not go.

"I think it's a peanut," I reply.

He then tries several. "I'm going to try mine. Which do you think goes the goodest?"

"I think yours."

"I think yours." He now is diverted to climbing up the foot rail on the couch, turns an inhibited tumblesault so that his legs will not land on me. "Shall I do it again? Do you want me to?"

"Not too much." He now begins a story of a little boy who was left on the step and—"my Uncle Billy brought him home and we kept him, and he didn't have any Easter, and I gave him my chicken. His name was Bobbie." It turns out to be one of the little babies whom we had placed in this home.

Suddenly changing his occupation, "Me going to fight. Me always fights." Seizes the steamer rug, the pillow, and the stool, and rolls over and over with them on the floor. "You did, did you? Ain't that just too bad?" Kicks the chair. "Come on, boy, fight like anything! Gee, look where that darn pillow is. I bet the pillow is hot." As he lies resting, "Do you move the bed at night?"

"I don't sleep here, Jack."

"Where do you sleep?"

"Out in the country."

"Is it far?"

"It's about fifteen miles."

"Is it near where I live?"

"Not very. I think you'd have to take an automobile." He now decides, after a little more fighting, to play blind-man's buff. He comes groping toward me and feels of my shoulders and head. (I think it is an excuse for contact.) He comes crawling on the couch from the foot. "What is this? A bear? What's he going to do?"

"He's going to eat the paper."

"Go away, bear."

During this he has moved almost into my lap, but quickly gets off on the floor, yelling and crying, "I hurt myself."

"You fooled me once, Jack." He continues to whimper. In play I say, "What's the matter with the poor little boy?"

"I hurt my mouth."

"Oh, that's too bad, poor little boy. He hurt himself. What's he going to do about it?"

"I hurt my sore tooth."

"Did you really hurt your tooth, Jack, or are you fooling me?"

He peeks around at me and laughs. "Supposing I had, what would you do?"

"I'd believe you." He seems a little at a loss, looks at the time and sees how much there is left. "I have something for you to take to the country with you, Jack, if you don't want to play anything. It's in that envelope on the mantelpiece."

He examines it with much interest, but doesn't know what the little packages are. Finally he says, "I think it is for the garden."

"Yes, they are seeds. Some are flowers and some are vegetables."

He doesn't understand about seeds, evidently has no idea how things grow, but is very much thrilled. Especially likes the big ones, like the package of corn. Wants to know just which package has the littlest seeds in it, and what will happen if you open them. He counts them. Then puts them away again. "You didn't want to tell me at first that they was up there, did you?"

"No, I thought you would like to have your play out first."

He takes the seeds out and goes over them once more. There is in the envelope also an advertisement which came in the mail—a boat that moves across the ocean. This is very fascinating to him. "I wonder if we got one at our home, too?" Finally he says, "It must be time for me to go."

"You are right, Jack, it is."

"I'm going to take these home, and I'm not going to let the little girl open them, either."

"If you think that she will, you can give them to Mrs. T. to keep."

"No, she isn't allowed to go in my room."

"It is time, Jack."

"I thought it was time. We talked a long time." He is very sweet about helping to fix the room. "I'm doing most of the work this morning. It's a good thing I'm fixing this up because the lady would think it was terrible if she found it this way."

"I think you are fixing up the room as a present, Jack." He doesn't quite understand that. Thinks it isn't much of a present. "But I like it, Jack. I think it is a good present." He will not take his marbles. He is leaving those as a present for me.

"Did these come in the mail, too"—referring to seeds— "like the boat?"

"No, indeed. I bought them in the store for a present. They cost five cents apiece." [35]

"How much is that altogether?"

"There are eight packages, that makes forty cents." Jack is impressed and very pleased.

"Are there other kids coming here?"

"There haven't been any kids for a long time."

"They don't come much? Not like I do?"

"No, not so often as you do." Finally he goes out the door, quite composed but sober. I explain to him very carefully that he will not be able to come on Tuesday because it's too near Monday, but maybe he can come by the end of the week if he still wants to. He remarks something to the effect that maybe he will be too busy to come, but it is very difficult for him to admit this.

[35] On the basis of technique, I cannot justify the giving of a present. I only know it seemed necessary and right to me in this case and at this point. I did it as an expression of myself; a desire to give a tangible something.

From Visitor's Record
May 9, 1932

(Miss H. was ill, so Jack was introduced to Mrs. R., who now takes over the visitor's record, as well as the supervision of Jack in his foster home.)

When I called for Jack in the play-room, he put on his coat and hat without any question. At once he wanted to spend a quarter he had been given, and was so insistent that I stopped in a town en route to let him spend it, which he did, but with no real interest.

He was excited over the first cow, shouting, "Ooh, cowie, ooh, cowie!" at the top of his lungs.

After arriving at the foster home, Mrs. S. soon won Jack with the warmth of her welcome.

"I want to see everything you've got," he announced.

"Come on, then," she replied. "I have the very thing for you to see," and led us to the cellar, where there was a large incubator, with eight hundred eggs just beginning to hatch.

I explained to Mrs. S. about Jack's forthcoming trip to town, telling her that it would be just as well for Jack to become so interested in the farm that he could give up these trips to Philadelphia. When I went, Jack waved good-by, not very gaily, and as I drove out the lane I saw him trotting along at Mrs. S.'s heels into the barn.

I. R.

From the Visitor's Record
April 13, 1932

On the trip to town Jack was very ingratiating.

"You didn't think I wanted to come, did you?" smiling slyly as though he had put one over on me. I said I merely

wanted to know if there was something else he would rather
do with this day than come in to see Dr. Taft. He assured
me that there was not. On the way out he talked about the
farm, Auntie, and the dog Patsie, with great sense of
possession. He said he was to see Dr. Taft two Fridays
from to-day. I told him I would drive him in if I could.
I would let him know. I again emphasized to Mrs. S. our
desire to have these visits eliminated through new interests,
but as long as Jack really wanted to come, I would try
to bring him.

I. R.

May 13, 1932, Friday—Thirtieth hour

The arrangement with Jack had been that he might come
in on Friday of his first week in the country, if he wished.
We rather hoped he would not want to, but it has been
a very rainy, lonely week, and he did want to come. He is
sitting on the step when I return from lunch. There is
nothing unusual about his greeting except that he looks at
me a little strangely, as if to see whether I were the same
person. His first remarks are about the Lindbergh baby.
He seems quite upset and very much puzzled as to what the
man found and how. "I heard about it on the radio last
night. What would you like to do to those men?" he asks.

"I think I should like to see them punished, Jack."

"Well, I'd like to see them killed. Shut them up in jail for
a while, and then put them up against a wall and shoot
them." (Some of this violence is for me.)

He goes at once to the desk and begins to fly his airplanes. All of a sudden he remarks, "I haven't seen you
for a long time, have I? When shall I come again? To-
morrow?"

"Not to-morrow, Jack."

"Why not?"

"I haven't any time to-morrow, and you couldn't come
in again so soon. You live too far out in the country."

"I haven't planted my seed yet."

"No, I suppose not. It has been too wet."

"Yes, and too cold."

"I think you've lost a tooth."

"Yes, I have."

"Did you pull it or did someone else do it?"

"They done it. Where was you when I was waiting? You took so long. Was you at lunch?"

"Yes, I went to lunch and to the bank."

"Well, how far away is the bank?"

"Two or three blocks." During this conversation he is flying the airplanes.

"Do you know what? Miss H. is going away." (Miss H. is the person in charge of the play-room at the Children's Aid Society.)

"Yes, I know."

"She's going to cross the ocean, and it's going to take her nine days." There are a few more words about crossing the ocean and boats. I begin to sneeze and blow my nose rather violently. After a bit of this, he remarks, "Was you crying?"

"It's just my nose. Did you think I was?" (He hoped it. Would like me to show feeling.)

"Well, your eyes were red." He is chasing up the airplanes vigorously, hunting for them in all the corners, and remarks, "Everything is so clean. It's all cleaned up."

"Whether this was a sense of change, I do not know. Certainly things were not clean.

"We have a dog named Patsy, and maybe he wasn't sick when I went away! He looked as if he was going to cry."

"What kind of dog is this?"

"It's a kind of a police dog."

"Does he live in your new home?"

"Yes."

"He'll be waiting for you when you get back, I suppose."

"When we came he was trying to jump over Mrs. R. to get to me."

"Do you have anything else besides dogs at your house?"

"Yes, we have horses and dogs and cows and chickens. Me have a good time, don't I?"

"It sounds like it."

By this time he is getting louder and louder and more and more rough. As he is ransacking the desk, he suddenly catches sight of two framed photographs on the wall which he has never noticed before. "Oh-h-h, it's a lady bare."

"Well, what of it, Jack? That's a picture of a statue."

"She hasn't got anything on."

"No, she hasn't. Didn't you ever see a statue? They are made of marble, you know. Haven't you seen the man on the horse in the park?" This apparently does not interest him.

He starts in on the pencil-sharpener. "I wish you'd give me this for the country. Will you?"

"No, Jack. If you want one, you will have to get your own."

"But you gave me something once."

"I know I did, but I wanted to give you that. It was a present. If you want a pencil-sharpener, you must save your own pennies. This one doesn't sharpen very well anyway. A knife would be better."

"Well, what do *you* use it for?"

"I can use it a little better than you can."

"Who lives at your house, Jack? Are there any other children?"

"Yes, there are four—two girls and two boys."

"Are they older than you?"

"Well, one boy is almost a man. Is that older than me?"

"It certainly is."

"Is me almost a man?"

"I wouldn't say so, Jack. You are almost a big boy, but not a man." All this time he is trying to sharpen the pencils.

"How much does this cost?"

"Oh, I imagine five or ten cents."

"If I give you a nickel, will you give it to me?"

"If you really want to spend your nickel for it, you may buy it."

He hesitates. "Perhaps I could buy one somewhere else."

"I am sure you could."

He seems to be at a loss as to what to do. "Can I bring anything here to play with? Can I bring a wheelbarrow?"

"Why in the world would you want a wheelbarrow here? There's no dirt here. It would be better to have it at home."

"Well, I want something to play with. I want to load it up with something."

"This is no place for a wheelbarrow. You know, Jack, I really think that you have a better time at home than you do down here. That's the trouble."

"But I like to play here, too. Can I take this with me?" picking up his own egg-beater.

"Certainly; it's yours."

"I thought you wanted it."

"Why, it's yours, Jack. There's no reason why you shouldn't take it."

"Have you got a little tiny board?"

"I don't think so, Jack. What do you want it for?"

"I just want to know if you have one." He rummages around and decides to use the blotter for the board. Then he gets out the baby doll and the bed and coach. "Has there been anyone here since I was here?"

"There have been ladies."

"No children? No boys?"

"No, only grown people."

"Didn't they bring any children with them?"

"No."

He now props the blotter upon the stool to form an inclined plane, and the rest of the time he plays at sliding the doll up and down this plane. "Last night I fell out of bed. When I woke up, I was sitting up sleeping, and at last I got awake and I called."

"Who came?"

"My aunt I'm living with." He begins treating the baby very roughly, sending her on all kinds of dangerous expeditions, landing her on her head, tossing her in the air. He speaks for her in a squeaky voice, "I don't like to be all wet." Cheerfully, "She fell into the tub with her clothes on, and splashed her mother in the face. Boys! she hopped up out of bed. Boys! she had a nice ride. But she didn't have such a nice time falling over."

"Jack, I think that one must have killed her."

"No, she landed on her mother's mattress, but I guess she did get killed this time. She landed on ice. Boy! that was an accident."

"Who is she, Jack?"

"Oh, she's a baby, and her mother's giving her away." He throws baby, bed and all as violently as he can, and breaks the bed. He falls into a fit of coughing, almost choking himself with the effort. "I have a very bad cold."

"No, I don't think so, Jack. I think you are afraid because you broke the bed."

"Yes, I am. Will you do anything to me?"

"No, it's just too bad that you have no bed to play with now." I am taking notes rapidly and look very serious.

"Do you look mad?" he asks.

"I'm not mad, Jack. It was a pity to break the bed, that's all."

"Will you let me come any more?"

"I'm not going to do anything about it, Jack. You seem to feel pretty rough to-day, don't you?"

"Well, I'm just happy to get home."

"What do you mean by home? Do you mean here?"

"Uh huh." After a pause, "Are you mad at me?"

"No."

"I thought you were mad at me." He is now throwing the doll around in the waste-paper basket, getting rougher and rougher as he plays. "Would you like to be that baby?"

"I don't think I would."

"Well, I'm pretending it's you."

As the baby has an unusually violent fall, I remark, "Look where I landed."

"Your nose is bleeding and broke." [36]

"Jack, I guess you are mad at me because you haven't seen me for so long."

"You won't like this bed," throwing the baby into the big box.

"I'm glad it's the doll, and not me, really."

"I'm glad it's not you, too."

"It's just about time to go, Jack."

"When am I coming again? I'm coming next week."

"Jack, I'm sorry, but I am not going to be here next week. I'm going to be away. So you can't come next week." He is much confused by this, and I have to repeat each day by itself. Still he doesn't understand, or will not. Finally he accepts the fact that if he comes, it will have to be the week after this next one, and he says it over after me. "I do not know when you can come even then. You will have to ask Mrs. R. and see if she can bring you, but I could see you the week after next, if you like. Now it's time to clear up the room."

"I'll pick up the airplanes and you'll do everything else," says Jack. He pauses in front of the desk, and once more looks at the pictures. "Oh, look what that lady's got up there."

---

[36] This is the inevitable destructiveness which is engendered by the pain of separation, however much one accepts the will to go, but it is balanced by an equally real positive feeling.

"What do you mean?" I take down the picture and give it to him so that he can show me.

"What's that?" pointing to her breast.

"It's the lady's breast. You can see it on this other picture perhaps."

"What's it for?"

"It's where the baby gets the milk."

"But I thought they were dry."

"Yes, so they are sometimes. But when there's a baby, then they have milk in them. Didn't you ever see a cat with kittens?" Shakes his head. "Did you ever see a dog with puppies?"

"No."

"Well, have any of the cows out at your house calves? You know where the milk comes from on the cow."

"We do have to clear up this room, Jack. See if you can't help."

Reluctantly he picks up a few papers. "I have to take a nap," seating himself on the couch. "Tie my shoe." I pay no attention. "Tie my shoe. Please tie my shoe." I finally decide it is easier to do it as the time is getting short. As I bend over, he points to my necklace, "What's that?"

"Amethysts." He repeats it after me.

"You have something like the lady."

"Yes, of course I have, Jack. All ladies have breasts. Didn't you know that?"

"Yes, but I didn't know milk came from them."

"Your mother has breasts, too, and when you were a baby, that was how you were fed, probably."

He is very reluctant to go, and I finally have to turn him out, telling him someone is coming.

"Who is it?"

"A lady."

He goes to the toilet on his way out, and rings the bell violently as he goes through the front hall, shouting good-by over and over.

Letter from Mrs. S. (foster mother)
May 23, 1932

I think Jack is coming along fine and is as busy as a bee, but he would like to have the trip to Philadelphia this week. I think it would be well to give him this one and then not promise any more. It is funny that he holds me to a promise like a leech. Even after a long night's rest it is just as fresh in his mind.

From Visitor's Record
May 26, 1932

Jack was playing in the back yard when I called, and seemed most disinterested in dressing to go. Mrs. S. feels that Jack is really ready to stop coming to town. When she told him this A.M. that to-day was the day (Thursday) and not to-morrow, he was quite upset, and had other things to do, but a promise is a promise to Jack. On the way down, I said I was going away for five weeks and would not be able to bring him in. Later he said, "You know I wouldn't be able to come anyway, because there are lots of things I'm going to do to help Auntie and Uncle Wilmer, and I will just be too busy. I'm going to tell Dr. Taft that you will be away for a long time and that after that I'll be busy." Later he asked, "How many Saturdays will you be away? Can I come when you get back? I am going to tell Dr. Taft that you are going to be away and that you will bring me in when you get back." I said, "All right."

I. R.

May 26, 1932, Thursday—Thirty-first hour

Jackie is coming down the elevator as I am about to go up to get some paper to take notes. I speak to him cordially. He seems a little confused. "I'll be down in a minute, Jack." When I come down, he is waiting at the foot of the elevator.

..

"What did you go upstairs for?"

"Something I forgot—paper and pencil." He is looking very well. "You are all sunburned. Have you been playing outdoors with Patsie?" I ask.

"How did you know her name was Patsie?"

"Because you told me."

"Oh, yes, I know, and she's a girl."

"Did Patsie miss you when you came away this morning?"

"She didn't see me go." He makes for the airplanes at once. "Are they here yet? Yes, they are. They are asleep."

He gets out the doll and the coach for a few minutes, and then goes back to the airplanes.

"A little girl said to me, 'You'll be late to dool (school).' "

"Is she your playmate?"

"No, she used to be." I could not get the connection of this.

"Have you a playmate?"

"No, the big boy won't play with me."

"Well, you have Patsie. How is your garden, Jack?"

"It's coming up. I planted some of the things. Something's going to be six feet high." He couldn't remember which flower it was; wanted to know just how high the corn would be. He is flying the airplanes and claiming my attention every minute. "Mrs. R.," saying the name carefully, "is going away, so I will not be able to come down here for a long time."

"Well, Jack, you will have grown up when I see you again." A little more playing, and then out of the blue, "We got cows, horses, chicks, and guineas. Guineas!" with pride and emphasis.

"You don't mean it! Did you ever eat a guinea, just like a chicken?"

This starts him on a long story about kicking a dead chicken, which I could not make out. After a while, "Did you think I wasn't coming to-day?"

"I wasn't sure, Jack."

"I thought when I saw you in the elevator you didn't know I was coming."

"Well, I didn't know but what you would be having too good a time in the country to come in."

"I told you I'd come."

"How do you like the country?"

"All right, thank you." He laughs. "Did you hear me?"

"Yes, you are very polite, Jack." He is talking about the planes. "Me fly this airplane. Me," he says, laughing—"that's baby talk."

"So it is, Jack."

"Yesterday I took a bath in a tub—a big, round tub."

"You mean a wash-tub?"

"Yes."

"I used to use a wash-tub when I was your age, too."

"And I played with bottles—little, round bottles. I put them in the water and they made bubbles like a fish." At this point we interchange a good many "thank you's." He picks up my handkerchief. I return his airplanes. We vie with each other in politeness.

"You certainly are polite, Jack."

He gets very shy, and, looking at me out of the corner of one eye, says, "I am not polite, very."

"Neither am I, Jack, very."

Jack, hastening to make it right, "We are both polite a little." By this time he has returned to the rug and the pillows.

"Is there a man where you live, Jack?"

"Yes."

"What does he do?"

"He works on the farm. Sometimes he takes me to ride, and sometimes he buys me taffy. We got a baby cow at our house."

"Oh, you mean a calf."

"Why do you call it a calf?"

"Because that's what a baby cow is."

"We didn't buy it. It grew somewhere."

"In the cow, didn't it? What's it like?"

"It's all black, and its nose is white, and it was on Tuesday or Wednesday or Thursday."

"It came out of the cow, didn't it?"

"I guess so."

"I'm going to play Mom and Dad and Pop."

"What's that?"

"Well, I'm the Daddy, and Mom's the Mom."

"Who's the Mom?"

"Oh, you are the Mom." He gets out the rug and the pillows, and begins tumbling and rolling himself around in the rug. Hurts his leg, but doesn't cry. Makes me untie his shoes. Tries to put the rug over my head.

"Can't do that, Jack. I haven't time to do my hair over." I leave the room for a few moments and I hear him singing "Bob White" at the top of his lungs. When I return I say, "I thought I heard a Bob White around here." He outdoes himself calling, and I reply with "Wheat's most ripe."

"Is that what they say?"

"They are supposed to."

"Did you ever see one?"

"Yes, I think I have, but not for a long time."

"We heard one the other night. Tie my shoe."

"Are you such a baby you can't tie your own shoe, Jack?"

"Yes, I am. You tie it."

"All right, we'll tie the baby's shoe."

He is now investigating everything in the room, especially the desk. Finds my cigarette box again. "Do you smoke?"

"Yes." Finds one cigarette. Takes it up and pretends to smoke it. Would take it if I did not keep my eye on it.

"I'll never forget," says Jack, "the time I spilled that dish and it ran into the other one."

"That certainly was good, Jack."

He now begins working on locking and unlocking the

desk. "Here is the key," he says, "inside the desk. I said it was there, and you said it was there. We both told each other."

"Can you lock it?"

"She's locked. I couldn't do it before when I was here. I wasn't strong enough."

"You must be getting strong in the country."

"I am." Now begins to ask me for various things in the desk with great persistence—the powder box, the doll, the books. Finally comes to a piece of cloth that I brought down for him to sew on. "Can I have this?"

"What do you want that for? Is it just to make me give you something?"

"Well, can I have it?"

"It's the rag that you sewed, isn't it? Yes, you can have that."

"But I'm going to unstitch it," says Jack. (One last triumph—if it is unstitched, it will be the forbidden.) "Can I take this?" pointing to the egg-beater.

"Certainly. Don't you want your marbles, Jack?"

"I do. I have got a boy to play with now."

"Who is he?"

"Albert."

"Oh, the big boy."

"How did you know that?"

"Well, I just supposed it was. You said there was a big boy. It's time to go, Jack."

"Time to go to school?"

"Time to go for a ride with Mrs. R."

"Oh," with joy, "me going to see airplane! Me got thirteen marbles. Six and ten at home."

"Help me put away the things, Jack." As I pick up the baby and the coach, he kisses it good-by.

"I'm going to call this marble you gave me 'Pee Wee.' Isn't that a funny name?" He does very little helping, but complains loudly that I don't help him a bit. Thinks I ought to pick up the airplanes as well as do everything else.

"But, Jack, they are your airplanes, and you played with them." Reluctantly he collects them and throws them wildly into the desk. Begins to try to find some little thing that I will give him. Picks up a broken pipestem that is in the box.

"Can't I have this?"
"No. You don't want it."
"Can't I take it?"
"No."
"Why not?"
"Because I don't want to give it to you." Puts it in his mouth and will not hand it over. Finally after much emphasis on my part he spits it into my hand. "You'd better go wash your hands, Jack. They are pretty dirty." He goes out muttering something about "mean." "I'm a mean woman, Jack, because I won't give it to you." (Hard-hearted as this seems, it is easier for Jack this way.) When he comes back, after long waiting, he is quite rough. Picks up a bunch of paper towels and starts to destroy them. "You are trying to be bad, aren't you, Jack?" Instead, he rushes out without his coat, yelling good-by from the hall. I go to the window and from that point he is willing to take the coat. "Good-by, Jack. Give my love to Patsie."

"She'll come up and kiss me when I get home." He goes with a very sweet expression on his face, apparently reconciled to departure.

Report from Visitor
November 5, 1932

Jack has made a good adjustment in his foster home. Enuresis is lessened. There has been no rejection of school thus far. Visitor's inquiry regarding Jack's attitude toward coming to Philadelphia brought out the following response from the foster mother. "You're the forgotten woman. He never mentions you or Dr. Taft or any of his old friends any more."

IV. COMPARISONS AND INTERPRETATIONS

The record of Jack, because it is longer and because Jack is a more self-conscious, verbal, emotionally sensitive child, is more difficult to follow as a whole than the first record but contains the same general movement which consists first of the conflict between the desire to come and the fear of coming, and second of the struggle between the will to go and the fear of going. In each single hour one can trace a miniature therapeutic experience with its minor acceptances and resistances, its fears and its satisfactions.

Jack is freer to feel than Helen, more able to direct his attitude toward me fairly consciously while confining his behavior to objects. He is also much more alive to my response, to the possibility of retaliation on my part, in feeling as well as in action and distinctly conscious of the likelihood that he is not the only one that his coming may not be as important to me as it is to him. Helen asserts her own will, however negatively, with far more confidence and power to defy or deny the attitude of the other, while Jack is caught in his necessity to make sure of the other before he can trust himself. What Helen needs most, therapeutically, is to yield to accept the defeat of her own will in a deeper need to submit to the claim of the love object after which she may be enabled to be herself more positively with less denial and defiance. Jack, on the contrary, has the task of learning to affirm his own will despite the pull of the love object or the temptation to assert himself indirectly through possession and domination of the other. Helen resorts to a bold negative self-assertion first, a flouting or overpowering of the other. Jack seeks a more subtle appealing domination or justification through love identification and must learn to act for himself with less regard to the effect in terms of outside approval or disapproval. To put it one-sidedly, Helen must learn to be good for herself, Jack to be bad on his own responsibility.

As a more conscious child, sensitive in fear as well as need to the reactions and personal qualities of other persons, John is for that very reason far more aware of himself and his own motivation. He cannot escape fear and guilt or the need for the other as Helen does in action. He is too conscious of all the possibilities, defeat, rejection, loss, and his own inability to control the environment. More frank to feel and express his resentments on the spot, to betray jealousy and the desire to be first, Jack is also better able to confess the positive emotions which are so difficult even for an adult to admit and to see the therapist as a person apart from himself. His activities are not so much the direct projection of unrestrained impulses as they are the symbolic expression of emotions of which he is often quite aware as when he mistreats the doll as a substitute for the therapist, with no effort to deny it or frankly reveals the nature of his interest in hitting the lights. He exhibits also a creative, purposeful activity, a playing which may start out as a symbolic or purely provocative reaction and soon becomes interesting in and for itself. He has a positive, planful exercise of will directed to objects which Helen seems to lack markedly, a capacity for enjoying the ordered use of his own powers quite apart from the relation of his play to anyone else.

To this most favorable trait is added a willingness to learn, to take concrete help in tackling a new problem, like sewing or cutting, without giving up too completely to superior knowledge and skill or rejecting it in pure negativism. Yet in school John presents a real problem in his refusal to conform or to learn. This would be the case, I believe, only with a teacher who entered into a will conflict at the start in which case John could resist indefinitely and with infinite variety of medium. With an understanding, skillful teacher, John might easily find in school another source of therapy as genuine as any which the professional therapist could offer. In Helen's case I was dubious as to results; with John whose experience is not only longer in time but far deeper in feeling I have not been able to doubt. What is living if not a prolonged struggle to achieve a reasonable balance between acceptance of limitation and refusal to be limited, between admission of need for the other and a maintenance of the value and final separateness of the individual self? Any experience which helps a child to find himself within limits he can affirm is a releasing, learning, growth experience.

In every hour of this record, if you look closely, you will see Jack feeling his way against an opposing limit, resisting, teasing, coaxing, pleading, fighting fiercely, exerting his strength to the utmost to overcome my refusal and then after a burst of rage, hate or despair, accepting it as just or at least inevitable and turning afresh to the free creative possibilities or the emotional satisfactions which the situation does afford despite its rejections and deprivations. "Yes, you always do let me play." We have to remember that all the time, while the individual is fighting against limitation, he is really dependent on its existence for his freedom to fight. If he actually overcomes a particular barrier then he must quickly find another or fear overtakes him. After all, he is a creature of limits, he *is* finite and to find himself able to overcome what he has taken for absolute power, is to be embarrassingly close to infinite responsibility, to be stronger than anything else and therefore to have no refuge left. No human being wants to be God all of the time.

Jack is amusingly prompt in his reaction to success. In the 10th hour when I suddenly and inconsistently give in on the rule about taking things home and tell him he can have the advertising booklet, he indulges in a short burst of elation over his victory and then out of the blue complains of feeling sick. He quickly tries to turn this into an instrument for controlling me. "I'll vomit again" threateningly, but if it had worked I think Jack would have been in a panic, the panic of the accepted lover, of the rebel without a cause.

The 11th hour marks the first climax of the love submission, registered in the singing of "Springtime in the Rockies," and this is quickly followed by a marked strengthening of the ego reaction, aggravated by my absence for two consecutive Saturdays. When I remind him, in the 15th hour (Thursday) that he won't see me for a long time, he only replies, "I'll still be happy" and admits under the sting of desertion that he'd just as soon not come any more. To make leaving a pure getting even is not the most constructive basis for ending a therapeutic relationship although it is better than nothing and the sense of injury which the therapist's irregularity or absence arouses may be a useful stimulus to the patient's will if he can be tided over the too violent impulse to go in his turn. I do not hesitate therefore to suggest at least one more visit to bring back the borrowed key, with the freedom to go then if he wishes. The violence of his rejection is amusingly evidenced in the throwing away of the envelope (mine) on his way to the car as reported by the case worker, with "a good riddance to bad rubbish" and a destructive stamping. It is not easy to get free of the entanglement with the love object without a little hate and for some individuals, a great deal.

So extreme a denial of the value of the therapeutic relationship as John allowed himself in the 11th hour is bound to be compensated for by an equally strong swing in the other direction which we find at its height in the complete acceptance of regression, not emotional but actual, in the 17th hour, the Thursday preceding a second omitted Saturday. The marked fear which is aroused by the acute consciousness of being caught in the therapeutic situation without seeing how it will be possible to bear leaving it (a charactersitic reaction to any unusual absence or to the approach of the ending) comes to the fore in the dream of robbers with the sense of utter helplessness which is expressed in an hour of feeling sick and lying feebly on the couch like a baby, fingers in mouth, a complete giving up of the autonomous will to lean upon the strength of the other. It is interesting to note that he leaves on this occasion without the usual joyful ceremony of flapping, ringing and final admonitions. The ceremonial, I take it, is an overcoming of the limitation which I impose in setting a daily ending. It is his creative use of the environmental limit, a working it over to his own ends, with a sense of control which extends to me, in that I carry it out in his terms according to direction "Say good by twice." To-day he is too sunk to meet reality creatively to exist on his own without the support of the maternal strength. He feels it only as alien and threatening.

After the second Saturday's absence, he has another ego swing (18th hour) but less extreme. He expresses boredom, threatens not to come for a week but takes it back of his own accord and after an hour of destructive expression returns with zest to his ceremonial of leave-taking. From this point on Jack struggles with the problem of the final going which is rapidly drawing nearer. He knows he is to move to a new home in a few weeks and while he will not admit it overtly, assumes that he will not continue to visit me: "You won't see me very long" (21st hour) as a means to gain his end and "That's why I decided to come (on Saturday) 'cause I got only two more" (25th hour). Leaving, separation, growth has to be accomplished inside. The other person cannot take it over if he would. Yet the patient feels at times, inevitably, as if too much were being expected of him. He cannot do it himself, the other must be made to assume the burden by refusing to let him go or by forcing him out. A final show-down is demanded before the patient reluctantly assumes responsibility for his own growing will to be free, to be himself. After many ups and downs, explorations and testings of my patience mingled with spurts of angelic behavior and consideration of my wishes, Jack finally forces me to the wall in one last crucial conflict, in the 23rd hour. It is a terrific struggle and I am free to confess that it takes all the courage and firmness I can muster to hold out against the irrefutable logic, the winning sweetness, the desperate pleading for just one thing, "just a little thing. You won't be bad if you give it to me and you won't be bad if you don't give it to me either." When he is forced to realize that he cannot get anywhere through domination of me, the pain of inevitable separation and separateness breaks over him and for the first time he cries with genuine emotion although he recovers quickly and soon seeks to turn the tables on me by asking if he can stay away Saturday. "Would it hurt your feelings if I didn't come?" His own hurt feelings make him aware of mine and also are more easily borne projected upon the therapist than in the self.

After this bitter struggle in which limitation is accepted more deeply than ever before, Jack springs into a new creative possession of the situation and maintains it more or less consistently to the last visit. The paper airplanes provide a perfect solution for his problem, as they are within his control, do not threaten me or the office furniture, yet command my constant attention better than any play he has discovered. We now see a growing acceptance of going, a taking over of the responsibility as to future visits. He wants to feel free to come but also free to decide whether he will or not, replying to my well meant suggestions with an impatient "*I'll* tell *you*," and yet to the end finding some positive value in every contact. The spot where I come nearest to repeating the pedagogical slip of the first record is when Jack so cheerfully fails to return the borrowed nickel. The moralist almost gets the better of me at that point in the instinctive feeling that no child should get away with such behavior, it isn't honest. But actually, why not? Is it not rather a necessity that in some way, somewhere the child should conquer in concrete terms, just as every patient conquers in finally completing the experience his way, regardless of the therapist. But the child has to act it out, to overcome the therapist by some little trick, to win out where he has had to give in so often. In neglecting to pay his debt Jack holds out effectively against me and his own fear of disapproval, which, I maintain, in this instance and in this situation, is highly therapeutic for him.

In a growing realization of his own desire to go, like many an adult, Jack becomes insistent on the need for fidelity in the other. "When I move you come back here, because I'm coming to see you. You be sure to come back here and you make it Tuesday and Wednesday and Thursday and all like that." Also he is anxious to feel that he is the only one, or at least unique in some way—"They don't come much (other boys), not like I do." He is able now to admit that he wants *me* to care and is much surer that I do, since he likes the new self he is beginning to experience. "Say you love me truly," shyly but with real feeling

(28th hour) and as he leaves "be sure"—with deep meaning. The awareness of difference which always follows the acceptance of separation can be detected clearly in the *27th hour* when he remarks on my looking fat when he first came. "Do *I* look fat? Was I fatter?" he inquires. It is his feeling of change in himself and his new sense of me as an outside object. I should interpret his sudden interest in the breast, in the picture and with reference to me (30th hour) as a recognition and acceptance of difference, perhaps sex difference in physiological terms, an admission that the mother has something which he does not, a breaking up of too complete identification which is made possible by this new willingness to be himself.

In the symbolic birth struggle of the 20th hour, "I'm getting born, I don't get hurt," Jack strikes the key note of a therapeutic experience with a favorable outcome. He has taken over the birth fear and transformed it into an ego achievement. To give up the therapeutic tie may be painful, but Patsy (the dog) is waiting to kiss him when he gets home. Patsy is part of a healing reality which is even better than what he has left behind. Patsy responds to affection, Patsy really does care, and Uncle W. needs his help on the farm, perhaps he (Jack) will "be too busy to come," after vacation. This is as it should be, the patient goes on to a new world which needs him as he needs it. It is the therapist who is abandoned, who, like the scapegoat, takes upon himself the death aspects of the birth process, and becomes the repository of the outworn self.

CONCLUSION

THE FORCES THAT MAKE FOR THERAPY

On the basis of these concrete pictures of relationship therapy, I should like to present in conclusion, briefly, what seem to me to be the sources of the therapy,[1] to be derived in these contacts. Therapy is a process in which a person who has been unable to go on with living without more fear or guilt than he is willing or able to bear, somehow gains courage to live again, to face life positively instead of negatively. How is this possible? If one thinks of an exact scientific answer to the question, I must confess that I do not know; that, at bottom, therapy of this kind is a mystery, a magic, something one may know beyond a doubt through repeated experiences but which in the last analysis is only observed and interpreted after the fact never comprehended in itself or controlled scientifically any more than the life process is comprehended and controlled. Yet it is possible to describe it theoretically in philosophic or psychological terms although one realizes that the description will be of no therapeutic value to any patient and of no immediate avail to any therapist who must play his part at the moment without rehearsal or prompting.

From the point of view here presented, the source

[1] See Rank, "Genetische Psychologie," Vol. II.

of failure in living lies primarily in fear as a quantitative factor, and the effect of this fear upon the balance
which is required to accept and maintain the conflict
inherent in the life process on a comparatively constructive basis, at least sufficiently so for growth to
go on. Fear is a necessary part of all experiencing, a
consequence not so much of immediate external danger
as of the inherent ambivalence of the human being
who must always be pulled in two directions, must always long for and avoid the problematic situation,
must fear stagnation even while he resists his own impulse to growth. In other words fear is inherent in
individuation and self-consciousness, in the necessity
to be both part and whole.[2]

That the growth process is never wholly pleasant is
self-evident. Because we do not control it, it involves
always some reluctance to let go what has been, some
fear of the unknown that is to come. Change of any
kind, be it organic or purely external, partakes of the
same dual value; holds within it the possibility not
only of desirable acquisition but of loss. At bottom,
all growth or change like the birth process [3] which is
its prototype, is seen to contain the elements of death
as well as life. As a rule the death aspect is only partial and is more than compensated for by the new life
created thereby. Yet always there is the lurking possibility of total loss, of the final passing out of this
particular individualized form of life which, in truth,
is its ultimate fate. However speculative it may sound
and however differently it may express itself in any

[2] See Rank, "Technik der Psychoanalyse," Vol. III.
[3] See Rank, "Trauma of Birth."

particular case, the fact remains that always, at bottom, every serious blocking in a human life is the expression of an unsolved or rather unaccepted conflict between the will to become more and more individualized, to develop one's own quantum of life, and the reluctance to pursue whole-heartedly a course which is beyond control by the individual will and which inevitably leads to the annihilation of this dearly bought individuality.

The possibility of healing for those who are caught in the fear of living, because of undue violence, interference with, or difficulty in, the earliest growth experiences, perhaps even before birth, experiences which are somehow not outweighed or compensated for by later successes and satisfactions, lies primarily in the fact that to live with enough satisfaction to want to keep on, is natural. We are after all living creatures, part and parcel of this so strange and ambivalent process called life. Somewhere in each and every human are the very impulses and needs which make duality of aim and direction exactly right, the only reality for which we are fitted or which we could accept. We fail to recognize this inherent fitness when the quantity of fear aroused by the fate of initial strivings is so extreme that paralysis or over-compensation occurs. The balance between self and other, part and whole, life and death, becomes too one-sided and the individual is thrown too far into a denial of the impulse to move or an over-insistence upon movement, into a self-depreciation or over self-assertion, into rejection or over-estimation of his fellows.

Fear, which is attached to a too prolonged static

condition as well as to whatever breaks up or threatens a cherished wholeness, whether it be an external danger, a flaw in the solution of a problem, a fateful person or an inner unrest, is a necessary accompaniment of living. Only when it is so great that it chains the individual to one or the other aspect of the process, to the exclusion or attempted exclusion of the other, does it become pathological. If the human being cannot enjoy the experience of completion and wholeness either for fear he will stick in it forever or for fear that he will not be able to keep it, then he needs help, not to root out fear but to reduce it to reasonable proportions so that it may function effectively as part of the life process, to spur or to check as the situation demands, instead of acting as an irrational block to living. The antidote for fear is successful experiencing. The fear of being caught in wholeness, in union with the other, can be reduced only when the impulse to unite completely is lived through deeply enough to convince the individual that since it has not, it need not destroy him. The fear of moving, of breaking away from the warmth and safety of a wholeness thus attained, is lessened only when release from external interference permits the impulse to movement, to development, to become dominant, so that the individual discovers in himself the possibility of a wholeness of his own making which is even more satisfying than the wholeness of union and frees him from a too binding dependence on the other.

To conquer the problem of living then, in so far as this is possible, is to learn to accept it as process, to achieve a freedom and a balance which permits the shattering of any particular wholeness, without mistaking it for total disruption and finds in the break-up of the old, not merely loss but the material for new creation. The person who has finally achieved a balance between the claims of self and reality so flexible and responsive that it can no longer be seriously disturbed by living, has perhaps carried through his impulse to individuation to a fulfillment which permits of dying as a final expression of the as yet not-fully-realized impulse to unite, to lose the self as a part in the larger whole. That such a completeness of living is only a theoretical goal goes without saying, nevertheless, individuals differ unbelievably in the degree to which they approximate it. Is it not possible that much of what we call the fear of dying is largely the guilt for not having lived? Death, which is present in every moment of living from conception to the grave, must surely be a natural process too if not imposed from without.

It is this getting away from the sense of external violence and imposition to a convincing realization of inner forces which are not fearful and alien but belong to the own self as well as to external reality that is necessary for healing. The neurotic is caught in life as in a trap. Fear will not permit him to recognize his own creative power or to admit the destructiveness which he shares with the rest of life. He must be everything or nothing, all powerful or consumed with fear of a reality which is stronger than he, perfect or condemned to an intolerable imperfection. What he needs is to learn to flow with life, not against it; to submit willingly, to let himself be carried by its strength without giving up responsibility for being that particular part of the current which is uniquely himself, yet like enough to the rest to take the same direction, to be moved by similar forces. That he can be destroyed by life is true, and that, when threatened by destruction from without, he feels life as alien and fearful is true also, but it is equally true that even this life which can turn against him is like him, is bone of his bone and flesh of his flesh. Somewhere within him is the capacity to accept it, to go with it, to know on the one hand the joy and responsibility of the individual creative will in its wholeness, and on the other the need to submit as a creature, a part, to the domination of the all-powerful but sustaining whole. Otherwise there is no therapy.

Relationship therapy, then, is nothing but an opportunity to experience more completely than is ordinarily possible the direction, depth, and ambivalence of the impulses which relate the self to the other, to outer reality, and to discover first-hand the possibility of their organization into an autonomous, creative will. There are two, and only two sources of the feeling of wholeness to which we attach our sense of security in living, and which enable us to bear the anxiety that change and disruption occasion. One is the peace which the individual feels as part of a whole when he is sustained by a sense of organic union with the other, as the child is sustained in the mother's body, not annihilated, but held in a sufficiency of strength which is felt as its own. The second is the security and power which are acquired painfully by individual striving in the face of fear and partiality, through the slow growth and organization of the self, the creative will, whose strength partakes of and contributes to the great underlying forces of life. Love, sex union, religion, philosophy, the group, provide the natural substitutes for the primal sense of security which is derived from the beneficient aspects of the maternal strength before the disillusioning shock of birth, where the individual's share in producing so great a change is often wiped out or obscured by the impression of external attack and compulsion. Even sex may fail as a natural therapy for fear if the grim organic memory of that first too forced and violent introduction to autonomous living has not been softened by the tenderness and restoration of union at the mother's breast, followed by some sense of ego achievement in the weaning and early habit training. On the other hand the education of children, creative work, art, science, mechanics, are expressions of the organized individual will which has attained in itself and its own creativeness a wholeness that enables it to bear the fear of individuation and the separation from the whole.

The reason why these experiences in relationship which I have called therapeutic, work healingly for the individual, is that there is present always in every human being underneath the fear, a powerful, more or less denied, unsatisfied impulse to abandon the ego defenses and let the too solid organization of the self break up and melt away in a sense of organic union with a personality strong enough to bear it and willing to play the part of supporting whole. The therapist, who agrees to live for this limited time in the interest of the patient, who gives up temporarily the projection of personal needs and impulses in order to allow the patient to work through his own unmolested, provides an opportunity which is unique and irresistible in that it permits a realization of wholeness and security as part of a protecting supporting medium like nothing in human experience unless it be the intrauterine existence. Many patients realize in this relationship for the first time a kind of cosmic ecstasy far beyond the sexual like that which the mystics describe, a oneness with life, an harmonious flowing into reality. That such an intense emotional realization of one human impulse should arouse equally intense fear goes without saying. It is the final overcoming of fear, fear of loss of the self, and fear of the loss of the other, to the point of taking the experience regardless of consequences, that constitutes the first victory for therapy.

With children, the struggle against yielding, in terms of a projected will conflict is evident enough, but the child is less capable of emotional awareness than the adult, and expresses the positive joy of an accepted impulse to union very shyly and indirectly. Rather he acts out his regression in infantile behavior and real dependence on the therapist, while the adult with help is able to reach his fulfillment emotionally, with the relief of verbal expression. The yielding and submission which mark the climax of the initial clash of wills between patient and therapist, are tolerable only because, as the patient finally comes to see, they are an expression of his own nature which he has been fighting as if it were being imposed upon him by the therapist. To accept defeat then is really to conquer, to overcome fear sufficiently to be able to yield to the impulsive self and the sweep of the life forces.

The success of this half of the therapeutic experience depends on two factors: one, the degree of fear which the patient has to overcome; and second, the ability of the therapist to keep from interfering, to exert no compulsion beyond that needed to maintain his own integrity in the situation, and to be able to accept without fear, denial or sense of personal involvement, the full value of the love experience for the patient. The patient does not need to be warded off, except as he demands response in kind or carries his impulses into unacceptable action. He will not cling forever unless he meets counter-resistance in the therapist. His own will to selfhood which has been held in abeyance during this phase of domination by the love forces, will now of its own accord begin to restore the balance and initiate the movement which leads to separation. The therapist has only to recognize it, to admit its rightness and reality when the patient is too confused by guilt to confess it openly.

There remains, then, one further experience to be gained from the therapeutic relationship, without which it becomes a trap as truly as the previous life experiences of the patient, and that is a constructive, creative leaving of the therapist and the therapeutic situation which will diminish the fear of individuation, since to leave convincingly is to find that one can bear both the pain and the fear of withdrawal from a depth of union never risked since birth or weaning and to discover within the self a substitute for the lost wholeness. No particular therapeutic relationship presents such a clear positive picture, since it always has in it all the uniqueness, unexpectedness and ambivalence of real experience which is lost the second it is abstracted. The interaction between the will to unite and the will to separate is continuous from the first moment to the last. In every hour there will be minor yieldings and minor withdrawals. Underneath these shorter surface movements the patient as well as the therapist feels a deeper current which flows with a different time span but with the same interplay of conflicting tendencies. The week has its own ebb and flow, just like the hour and yet there is a general trend in terms of a still longer span, which carries the love impulse to its climax of acceptance and brings the ego strivings to the final point of rejection of the supporting relationship and assertion of the independent self. The hours and weeks which are dominated by the growing power of the transference emotion are never without resistances and rejections on the part of the ego, nevertheless as this is lessened, the total character of the separate parts changes also. The twentieth hour does not feel like the fifth or the tenth. The union which has been attained through hours and weeks of minor destructions and re-creations is fairly strong and elastic enough to contain considerable difference without shattering. Therefore when the sense of wholeness in the transference emotion is most complete, it is also most able to bear the already included and tolerated impulses to separation. It is at this point of greatest security, that the second trend in the relationship can begin to make itself felt and gradually as the ending becomes a reality which is more and more accepted in terms of the need of the patient to be free, to exercise his own strength, the hours and weeks take on a different coloring under the now frankly enjoyed assertion of the growing ego, which by living through the therapeutic relationship, has come into possession of its own strength as well as its weakness.

Time, then, as arbitrarily utilized to limit the therapeutic situation, is nothing more than the external symbol, the tangible carrier, of the inevitable limitation in all relationship, which becomes tolerable here for the first time, only because the patient is allowed to discover it one-sidedly, in himself, in terms of his own will and nature. This discovery, which he makes and accepts in greater or less degree within a comparatively brief period, has no more final, fixed, guaranteed quality than any other growth experience. No therapeutic relationship, however valuable, can make up for years of refusal to live. The more the individual has been able to accept life before he comes to the therapist, the deeper and richer will be his experience in this particular relationship and the more effectively will he be able to connect it with the reality outside. The individual whom extreme fear and unfavorable circumstance have estranged from his fellows and deprived of the deeper human entanglements, may experience what for him at the level where he is, is a miracle of fulfillment and release, yet find himself with a long and painful period of living to be gone through slowly, by himself, in reality, before he is able to utilize to any marked degree the potentialities of the therapeutic awakening.

There should be no sense of failure, no critical attitude, either toward therapist or patient, if the patient comes a second or a third time, for a single contact or for a series of contacts in order to realize, at a point where his own development permits, the fullness of the experience which he was unable to bear at first; to yield himself once more to the feared love forces in order to seperate more completely than he had been able to do at first. In fact, I am ready to affirm the increased value of the therapeutic relation which is not cut off violently in complete separation, but rather carries over into reality, so that the growth process may be a gradual freeing, as it is biologically, with successive swings toward union and independence, until the individual naturally attains the balance which permits the therapist to drop out of his life, in favor of less one-sided relationships. To insist that the patient shall leave forever and never be heard from again, or even to imply that virtue lies in such a course, is to arouse the negative will conflict, and endanger at the last moment the therapeutic possibilities in what has gone before. The patient must not only be free to return as he is to go, but in certain cases may even need encouragement and some suggestion that it is better not to spend all of his strength in trying not to come; a second denial which might be almost as disastrous as the original blocking. The patient, like the rest of mankind, can learn to bear life only gradually. It is therefore no crime, but a sign of growth, that he is able to return in the face of fear, to experience more deeply and fully the life forces which he knows he has not yet accepted to the limit of his capacity and thus to acknowledge in turning to the therapist once more, not only his need for help but the new strength which enables him to take it.

In order to act upon this philosophy therapeutically, the therapist himself must be free of guilt and the pressure of self-interest sufficiently to be able to distinguish between the patient who returns merely to assure himself that there is nothing here that he wants and the patient who is trying to summon courage for a deeper experience. Only if the therapist is as ready to help the patient to get away as he is to show him his need to come back, can he bear calmly the accusations which both the public and the patient himself are quick to make, imputing ulterior personal or economic motives which can be settled only by his own conscience or, in the last analysis, by the efficacy of his method for the patient.

Relationship therapy, inasmuch as it is only an intensified, condensed growth experience, induced by specific conditions which combine unique freedom with unique limitation, can never exhaust itself within the brief period of actual contact, but on the contrary releases growth capacity which continues to effect changes in the person, more conspicuously and consciously of course in the years immediately following the experience. This does not imply an alteration in the fundamental pattern that characterizes the individual ego. The nature of that pattern, its peculiar form of response to life, is the essence of individuality and could not change materially without destroying the person as such. But the balance in the relation of the forces which constitute the self can shift in the constructive giving up of a therapeutic relationship;

the too extreme swing or the too one-sided expression of ambivalent impulses will be modified gradually to permit a functioning which, for the individual, is release to be himself, not a transformation in terms of an alien standard. For relationship therapy, like life, utilizes the forces already within the human being and therefore, in so far as it is effective, is never finished while the individual survives but continues to develop in time, the inevitable medium in which man creates, no less than the symbol of his final limitation.